A Navaho Medicine Man.
(After Harper's Weekly).

SHAMANS AND SHAMANISM

John Lee Maddox

DOVER PUBLICATIONS, INC.
Mineola, New York

Bibliographical Note

This Dover edition, first published in 2003, is an unabridged republication of the work originally published in 1923 by The Macmillan Company, New York, under the title *The Medicine Man: A Sociological Study of the Character and Evolution of Shamanism.* The original running heads have been retained for this edition.

Library of Congress Cataloging-in-Publication Data

Maddox, John Lee, 1878-
    [Medicine man]
    Shamans and shamanism / John Lee Maddox.
        p. cm.
    Originally published: The medicine man. New York : Macmillan Co., 1923.
    Includes bibliographical references and index.
    ISBN 0-486-42707-2 (pbk.)
        1. Shamanism. 2. Traditional medicine. I. Title.

GN475.8.M263 2003
291.1'44—dc21

2002041432

Manufactured in the United States of America
Dover Publications, Inc., 31 East 2nd Street, Mineola, N.Y. 11501

LIST OF ILLUSTRATIONS:

iv

CONTENTS

ABBREVIATIONS.

Am. Jour. Pharmacy	American Journal of Pharmacy.
Am. Jour. of Psychology . .	American Journal of Psychology.
Am. Med. Ass.	American Medical Association.
Am. Pharm. Ass.	American Pharmaceutical Association, Proceedings of.
Am. Phil. Soc.	American Philosophical Society, Proceedings of.
Aust. Ass. for Adv. Science .	Australasian Association for the Advancement of Science.
Bur. Eth.	Bureau of American Ethnology.
Cat. N. A. Indians	Catlin, Letters and Notes on the Manners and Customs and Conditions of the North American Indians.
Contrib. North Am. Eth. . .	Contributions to North American Ethnology.
Dic. de Mat. Med.	Merat et de Lens, Dictionnaire Universel de Matière Médicale.
Encyc. Brit.	Encyclopedia Britannica.
Healing Art	Berdoe, Origin and Growth of the Healing Art.
Hist. Veg. Drugs	Lloyd, History of Vegetable Drugs.
Informat. Respect. Indian Tribes	Schoolcraft, Historical and Statistical Information Respecting the Indian Tribes of the United States.
Internat. Cong. of Anthrop. .	International Congress of Anthropologists.
Jour. Am. Folklore	Journal of American Folklore.
J. A. I.	Journal of Anthropological Institute of Great Britain and Ireland.
J. A. Soc. Bengal.	Journal of the Asiatic Society of Bengal.
J. A. Soc. of Bombay . . .	Journal of the Anthropological Society of Bombay.
Med. Naturvölker	Bartels, Die Medizin der Naturvölker.
Peters' Ancient Pharmacy . .	Peters, Hermann, Pictorial History of Ancient Pharmacy.
Prim. Cult.	Tylor, Primitive Culture.
Prin. Soc.	Spencer, Principles of Sociology.
Pop. Sci. Monthly	Popular Science Monthly.
Saxon Leechdoms	Cockayne, Saxon Leechdoms, Wort-Cunning and Star Craft.
Trans. Linn. Society	Transactions of the Linnean Society.
Useful Drugs	American Medical Association's Handbook of Useful Drugs.
W. African Studies	Kingsley, West African Studies.
Yale Med. Journal	Yale Medical Journal.

FOREWORD

The most satisfying outcome of any scientific study is the conviction that truth has prevailed, and so, presumably, will prevail. And in no other range of observation is this conviction more gratifying than in the field of social phenomena. The beginnings of what we now most prize have been childish, laughable, grotesque, revolting, or downright horrible. But this was not because men were wrong-headed and perverse; it was simply because they did not know, as the child does not. They were doing the best they could, under the circumstances. They had wrong premises from which they deduced, logically enough, conclusions that were wrong. With no external or adventitious aids, they sized up the problem of living as it appeared to them and evolved a life-policy which they put into practice.

In this practice the adequacy of the theory was always challenged by and tested on the actual conditions of living. However strongly supported by tradition and by what we call superstition, the theory could not indefinitely stand if it involved maladjustment to these conditions; and even if adjustment had been, for the moment, secured, it presently turned, with the inevitable change of the life-conditions, into maladjustment. Of a consequence it was provided that life-theories should be subject to correction just as it is provided that bodies fall toward the earth's center.

But if the correction of error is provided for, then it matters little what you start with, if there is time enough

— and there is no lack of that when it comes to cosmic processes. You are sure to work out toward the truth. Wherever you take hold of the social fabric, you find its strands, dependable enough now, running back into a snarl of the fantastic and irrational. Out of this unpromising and often ridiculous beginning has come all that we now value; and without those beliefs which we wonder at as we reject them, but which spurred our forebears to an activity without which there would have been no observation and verification, we could not have been where we now are. It is no small service to the race to demonstrate that truth comes out of the automatic correction of natural error, and not otherwise; for it gives a true perspective of human life and a clearer understanding of what we are doing and can do to live better in the future. It is also possible, in the light of such knowledge, to believe that the process will never end while men live on earth. Social evolution teaches us that the race began in destitution and error and has, by the exercise of its own powers, and not by outside aid, for the most part unconciously, worked itself up to what we now prize and call culture or civilization. There is no more reason to believe that this process will ever stop than there is to believe that arbitrary intervention ever interrupted its course in the past.

This is the broadest generalization to be derived from studies like the one before us; and it represents their

FOREWORD

widest human interest. Here we have a thorough study of an outstanding functionary in evolving society—a complex type out of which have developed numerous special types that are well-recognized and highly valued social assets in the present. Any such study, when well done, contributes strongly to our understanding of the evolution and life of human society.

So far as I know, there exists no other study of of the shaman which compares, at the same time in fullness and breadth of perspective, with that of Dr. Maddox. He has carefully given due credit to other fine monographs which have treated the subject less completely or from a point of view less comprehensive. Doubtless a number of ethnographers, from their field-experience, know the shamans of this and that tribe or region much more intimately than is possible for the student of their accounts; but there are few field-observers who attain the perspective possible to the worker in the study who reviews a wide literature and applies to it the comparative method. What the latter loses in exactness of detail he more than balances by the sweep of his survey.

It is this sort of study that is most needed at present for the upbuilding of a science of society. Here is a book that adequately treats a very important chapter in social evolution. It is in line with the best modern work, and I believe that the industry and scientific candor of the author will inspire confidence. Scientific students of society

FOREWORD

will now have at their service a treatise which will not
have to be substantially altered for a long time to come.
And many a general reader will experience much enlightenment while he turns the following pages.

A. G. Keller, Professor
of the Science of Society
in Yale University.

PREFACE

When the author began his studies in the social sciences there was in existence no adequate treatment of the subject with which this book is concerned. Surveys of the topic, excellent and suggestive, but unsystematic, had been made by Herbert Spencer in his "Principles of Sociology," by Dr. Max Bartels in "Die Medizin der Naturvölker," by the late Captain John G. Bourke, of the United States Army, in "The Medicine Men of the Apache," and by others; these monographs, moreover, were written some years ago. It was, therefore, with the double purpose of bringing the subject abreast of the times, and of treating it in a systematic manner, that the substance of the present volume was written, originally in the form of a thesis for presentation to the faculty of Yale University in partial fulfilment of the requirement for the degree of Doctor of Philosophy.

The study of shamanism, however, pursued in the preparation of the dissertation, proved so interesting, that the author has felt constrained to devote time, not occupied in other duties, to the effort to develop the original survey of this important topic in a manner worthy of its significance. Many helpful criticisms of the original thesis in the meantime have been received, both from field experience and from other sources; much new material

PREFACE

has been gathered; the matter, both new and old, has been rearranged; and the following book is the result.

It is a pleasure, in presenting this study, to make acknowledgements to men who have had much to do with its production. Thanks are especially rendered to Professor Albert Galloway Keller, Professor of the Science of Society in Yale University, for a new point of view regarding the science of society, and for direction of effort along lines of proper research in the fields of Anthropology and Sociology whereby the evolutionary character of the activities of the medicine man has been ascertained. It was fortunate, furthermore, for the writer to have been able to work for a short time with the late Professor William Graham Sumner of Yale University, and to have caught some measure of his inspiration. After his death, through the kindness of Professor Keller, there were placed at the disposal of the author the notes and references, which had been collected during many years of labor on the part of Professor Sumner. It is with a deep sense of gratitude that this acknowledgement is made, since, had it not been for the privilege of utilizing the Sumnerian collections, much of what follows could not have been written.

Thanks are likewise expressed to Dr. Oliver T. Osborne, Professor of Therapeutics and the History of Medicine in Yale University, and to Professor John Uri Lloyd, of Cincinnati, Ohio, for helpful suggestions, and for material bearing on the history of drugs.

PREFACE

The author would finally record his obligations to Miss Marjorie Ward of Chicago, Illinois, for helpful criticism of this book when it was in manuscript form, and to Dr. J. B. Clayton, of the Bibliographical Department of the Library of Congress, for his generous services in superintending the checking of the accuracy of the references. Owing to enforced exile from the vicinity of the great libraries, it was impossible for the absentee to do the work which Dr. Clayton so cheerfully undertook and so ably performed.

It remains to be said that it was the original purpose to elaborate a treatise on "The History of Medical Remedies," but after much research the writer has found this to be impossible, owing to the fact it has never been feasible to spend two or three years in residence at a library especially adapted to the purpose. It is his hope, however, at some future time, to take up that subject in addition to a study of the medicine man in his capacity as priest, and treat both topics exhaustively in the manner outlined in this book, making use of the present volume as a background and initiation.

J. L. M.

At Sea,
November 15, 1921.

CHAPTER I

INTRODUCTORY.

Carl Schurz, while Secretary of the Interior, said of Ouray, a Ute head chief, "'He is the most intellectual man I ever met!'" [1]

Savage peoples, although they lack the culture of the schools, are not altogether without mental equipment. Great chiefs appear from time to time, who, through force of intellect and character, exercise wonderful influence and control over the members of their tribes. The greatest man of primitive times, however, is not the chief, but the religious leader. He frequently takes the initiative both in civil and religious affairs. This individual is the leading and successful factor among all savage tribes and nations. And yet he has had no biographer. Excellent sketches have been written dealing with one or more phases of his activity, in one or more particular tribal groups. But hitherto there has been no attempt to gather accounts of his character, methods, and functions from the ethnography of different peoples, living in different parts of the world, at different ages, to generalize therefrom, and thus present the portraiture of a strong personage, who, call him by whatever name you choose, is not limited

[1] Munsey's Magazine, April 1914, p. 534.

1

to any race or time, but is the dominant element of
society in its undeveloped state among all peoples and
at all times. It is the present purpose, therefore, to set
forth an accurate account of the greatest and most roman-
tic figure of savage life, with the intent of showing that
man, wherever found, as regards religious sentiments and
customs, reacts in a similar manner against his environment; and that, consequently, the conditions which produced the medicine man among the North American
Indians, produced the shaman of the Yakuts, the mulogo
of the Uganda tribes, the ganga of the Zulus, and the
angakok of the Eskimos—these being different names
describing the same individual, whose characteristics,
methods, and functions, though they may differ in detail,
yet on the whole are the same wherever you find him.

To this end it will be necessary to bring the background into perspective. Man lives under a three-fold
environment. The physical and animal world affects him
in his search for food, and so comprises what may be called
the natural environment. His relations with his fellow
men complicate his relation to his natural environment,
and constitute the social environment. The world of ideas
concerning the facts and experiences of life complicates
yet more his relationship to the other two environments.
Among primitive peoples, this third environment is composed almost entirely of the notions of man concerning
ghosts and spirits, and may be called the imaginary environment.[1]

[1] Keller, "Societal Evolution," p. 260; pp. 133 ff.

Whence came the idea of an imaginary environment? It is superfluous to say that primitive man was overtaken by the ills and pains of life. Before man became man, the earth was swept by hurricane, tornado, and pestilence. Animals sickened and died. Ills and bad luck are necessary concomitants to earthly existence.

Ability to reason is not pronounced in the animal world. As a matter of fact, therefore, when pain and death attacked the forms of life below the human, there was nothing for the unfit to do but succumb. When a lion pounced upon a deer, the deer would not have sufficient inventive genius to defend himself by means of twentieth century methods. When a wolf was smitten with disease, he had no idea that the way to preserve life is to destroy the germs of disease. And so the only possible event under the circumstances was the death of the unfit. For milleniums, therefore, plants and animals suffered and died without thought or question, thereby making room for superior forms of life. These superior forms, because of their inability to adapt themselves to their environment, had, in turn, to submit to the inevitable, and thus the process of the struggle for existence and the survival of the fitter continued.

After aeons of struggling, suffering, dying and surviving, there came forth, by reason of some alteration in the germ plasm, a being who did not meekly, uncomplainingly, and without question, yield to the claims of natural selection. Who was this highest product of nature? For ages he has been called "Man." In his first stages of existence,

man had no idea of the law of causation.[1] And yet he was
beginning to think, else he would not have been man.
What awakened his reflective powers? The ills of life, to
which animals had submitted without interrogation. "The
minds of men always dwell more on bad luck. They accept
ordinary prosperity as a matter of course. Misfortunes
arrest their attention and remain in their memory." [2]
When failure, loss, and calamity overtake an individual who
is capable of thinking, there are three possible attitudes
in the premises: indifference, agnosticism, and faith. It
is impossible for man, in a primitive stage of culture, to
adopt an attitude of indifference regarding his woes.
Neither can the savage make agnosticism his life philosophy. The nature man, therefore, has recourse to the
third possible expedient, that of faith. He believes his misfortunes to be due to agency;[3] he ascribes his bad luck to
the imaginary environment. It is characteristic of childish
and untutored individuals to refer phenomena for which
they are unable or too inert to give a satisfactory reason to
the aleatory or luck element.* And the imaginary world
of ghosts and spirits is nothing more and nothing less
than the personification of the aleatory or luck element.

Primitive man arrives at the conclusion that the ills
of life are due to agency by the simple process of

[1] Encyc. Brit., Eleventh Edition, Vol. II, p. 6.
[2] Sumner, "Folkways," p. 6.
[3] Sumner, "Folkways," p. 7; Bartels, "Med. Naturvölker," p. 10.

* A full treatment of this subject by Professor A. G. Keller,
of Yale, appeared in the "Scientific Monthly," for February,
1917, pp. 145—150, in an article which has for its subject,
"The Luck Element."

reasoning from the known to the unknown. He sees his companion done to death by falling trees, by animals, or by human agencies. What, then, more natural than that he should ascribe all deaths to agency?[1] If the agents are not always visible, there must be invisible enemies, malicious and vindictive, to whom suffering and death are due.

This solution of the problem of suffering is substantiated by dreams. As they repose in sleep, nature people see their imperious and implacable ancestors, who convey the information that they are yet alive, and even more powerful and malevolent.[2] They punished their descendants when living. They do the same, in an intensified degree, after death. Hence the living experience loss and pain.

If they do not dream of inimical ancestors, primitive peoples see in dreams other enemies, now gone to the spirit world, and perceive that these continue their hostile action. When the dreamers awake, no foe is near. They then recall that the bodies of the enemies dreamed about no longer exist.

According to the primitive method of reasoning, therefore, although the material bodies have disintegrated, the souls of these enemies must still be alive and near at hand, and hence the inevitable causes of the woes of the persons against whom they vented their spite before death. And so in the imagination of savage tribes the air becomes

[1] Vide pp. 14, 120, 167.
[2] Keller, "Societal Evolution," p. 60.

peopled with spirits, who inhabit a world similar to this earth. Thus, among the Ewe-speaking peoples, everything in the next world is the same as in this, including mountains, rivers, trees, animals, men, family life, and form of government. People in the other world carry all their physical imperfections.[1] Among the Zulus the ghosts of the dead are thought to be friendly or hostile, just as they were before death.[2] The Tshi-speaking peoples believe that life in the other world is the same as in this, because a man frequently sees in dreams the images of the dead who appear, in dress and in behavior, precisely as in their previous life.[3]

Granting the major premise of nature man that he is at all times surrounded by invisible foes, which vent their spite at every opportunity, a person has a philosophy of life to which he can turn as a solution for every perplexity and difficulty. Every man must experience misfortune. The savage is no exception. What more natural than that he should apply his life philosophy, and ascribe the occurrence of bad luck to the activity of the malicious daimons of which the air is full!

While it may be said in general that the savage attributes all misfortune to ill-disposed daimons, it is with reference to the occurrence of sickness and death that the application of the daimonistic theory is most apparent. Everybody conversant with the ethnography of primitive peoples knows that, even in the most remote

[1] Ellis, "Ewe-Speaking Peoples," p. 107.
[2] Encyc. Brit. Eleventh Edition, Vol. II, p. 6.
[3] Ellis, "Tshi-Speaking Peoples," p. 158.

times, when the experience of disease and death provoked
the question, Who did this to us? the life theory of the
savage furnished the ready answer that these ills were due
to the baneful or ill-disposed influence of the inhabitants
of the imaginary environment.[1] The language in which
this answer would be clothed might, to the untrained
thinker, convey a quite different impression, but on careful interpretation it would be found at bottom to express
no other meaning.[2]

In order to establish beyond question the explanation
of primitive man regarding the occurrence of bad luck,
especially with reference to sickness and death, attention
is here directed to the various ways in which this fundamental idea is expressed by different peoples who live
or have lived in various parts of the earth.

Among some tribal groups sickness is attributed
to the influence of an offended ghost. This being,
although not yet a god, is endowed with superhuman
faculties, by which it may benefit or harm the living.
According to the Finns, the souls of the dead waylay men,
in order to kill them and eat their hearts and livers. The
spirits will spare not even their nearest relatives. Smirnov
tells of an old man who, in dying, cautioned his young
wife not to follow his body to the grave lest his ghost devour her. When she disobeyed, she was saved only by pronouncing the name of God.[3] Similar is the belief of the

---

[1] Sumner, "Folkways," p. 30.
[2] Bartels, "Med. Naturvölker," p. 10.
[3] Smirnov, "Congrès International d'Archéologie Préhistorique
et d'Anthropologie de Moscou", XI, 1893, p. 316.

Australians that sickness is caused by a ghost that is eating
the liver of the victim,[1] and the belief of the Tasmanians, in
the case of gnawing diseases, that the one who is ill has, by
unknowingly pronouncing the name of a dead man, caused
the spirits of that deceased person to enter his body and
devour his vitals.[2] So, too, the Zulus will try to propitiate
with the sacrifice of an ox the dead ancestor of whom a
sick man dreams, and who must, therefore, be the cause of
his trouble.[3] Some tribal groups of Samoa think that illness
and death are brought about by souls of the dead that
creep into the heads and stomachs of the living.[4] And
in the same fashion, the Amazulu, as Callaway writes,
believe, when a man has been sick for a long time, that
he is "affected by the 'Itongo,' or affected by his people
who are dead."[5]

Another phase of the daimonistic theory of sickness
and death is the idea that these misfortunes are due to
spirit possession. As Spencer has shown, nature man believes, that during dreams, fainting-fits, swoons, trance,
and like phenomena, the soul, or other self, is temporarily
absent from the body, hence these unusual experiences.[6]
The Omahas, for example, according to one authority, say,
when a man faints and recovers, that "he died [fainted]
and went to his departed kindred, but no one would speak
to him, so he was obliged to return to life" [to recover

[1] Tylor, "Anthropology," p. 354.
[2] Encyc. Brit. Ninth Edition, Vol. VII, p. 61.
[3] Ibid.
[4] Ibid.
[5] Callaway, "Religious System of the Amazulu," p. 269.
[6] Spencer, "Principles of Sociology," I, pp. 145—152.

consciousness].[1] During the supposed absence of the soul, when the body twitched in a violent manner, and the question was provoked, Why this strange behavior? primitive man gave the best answer he could. He had no idea that a mere subjective state, or a deranged digestion, or a disordered condition of the nerves could produce such an effect. He brought his world philosophy to bear upon the situation, and accounted for the phenomena by affirming that, while the soul of the unfortunate person was away, one of the many inhabitants of the imaginary environment had usurped possession of the body.

If it is within the range of possibility for the soul not only to absent itself from the body, but also to re-enter it, as, for example, in dreams, likewise it must be possible for another spirit to enter the body, torture it, make it sick, and do it even to death. In cases of falling sickness, when the patient fell to the earth, foamed at the mouth, bit his tongue until the blood flowed, and his legs and arms were torn with convulsions, the best reason that the savage could give for such behavior was that the unfortunate individual was possessed by another spirit. His own spirit would not treat his body in such an outrageous manner. One or more of those malevolent beings, therefore, whose name is legion, and who are ubiquitous, must have taken possession of the luckless individual, either to punish for misdemeanors, or maliciously to cause all the suffering possible. Tylor notes that "the history of medicine goes back to the times when epilepsy, or 'seizure' [Greek,

[1] Fletcher-Laflesche, "The Omaha Tribe," Bur. Eth., 1911, p. 589.

ἐπίληψις] was thought to be really the act of a daimon seizing and convulsing the patient."[1] The prevalence of this disease in East Africa is believed by some writers to be responsible for the origin of the daimonistic possession theory.[2]

Primitive peoples explain insanity in a similar manner. Any person who observes the symptoms and conduct of an insane man, acting no longer like himself, seeing with other eyes, and hearing with ears other than has been his wont, will readily comprehend that to the childish mind of the savage, the most natural way of accounting for such phenomena is that of possession by a vicious spirit. And so it is said that the Samoans and Togans believe madness to be caused by the presence of an evil spirit.[3] In Sumatra lunatics are considered possessed.[4]

When one adds to these considerations the fact that an insane person sometimes manifests almost superhuman strength—being able, of and by himself, to defy the efforts of three or four strong men to manage him—the inference is plain that the unlettered and untutored savage must draw upon his philosophy of life for explanation, and believe that a daimon of power and might possesses the body of the ill-fated victim of insanity.[5]

Reasoning from the greater to the lesser, it is not difficult to understand that, since the savage conceives extraordinary mental and physical disorders to be due to

[1] Tylor, "Anthropology," p. 15.
[2] Spencer, "Principles of Sociology," I, p. 227.
[3] Turner, "Nineteen Years in Polynesia," p. 221.
[4] Spencer, "Principles of Sociology," I, p. 230.
[5] Ibid., p. 231.

daimon possession, he must consider disorders of a less violent, though not less fatal kind, to be likewise occasioned. In fever, both physical and mental disturbances are present. According to primitive belief, both are due to the same cause. Since malicious spirits are responsible for one kind of sickness, it follows that in all diseases an ill-disposed daimon has taken possession of the body, venting rage, wreaking revenge, or inflicting punishment upon its temporary habitat.[1] Thus, as already alluded to (p. 8 supra), in the Australian-Tasmanian district, disease is accounted for by the fact that daimons creep into bodies of men and eat up their livers.[2] Among the Dyaks, every kind of sickness is thought to be due to spirit possession. When they inquire of a small-pox victim concerning the state of his health, they ask, "Has he" [that is, the spirit] "left you yet?"[3] After an attack of illness, the Dyaks change their names, so that the daimon who caused the sickness may not recognize them and continue his malignant invasions.[4] Among the Patagonians, every disease is believed to be due to spirit possession.[5] To the Negritos of Zambales, Philippine Islands, all places are filled with spirits, which bring about every sort of adversity —failure of crops, bad luck in hunting, and illness. Before disease can be cured, the spirit that has caused it must be forced out of the body of the sick

[1] Spencer, "Principles of Sociology," I, p. 231.
[2] Grey, "Journal of Two Expeditions of Discovery in Australia," II, p. 337.
[3] St. John, "Life in the Forests of the Far East," I, p. 62.
[4] Ibid., p. 73. [5] D'Orbigny, "L'Homme Americain," p. 93.

man.[1] The Dakotas, according to Schoolcraft, think that
spirits inflict punishment for misconduct. These beings
are able to send the spirit of a bear, deer, turtle, fish,
tree, stone, or dead person into the bodies of the living,
thereby causing disease. The method of the medicine man
as to treatment consists in the recital of charms, and suction applied to the seat of the pain to draw out the spirit.[2]
In the West Indies, at the time of the discovery of America,
a native medicine man affected to extract the disease
daimon from the legs of his patients, and to consign it
to the mountains or to the sea.[3] In Egypt, at the present
time, one must always get permission of the "jinn" or
spirit to pour water on the ground, lest he accidentally
douse a daimon and be smitten with sickness for the
offence.[4] The Land Dyaks believe that spirits cause sickness by wounding their victims with invisible spears.[5]
Among the Matira, all sorts of maladies are thought to
be caused by spirits.[6] Among the Arawaks, pain is called
"the arrow of the evil spirit."[7] In New Zealand, it is
believed that different daimons share amongst themselves
the body of man, and that each daimon undertakes to inflict
pain upon the part committed to him.[8] In Cockayne's
"Saxon Leechdoms" is the following instruction: "Against
a strange (or unnatural) swelling, sing upon thy leech finger

[1] Reed, "Negritos of Zambales," p. 65.
[2] Schoolcraft, "Information Respecting the Indian Tribes of the
United States," Part I, p. 250; Part II, p. 179.
[3] Pinkerton, "Voyages," XII, p. 85.
[4] Encyc. Brit., Eleventh Edition, Vol. VIII, p. 5.
[5] St. John, "Life in the Forests of the Far East," I, p. 178.
[6] Tylor, "Prim. Cult.," II, p. 126.
[7] Brett, "Indian Tribes of Guiana," p. 362.
[8] Black, "Folk Medicine," p. 11.

(third finger) a paternoster, and draw a line about the sore, and say, 'Fuge, diabolus, Christus te sequitur; quando natus est Christus, fugit dolor;' and afterwards say another paternoster, and—'Fuge, diabolus.'" [1]

A common aspect of the spirit notion about disease is that a daimon may steal away the breath, causing the body when separated from the soul to sicken and die. It has already been explained that fainting fits and trance are accounted for by the supposed absence of the soul from the body.[2] In some cases, weakness, failure in health, and death are likewise explained. Thus, among the Fijians, "when anyone faints or dies, his spirit, it is said, may sometimes be brought back by calling after it; and occasionally the ludicrous scene is witnessed of a stout man lying at full length, and bawling out lustily for the return of his own soul."[3] In the Moluccas, when a man is sick, the belief is that some daimon has carried away his soul to hell where the daimon resides.[4] When a Karen becomes sick, languid, and pining because his soul [lå] has left him, his friends with formal prayers invoke the spirit to return.[5] In civilized America, sermons have been preached, within the last twenty-five years, from the alleged Scriptural text: "The first death is the separation of the soul from the body; the second death is the separation of the soul from God."

Another feature of the ghost theory is that disease and death can be invoked by magic, sorcery, or witchcraft.

[1] Cockayne, "Saxon Leechdoms," I, p. 394. [2] Vide pp. 8—9. [3] Williams, "Fiji and the Fijians," I, p. 242. [4] Frazer, "The Golden Bough," I, p. 271. [5] Tylor, "Prim. Cult.," I, p. 395.

According to this notion, the medicine man secures the
assistance of divinities to accomplish his evil purpose, or
controls the spirits in such a way as either to revenge
himself on enemies, or to punish those guilty of insub-
ordination.[1] In order to make more clear the primitive
idea of the power of the medicine man as magician to work
harm, the following cases are cited. The Australians ascribe
sickness to the invisible projection into the body of
substances such as quartz crystals;[2] the Omahas, to
the projection of worms, removable only by magic
formulas.[3] In Samoa, every dangerous sickness, every
accident, and every death was ascribed to sorcery;
and not infrequently suspected persons were murdered,
because it was thought that they had inflicted injuries
on other individuals.[4] To the Cherokees disease
and death are caused by malign influence, whether
of witches, the spirits of animals, or the ghosts
of the departed. Haywood, writing in 1823, states:
"'In ancient times the Cherokees had no conception
of anyone dying a natural death.[5] They universally
ascribed the death of those who perished by disease to
the intervention or agency of evil spirits and witches and
conjurors, who had connexion with the Shina (Anisgi'na)
or evil spirit..... A person dying by disease and charg-
ing his death to have been procured by means of witchcraft or spirits, at the instigation of any other person, con-

[1] Lehmann, "Aberglaube und Zauberei," pp. 21—22.
[2] Howitt, "Australian Medicine Men," J. A. I., XVI, p. 26.
[3] Fletcher-Laflesche, "The Omaha Tribe," Bur. Eth., 1911, p. 583.
[4] Ella, "Samoa," Aust. Ass. for Adv. Science, 1892, p. 638.
[5] Vide pp. 4—5, 120, 167.

signed that person to inevitable death.'" [1] In some tribal
groups, it is believed that if the magician gets possession
of anything belonging to a man—nail-parings, hair, spittle,
a drop of blood—he can inflict on the owner any evil
he chooses. Thus, regarding the Amazulu, Callaway
writes, "Sorcerers are supposed to destroy their victims by taking some portion of their bodies, as hair
or nails, or something that has been worn next
to their person, as a piece of old garment, and adding
to it certain medicines, and then burning the whole in
a secret place." [2] Frazer says that "an Australian girl,
sick of fever, laid the blame of her illness on a young
man who had come behind her, and cut off a lock of her
hair; she was sure he had buried it and it was rotting." [3]
The Tannese think that the burning of the "nahak"—or
rubbish, such as refuse of food—will cause sickness or
death, and they are, therefore, careful always to bury
their "nahak" or throw it into the sea, so that it may not
fall into the hands of their enemies.[4] The sorcerers in the
Marquesan Islands were thought to be able to destroy
a victim by burying his hair, spittle, or bodily refuse,[5]
and the magicians of ancient Peru, it was imagined, could
injure people by working hocus pocus on blood taken
from them.[6]

There is a belief among some primitive peoples that
if a sorcerer learns the name of a person, he can bring

[1] Mooney, "Sacred Formulas of the Cherokees," Bur. Eth., 1891, p. 322.
[2] Callaway, "Religious System of the Amazulu," p. 270.
[3] Frazer, "The Golden Bough," I, p. 377.
[4] Turner, "Nineteen Years in Polynesia," pp. 89—91.
[5] Frazer, "The Golden Bough," I, p. 376.
[6] Spencer, "Principles of Sociology," I, p. 246.

upon that individual all sorts of evil. The Celts and other Aryans thought that the name is not only a part of a man, but the most vital part—his soul or life.[1] The Australians, too, because of this alleged identification of the name with the soul, think that an enemy who knows the name of a person has power to harm him.[2]

The dread of the power of the magician is responsible for some curious notions in Australia. Several tribes believe that wizards can, while a man is asleep, remove the caul-fat from under his short rib, causing him no pain, but effecting his speedy death.[3] Men in the Kernai tribe have died in the belief that an evil power had stolen this fat despite the fact that no marks were to be found on their bodies.[4] Here the fat, like the name, is apparently identified with the soul; hence the notion that by removing the fat the medicine man also removes the soul from the body, which circumstance, as has already been seen, is held to account for sickness and death.[5]

There are primitive notions regarding the causes of misfortunes and calamities, sickness and death, which it is well nigh impossible to classify. Yet it is not difficult to perceive that the ghost theory underlies each of them. When the author resided in the Philippine Islands he learned that the Visayans, fearful, lest the "asuangs" [spirits] should creep into houses and destroy newly born babes, are accustomed to smear the doors and windows of their dwellings with garlic for those invisible enemies

[1] Rhys, "Welsh Fairies," Nineteenth Century, XXX, pp. 568 ff.
[2] Howitt, "Australian Medicine Men," J. A. I., XVI, p. 27 (Note).
[3] Berdoe, "Healing Art," p. 17. [4] Howitt, "Australian Medicine Men," J. A. I., XVI, pp. 53—55. [5] Vide p. 13.

cannot abide its smell. It is held by some nature people that an animal, or the spirit of an animal, can enter the body of a man and affect it for evil;[1] others say that bad winds are causes of sickness;[2] others, water sprites; others, the influence of charms; others, the infringement of the taboo; still others, the withering glance of the "evil eye,"[3] and so on through a well nigh inexhaustible list.

If "supernatural agent" or "agents" be substituted for "daimon" or "daimons," it is evident that the spirit theory of "bad luck," in general, survives in semi-civilized and even in civilized times.[4] In ancient Chaldea, all diseases were accredited to the influence of daimons. That is the reason for Herodotus finding no physicians in Babylon and Assyria. There was nothing scientific about the medicine of those ancient peoples; "it was," as Lenormant has said, "simply a branch of magic, and was practiced by incantations, exorcisms, the use of philters, and enchanted drinks."[5] In Exodus, 15:28, Javeh is declared to visit men with adversity for breach of his commandments. In the first book of the Iliad, all are represented as sick because the daughter of the priest of Apollo had been stolen. The god has sent sickness from the motive of revenge.[6] In India, the goddess of small-pox, "Ma-ry-Umma," is supposed to incarnate herself in the disease. When vaccination was first introduced among the natives of India

[1] Bartels, "Med. Naturvölker," pp. 21—22. [2] Ibid., pp. 41—42. [3] Ibid., pp. 43—44. [4] Spencer, "Principles of Sociology," I, p. 232. [5] Lenormant, "Chaldean Magic," p. 35. [6] Keller, "Homeric Society," p. 180.

they objected on the ground that the deity might be offended, since for people to render themselves immune to small-pox would imply an objection to her becoming incarnate among them.[1] Among the Tartars, all sickness is caused by a visitation of a "Tchutgour" or daimon, and the first duty of the physician is to exorcise the daimon.[2] Pythagoras taught that the air was full of spirits, which were responsible for disease and death.[3] Among the Romans, the Laws of the Twelve Tables contained the provision that no man should by incantation conjure away the crop of grain of another person.[4] The ancient Britons, thinking that all diseases proceeded from the wrath of the gods, found their only help in beseeching the priests to intercede for them.[5]

Throughout the Middle Ages belief in daimons, witch-craft, and supernatural agents as disease provokers abounded. John of Gaddeson (cir. 1290), an Oxford man, and a court physician, for example, prescribed for epilepsy that the patient, after fasting, confession, attendance at mass, and after special prayers by the priest, wear around his neck the text of Scripture, "This kind goeth not out but by prayer and fasting."[6]

The ravages of syphilis, which swept over Europe towards the latter part of the fourteenth century, were considered a scourge used by God to punish men and turn them away from unrighteous living.[7]

---

[1] Paris, "Pharmacologia," I. p. 32. [2] Huc, "Travels in Tartary," I, pp. 75—76. [3] Berdoe, "Healing Art," p. 162. [4] Encyc. Brit., Article, "Witchcraft," Ninth Edition, Vol. XXIV, p. 619. [5] Strutt, "Chronicles of England," I, p. 279. [6] Berdoe, "Healing Art," p. 237. [7] Roswell Park, "An Epitome of the History of Medicine," p. 136.

Aubrey records a favorite remedy which was used in the sixteenth century for sweating sickness. "Say every day, at seven parts of your body, seven paternosters, and seven Ave Marias, with one Credo at the last."[1] Here the ghost theory is clearly implied, for supernatural aid is sought as a means of recovery. In 1604, a law of the English Church forbade the clergy to cast out devils without a special license from the bishop;[2] and the belief that people were possessed by evil spirits continued far into the eighteenth century. That the daimonistic theory prevailed in America throughout the entire colonial period, the hanging of alleged witches in Salem, Massachusetts, in 1692, is but one of many proofs. Even today, misfortune, sickness, and death are often ascribed to spirit agency. Peters writes: "An eminent professor of medical jurisprudence in an American college, in October 1888, publicly stated that insanity of the sexual perversion type was an evidence of possession of the devil."[3] Not infrequently the belief is expressed that people who are killed while on Sunday excursions or boating trips meet their deaths as a result of divine vengeance for breaking the Sabbath, and this belief has only an altered idea of the supernatural being to distinguish it from the superstitions of savage tribes.[4]

The present day theory of disease is that of the invasion of the body by devils—that is adversaries—or

[1] Aubrey, "History of England," II, p. 296.
[2] Lee, "Glimpses of the Supernatural," I, p. 65.
[3] Peters, "Pictorial Pharmacy," p. 128.
[4] Spencer, "Principles of Sociology," I, p. 234.

germs of animal and vegetable rather than of supernatural origin, not necessarily with any malicious intent, but driven by nature to seek for substance whereby to repair waste energy. Various ways of access to the usurped abode are utilized by these parasites—the water drunk, the food eaten, the air breathed, and the proboscides of insects. It remains for future generations to discover exactly how far on the road to truth the theory of the twentieth century has advanced beyond that of the savage.

SUMMARY. Man, the reasoning and speaking animal, reacted differently from all other forms of life against a similar environment, and was led by the ills of existence to reflection. In some cases the agent of his woes was visible—the falling tree, or the club of an enemy. Reasoning from analogy, nature man believed himself to be justified in assuming that all calamities were due to agency. The agents being in many cases invisible did not alter the fact. This opinion was re-affirmed by dreams, in which an implacable ancestor or an inveterate enemy assured the sleeper that the relationship between them had not been changed by death. Man thus arrived at the idea of another world, which in every respect duplicates the present world. The savage, in other words, constructed in his own mind the idea of an imaginary environment, the inhabitants of which are the ghosts and spirits of the dead. These spiritual beings possess the same dispositions, passions, and animosities as when living. To the ghostly inhabitants of the other world nature man refers the agency of "bad luck." In order to present in a concrete manner the primitive explanation of "bad luck" in general, a typical example was taken, that particular form of misfortune about which, more than any other, men have thought, theorized, and speculated, namely, the existence of disease and death. It was found, on the whole, that the primitive theory of sickness and death is that of spirit possession. This belief takes a variety of forms. In some cases the evil is ascribed to the ghosts of the dead. In other instances a fully developed spiritual being is thought to have taken up its abode in the body of the victim for the purpose of tormenting him; in others still it is imagined that a sorcerer has subsidized a malignant spirit to work his evil purposes; and, once more, the "evil eye," the spirit of an animal, the entrance of bones, pebbles, splinters, or quartz crystals into the body are believed to be responsible for the destruction of life. The ghost theory survived throughout barbaric and far into civilized times. It is not entirely extinct at the present day.

Primitive notions regarding other-worldliness, the imaginary environment, and the aleatory element have been discussed somewhat at length for the reason that it would not be possible to understand the character and evolution of shamanism without first bringing the background into perspective. Given this proper foundation, however, the religion of primitive peoples, as well as the nature, evolution, and social influence of the medicine man can be readily comprehended.

CHAPTER II

THE MAKING OF THE MEDICINE MAN.

It was pointed out in the preceding chapter that when pain and misfortune were experienced by primitive man, and the question provoked, Who did this? his philosophy of life furnished the ready answer that he might thank the malevolent inhabitants of the unseen world for his ills, woes, and losses. Childish as such an explanation may appear, it furnished the starting-point for systematic thinking.

The second question provoked by painful experience was, Why are the gods angry, and what must be done to induce them to cease their inimical actions? The life philosophy of the savage here again supplied the "proper" answer.[1]

If it be borne in mind that in primitive thought the unseen world duplicates this world; that its inhabitants live as men live here; that they have the same wants, likes, and dislikes; that, in short, they are anthropomorphic beings possessing in an intensified degree the same attributes as before their deification,[2] it will not be difficult to understand that the various ways of dealing with the inhabitants of the imaginary environment, though they vary

---

[1] Sumner, "Folkways," pp. 30—31.
[2] Keller, "Societal Evolution," p. 60, and p. 260; also, cf. pp. 5—6 of this work.

according to the conception entertained by the weaker contestant respecting the nature and character of his adversary, are analogous to methods of dealing between man and man.[1]

Since ghosts and spirits are first conceived of as assuming an hostile attitude toward man,[2] it naturally follows that ways first adopted of dealing with them are identical with methods of dealing with mundane foes. When an enemy in the form of flesh and blood occasions trouble and disaster by reason of his rancorous conduct, the natural thing is to combat him. In like manner, when a malevolent spirit is responsible for misfortune, the normal course of procedure is to attempt to compel the spiritual enemy to cease its hostile attacks. And so it happens that various methods of exorcism are devised. In sickness, for example, nature man tries to frighten the daimon of disease by horrible noises, by threats and grimaces; or to disgust it by making the body a disagreeable habitat by means of fumigation or violent ill-treatment; or to expel it by the use of amulets and charms or by the recital of incantations. But the ordinary individual distrusts his ability, single-handed and alone, to deal with the superior powers of the unseen world. The consequence is that generally he will delegate this task to some person possessed of greater wisdom, knowledge, and power. And among savage peoples, the man who gains repute for dealing successfully with

[1] Spencer, "Principles of Sociology," III, p. 38.
[2] Lippert, "Kulturgeschichte," I. pp. 108 ff.

ghosts and spirits is an important personage. Sumner in support of what has just been said quotes the following striking passage from Michailowski: "Uncivilized people, who live under the immediate influence of nature and of blind chance, are interested above all in the means of escaping evil fortune and propitiating the forces of evil. They want protection from drought, lightning, storm, disease, death, and enemies. Not all can attain the means of winning good, and averting ill. Some persons are endowed with the requisite knowledge, and are thus fitted to be intercessors between their fellow men and the unknown powers. These are the shamans and their art is shamanism. The more developed the people the better defined is the position of the shamans, and the more systematic is the organization of shamanism. Although the system thus covers a wide range of civilization, yet the philosophy of life included in it has broad, common features." [1]

The name of the mediator between gods and men differs among different peoples. He is variously called the shaman, the angakok, the voudoo-man, the obi-man, the conjurer, the magician, the wizard, and the sorcerer, —to mention only a few of his many titles. For the sake of simplicity and clearness, however, he is here called "The Medicine Man." That was the appellation employed by the North American Indians to designate the representative of the unseen world, and it signifies "Mystery Man." In the life and thought of the aborigines of this country, anything

---

[1] Michailowski, "Shamanstvo," (Russian) Quoted from the Sumnerian Collections.

sacred, mysterious, or of wonderful power or efficacy is called "medicine". "Medicine," therefore, in the savage sense includes clairvoyance, ecstasism, spiritism, divination, demonology, prophecy, necromancy, and all things incomprehensible. Hence the medicine man is not only the primitive doctor, but he is the diviner, the rain-maker, the soothsayer, the prophet, the priest, and, in some instances, the chief or king.[1] He is in short the great man of primitive times.

Who is this important individual? What are his qualifications, and what is his training for office? What are the secrets of his power? What forces unite in his making? What is the method of his induction into office? These and similar questions suggest themselves in connexion with the present study, and apposite answers are necessary to an intelligent comprehension of shamanism.

In discussing the making of the medicine man, it may be set down, in the first place, that in a goodly number of instances his office comes to him by heredity. This is true of the Zulus and Bechuanas of South Africa;[2] of the Nez Percés, the Cayuse, the WallaWallas, and the Wascows, in America; and of some of the peoples of Siberia.[3] Among the Omahas, those who imparted religious instructions to the tribe formed a sort of hereditary priesthood, since this office devolved upon the elders, who usually were of the number eligible for the position of keeper.[4] The Navahoes on the other hand, following not

---

[1] Vide pp. 132—150. [2] Bartels, "Med. Naturvölker," p. 75. [3] Ibid.
[4] Fletcher-Laflesche, "The Omaha Tribe," Bur. Eth., 1911, p. 595.

a law but general custom, made the youngest son the
hatáli, or medicine man, on the ground that he possessed
more intellect and a better memory than any other member
of the family.[1] Of the Peruvians, Dorman writes that the
priestly office appears to have been hereditary,[2] and hereditary in families was the doctorship among the Dyaks[3]
and, to a certain extent, the priesthood of Nagualism.[4]
The power of the sorcerer in the New Hebrides,[5] like
the office of medicine man among the Guanas of Paraguay,[6]
was supposed to descend from father to son. Chiefly
hereditary, too, are the positions among the Pima Indians
of the "examining physicians" who are summoned in cases
of sickness, and of whom there are as many women as
men.[7] The post of shaman among the Chimariko
Indians, on the contrary, while it might be held by both
men and women, might or might not be hereditary,[8] and likewise, among the Negritos of Zambales, Philippine Islands,
admittance to the profession of medicine man might be
gained by one who had cured the sick, as well as by a member of the regular family of the "mediquillos" [doctors].[9]
But by the Saoras the power of the *kudang,* the man

---

[1] Matthews ,"The Night Chant, A Navaho Ceremony," Memoirs
American Museum of Nat. Hist. (Notes), p. 312.
[2] Dorman, "Primitive Superstitions," p. 384.
[3] Roth, "Natives of Sarawak and British North Borneo," I, p. 260.
[4] Brinton, "Nagualism," p. 29.
[5] Aust. Ass. for Adv. Science, 1892, p. 711.
[6] Hassler, "Die Bewohner des Gran Chaco," Internat. Cong. of
Anthrop., 1894, p. 356.
[7] Russell, "Pima Indians," Bur. Eth., XXVI, p. 256.
[8] Dixon, "The Chimariko Indians and Language," University of
California Publications in American Archeology and Ethnology, V, p. 303.
[9] Reed, "Negritos of Zambales," p. 66.

who held intercourse with spirits, was considered hereditary, not to be acquired by any one outside of the chosen
family.[1]

The notion of a divine call to the work of representing
heaven on earth is not peculiar to any one age, race,
religion, or state of civilization. Some savage peoples
believe in the necessity and reality of such a "call" as firmly
and as uncompromisingly as do the exponents of certain sects adhering to the Christian religion. The natives
of Victoria, for example, think that the spirits of deceased
ancestors search out those whom they desire to act as
medicine men. They meet them in the bush and instruct
them in all the arts needful for making them influential
in their tribe.[2] Among the Bilquila of northwest Canada,
the "chosen" fall into a sickness during which the gods
communicate to them an exorcising formula which they
must never divulge.[3] Kropf relates that the Kaffir medicine
man is called to his office by the supernatural powers, and
receives medical knowledge by revelation of the spirits.[4]
In some cases the peculiar behavior of a young man
is indicative of the fact that he has received the "call."
When a vague and indescribable longing seizes him, or a
morbid appetite possesses him, or he falls prey to an
unappeasable and aimless restlessness or a causeless
melancholy, the old men recognize these signs as the
expressions of a personal spirit of the highest order.

[1] J. A. Soc. of Bombay, I, p. 247.
[2] Bartels, "Med. Naturvölker," p. 76.
[3] Ibid.
[4] Ibid.

It not infrequently happens that fond and ambitious parents consecrate one or more of their children to the service of the gods. In some countries every family devotes a son to religious celibacy. On the Gold Coast, if several children die, sometimes the mother vows to devote the next born to the holy office, thinking that then it may live.[1] Among the Tibetans, Bishop writes, "a younger son in every household becomes a monk, and occasionally enters upon his vocation as an acolyte pupil as soon as weaned. At the age of thirteen these acolytes are sent to study at Lhassa for five or seven years."[2] Among the Western Iniots, the priests in office choose young children whom they train to be medicine men. Sometimes, even before a child is born, they will ask its parents to devote it to the sacred office. These parents must then fast, and pray to their ancestors to care for the future shaman. As soon as the child is born he is sprinkled with urine, and then his training begins. He is brought up to be unlike other children in speech, manner, and conduct, and with the title, "He who has been set apart," is led to believe and proclaim that he is made of different clay from the most of mankind. The neophyte is compelled to fast, to indulge in long and dreary vigils, thereby keeping his body under and bringing it into subjection, in order that it may without complaint obey the dictates of the mind and will.[3]

[1] Ellis, "Tshi-Speaking Peoples," pp. 120—121.
[2] Bishop, "Among the Tibetans," p. 88.
[3] Reclus, "Primitive Folk," p. 71.

When the author was living in the Philippine Islands, he heard that a few years earlier, in a barrio [village] some miles south of Manila, a famous "spit doctor" gained considerable notoriety by reason of his so-called wonderful cures. His account of the way he became a doctor is that one day while walking in the San Mateo mountains he became tired, and lay down at the foot of a tree to rest and refresh himself. Sleep overtook him, and a being with long, white whiskers appeared in a dream. After having made a few mysterious "passes," the ghostly visitor addressed him after this fashion: "Enchong, you are appointed chief doctor in these islands, and by virtue of this appointment you are empowered to heal all the sick that seek your aid. Spit on them, and you will secure their eternal gratitude." Returning to his native barrio, Enchong told everybody in the neighborhood of his dream, and the report soon spread abroad that his novel method of the treatment of disease by rubbing the sick with his saliva was infallible. In a short time the road leading to the house of Enchong was congested with carretelas [one-horse vehicles used by poorer classes], and not infrequently with conveyances of richer folk, crowded with sick persons, seeking the house of the doctor. When the civil authorities, however, became aware of the existence in their midst of that primitive method of the treatment of disease, they declared Enchong to be an insane person, and committed him to an asylum. And while the older inhabitants of Manila and vicinity continue to believe in the magical power of Enchong and his kind, it would seem that the younger generation, in part at least, have outgrown that kind and degree of superstition, for the Tagalog youth laughingly refer to him as "Doctor Laway," —Tagalog for "Doctor Spit."

On the Gold Coast, says Ellis, "the knowledge of the mysteries of the gods and their service is transmitted from generation to generation of priests; and their number is constantly being recruited by persons who voluntarily devote themselves, or are devoted by their relatives or masters, to the profession."[1]

From the accounts of travellers and other observers are to be obtained at first hand notions of nature people themselves as to the ways in which their medicine men are made. In Australia, for example, in the Makjarawaint branch of the Watgo nation, the necessary qualification for entering the calling of shaman was for an individual to be able to see the ghost of his mother sitting beside her grave. A boy thus talented would be taken in hand by a medicine man, smoked with cherry leaves, smeared with red ochre and grease, and otherwise prepared for his future work.[2] A medicine man of the Yakuts tells that he entered his profession through chance. He built a fire on the grave of a distinguished Tungus *shaman,* and the spirit of the dead took possession of him.[3] Miss Kingsley describes at length the process of shaman-making found in the Calabar region. "Every freeman," she writes, "has

[1] Ellis, "Tshi-Speaking Peoples," p. 120.
[2] Howitt, "South East Australia," p. 404.
[3] Sumner, "Yakuts," Abridged from the Russian of Sieroshevski, J. A. I., XXXI, p. 103.

to pass through the secret society of his tribe.. If, during this education, the elders of the society discover that a boy is what is called 'ebumtup'—that is, a person who can see spirits—he is usually apprenticed, as it were, to a witch doctor. He takes up his studies and learns the difference between the dream soul and the one in which 'sisa' are kept—a mistake between the two would be on par with mistaking oxalic acid for Epsom salts. He then is taught to howl in a professional way, and, by watching his professor, picks up his bedside manner. If he can acquire a showy way of having imitation epileptic fits, so much the better. In fact, as a medical student he has to learn—well, as much there as here. He must know the dispositions, the financial position, the little scandals, in short, the definite status of the inhabitants of the whole district, for these things are of undoubted use in divination and in the finding of witches, and, in addition, he must be able skilfully to dispense charms, and know what babies say before their own mothers can. Then some day his professor and instructor dies, and upon the pupil descend his paraphernalia and his practice." [1]

The sight of the unusual and unfamiliar fills the savage with feelings of awe. Whatever thing he cannot comprehend, whatever man he finds remarkable, he regards as supernatural.[2 & 3] The people of the twentieth century attribute physical or intellectual greatness to quality

[1] Kingsley, "West African Studies," p. 214.
[2] Schoolcraft, "Information Respecting Indian Tribes of the United States," III, p. 248; IV, p. 642.
[3] Winterbottom, "Account of the Native Africans in Sierra Leone," I, p. 222.

of brain fibre, or to genius; the savage, to spirit possession.
The Chippeways thus call anything that they cannot
understand, or anyone of their fellows who is unusual,
a "spirit." [1] Any capacity of an individual—physical or
mental—with which primitive man is not familiar,
causes him to regard the person with such peculiarities as
one possessed either by the spirit of a dead shaman, or
by a spirit of a departed ancestor, or by some other of the
myriad inhabitants of the unseen world.

The divergencies from normal, physical, and mental,
which various peoples have regarded as indications
of divinity, are many. Albinos, for instance, to some
savage races seem chosen by nature for the office of
priest. [2] There have been zealous advocates of Christianity,
of whom Origen, the celebrated Father of the Greek
Church, is the classical example, [3] who have made themselves eunuchs, taking literally the words of Christ: "If
thy right eye offend thee, pluck it out and cast it from
thee: for it is profitable for thee that one of thy members
should perish, and not that thy whole body should be cast
into hell." [4] But that there are persons of diseased
imaginations in all varieties of religious beliefs, stages of
culture, and physical and mental environments, is evidenced
by the fact that desexualization is sometimes regarded as
a necessary concomitant of religious authority. Castration

---

[1] Buchanan, "History, Manners and Customs of North American
Indians," p 228
[2] Bourke, "Medicine Men of the Apache," Bur. Eth. IX,
p. 460
[3] Newman, "Church History," Vol. I. pp. 280—282
[4] St. Matt. 19 : 12.

was required, for example, of the priests of Cybele;[1] and the *manang bali* of the Sea Dyaks, though a man, was garbed in the dress of a woman.[2]

Some peculiarity of circumstances of birth, or some especial mark of distinction—anything that differentiates a man from his fellows—may point to the fact that he has been chosen of heaven to represent it on earth. In Liberia, twins are regarded as especially designed for the office of medicine man. In Nias, those born feet first are considered specialists in cases of sprain.[3] In Korea, a blind son is a satisfaction to his parents, since he may become one of the *p a n - s u*, or sorcerers, and be assured of a comfortable living.[4] Among the Sea Dyaks, those who are blind and incurably maimed often support themselves by entering the priesthood.[5] Roth writes concerning those people: "I have now a blind man living with me. I had heard that the *manangs*, or spirit doctors, wanted to get hold of him, so one day I asked him if he really was going to become a *manang*. He replied, 'Yes, I suppose so; but if I had only my eyesight, catch me becoming a *manang.*'"[6]

Sometimes a person gains admittance to the goodly company of the elect by what may be called a process of natural selection. Thus a Pima Indian, in order to be-

[1] Depuis, "Origine de Tous les Cultes," II, part 2, pp. 87—88.
[2] Roth, "Natives of Sarlawak and British North Borneo," p. 270.
[3] Bartels, "Med. Naturvöker," p. 75.
[4] Bishop, "Korea," p. 402.
[5] Roth, "Natives of Sarawak and British North Borneo," I, p. 265.
[6] Ibid.

come a medicine man, had only to recover from a rattle-
snake bite on the hand or near the heart.[1] Similar was the
manner of selection in the case of a medicine man of the
aborigines of Victoria. This man fell to the ground from a
great height as a result of sitting on the portion of a
branch that he was cutting from a tree; but he escaped injury, and was rewarded for his stupidity by being made
a shaman.[2] In these cases it may be clearly seen that the
reason assigned by primitive peoples for the apparently
miraculous escapes is that of spirit protection or spirit
possession.

In the "Yakuts" of Sieroshevski is to be found a
description of the medicine men of that people which no
one can read without being impressed with their physical
peculiarities, and after reading he will cease, in a measure
at least, to wonder that the uncritical nature man should
regard these religious leaders as being possessed by the
gods. One of those persons "was sixty years old, of middle
stature, a dried-up muscular man, although it was evident
that he had once been vigorous and active. Even when
seen, he could still perform shamanistic rites, jump and
dance the whole night through without being weary.
His countenance was dark and full of active expression.
The pupil of his eye was surrounded by a double ring of
dull, green color. When he was practicing his magic, his
eyes took on a peculiar, unpleasant, dull glare, and an
expression of idiocy, and the persistent stare excited and

---

[1] Russell, "Pima Indians," Bur. Eth., XXVI, p. 257.
[2] Brough Smith, "Aborigines of Victoria," p. 465.

disturbed those upon whom he fixed it." [1] "Another *shaman*," says the same writer, "who was observed, had the same peculiarities of the eyes. In general, there is in the appearance of a *shaman* something peculiar, which enabled the author after some practice to distinguish him with great certainty in the midst of a number of persons. He is distinguished by a certain energy and mobility of the muscles of the face, which generally among the Yakuts are immobile. There is also in his movements a noticeable spryness." [2]

If the savage regards the physically abnormal as due to spirit possession, with what feelings of awe must he regard the mentally abnormal? He knows nothing of the laws of natural causation; it never occurs to him that the body has power over the mind, and that the mind in turn affects the body. With him skepticism and criticism are but slightly if at all developed; and he has not enough curiosity to prompt inquiry. The theory of natural causation necessitates growth, multiplication of arts, accumulation of experience, and familiarization, registration, and recognition of constant relations of phenomena. All this is not possible among primitive societies. For mental abnormality, therefore, nature man can do nothing but rely upon his world philosophy to furnish the "proper" explanation. This is the same as that assigned for the physically abnormal—the individual in whom are manifested unusual powers is regarded as a fetich, and hence is looked

---

1 Sumner, "Yakuts," Abridged from the Russian of Sieroshevski, J. A. I., XXXI, p. 102.
2 Ibid.

upon with feelings of respect, wonder, and veneration. Thus it happens that a man who is subjected to disorders of a strange and impressive character is sometimes chosen for a medicine man. Among the Patagonians, for example, patients seized with falling sickness were immediately selected for magicians, since they were believed to be chosen by the spirits themselves, who possessed, distorted, or convulsed them.[1] In Samoa, the office of medicine man was often held by hunchbacks or epileptics.[2] Ehrenreich says of the Karayá Indians of Brazil, "'Any one can become a medicine man who will present the necessary qualifications. Nervous persons, epileptics, and the like are regarded as especially adapted to the work.'"[3] The *shamanesses* of the Tungus were those who in girlhood had been addicted to a kind of foolish melancholy."[4] The priests of the Tshi-speaking peoples, according to Ellis, simulate convulsions and foaming at the mouth to give the idea of possession by a god. "Indeed," he continues, "all sickness is believed to be caused by superhuman agents who enter the body; but in the case, say, of an epileptic seizure, the natives have what they consider the strongest evidence of this. Consequently, the priests, in order to convey to the public the idea that a god has entered the body, simulate, as well as they can, the symptoms of a person in a fit."[5]

---

[1] Falkner, "Description of Patagonia," p. 117.
[2] Ella, "Samoa," Aust. Ass. for Adv. Science, 1892, p. 638.
[3] Bartels, "Med. Naturvölker," p. 179.
[4] Ibid.
[5] Ellis, "Tshi-Speaking Peoples," p. 148.

While it is true that men of inferior mental powers are sometimes chosen to represent the spirits, yet the medicine men wielding the greatest influence—an influence making for progress and advancement—have been individuals of intellectual parts. At Delphi, for example, Apollo was thought to speak through the mouths of feeble girls and women as a sign that it is no human wisdom and art that reveals the divine will. The mutterings of the priestess, however, were taken down and interpreted by attendant priests. Those priests were men of intelligence, and it was because of their activity in directing the placing of Greek colonies that civilization owes its lasting debt to the Delphian oracle.[1]

When a man of great intelligence adds to his mental resources an unusual fund of acquired knowledge and culture, the effect upon the savage mind is greatly intensified. In order to retain and augment his hold upon the people, the medicine man is under constant stimulus to acquire the ability to perform feats and effect results which exceed the ability of his constituents to achieve or even to understand. The consequence is that the attitude of the people toward him is that of reverence—which attitude is generally that of ignorance toward knowledge.

The unusual intellectual and physical phenomena exhibited by the medicine men excite not only awe, but fear. Among some peoples, it is said that it was the custom of ordinary individuals to fall flat upon their faces before the shaman. Other writers state that the fear of the medicine man is so great that in undoubted and repeated

[1] Meyers, "Ancient History," p. 179.

instances his curse kills as certainly as a knife. Among the Western Indians of this country, when a medicine man utters a withering curse on his antagonist, the latter knows that all hope is lost. Sometimes he drops dead on the spot.[1] Some Australian tribes believe that the curse of a powerful medicine man will kill at a distance of one hundred miles.[2]

As has been said already (p. 10 supra), primitive men attribute insanity to spirit possession. This disease of the brain, while perhaps most prevalent among civilized races, occurs as well among barbaric and savage tribes. But nature man knows nothing about brain diseases. No words in his vocabulary express such ideas. He explains the phenomena of insanity, therefore, in the easiest possible way, that is to say by the time-honored theory of ghost possession. When he sees an individual lying prostrate, refusing to eat, speaking to some one whom the bystanders cannot see, shrinking with terror from an invisible foe, talking nonsense incoherently, laughing without cause, the obvious inference is that one of those invisible spirits, of which the air is full, has taken up its residence in the body of the man.[3] That in Sumatra lunatics are considered possessed (p. 10 supra) is not surprising,[4] nor that in some parts of the eastern hemisphere madness is tantamount to inspiration.[5] The ancient Hebrews believed their prophets to be inspired. In

[1] Brinton, "Myths of the New World," p. 318.
[2] Curr, "The Australian Race," II, p. 610.
[3] Spencer, "Principles of Sociology," I, p. 229.
[4] Marsden, "History of Sumatra," p. 191.
[5] "Rambles in the Deserts of Syria," p. 190.

the ninth chapter of the second book of Kings there is to
be found the story of the anointing of Jehu as king of
Israel. Elisha commissions a young prophet to perform
that office, after which he is to pronounce a curse upon
the house of Ahab. After obeying the behest of his
master, the prophet is said to have fled from the house in
which the anointing took place. "Then Jehu came forth
to the servants of his lord; and one said unto him, 'Is all
well? wherefrom came this *mad* fellow to thee?' And he
said unto them, 'Ye know the man and his commission.'" [1]
Comment is unnecessary as to the connexion in ancient
Jewish thought between insanity and inspiration. The
word "huaka" in the Quichua language is the general term
for the divine. "Huaka runa" signifies the divine man, and
means one who is crazy.[2] Cook writes of meeting two
insane persons—a man at Owhyhee, and a woman at
Oneeheow—who, as was obvious by the attention paid
them, were regarded in that part of the country as inspired
by a god.[3]

Since an insane man differs from others because of the
indwelling of spirits, who in all the land is better fitted
to plead the cause of mortals with the gods? True, his
ways are different from the ways of other persons, but so
are the ways of the gods. The very fact, therefore, that an
insane person is unlike other men is proof positive that he
is by nature paramount. Being by virtue of his own divinity

[1] II Kings, 9:1—11.
[2] Middendorf, "Wörterbuch des Runa simi oder der Keshua Sprache."
[3] Cook, "Third Voyage," III, p. 131.

on intimate terms with the gods, and possessing a knowledge of their nature and disposition, he is excellently equipped for devising ways and means of procuring celestial benefactions. That this kind of reasoning often results in the elevation of a person who in popular esteem is mad to the highest position in the tribe may be inferred from an observation of Bartels to the following effect: "Through his shrewdness and turning to account of accidents, the medicine man manages to maintain his ascendency. Among the Baksa he is said to feign madness in order to give the impression that he is possessed by spirits."[1]

The medicine man not infrequently is a victim of hysteria. In this malady of the major description the patient gives vent to meaningless laughs, sobs, and cries. He often lies stretched out at full length, his hands clasped, his eyes closed, his body curved by a spasm. He may extend his hands supinely in an attitude of appealing terror, clutch spasmodically at the ground, shrink from some unseen enemy, fall back exhausted, nerveless, and to all appearances insensible. On recovery from the attack he is himself again with no recollection of what has occurred.[2] Modern science attributes these phenomena to "the loss of complete control exercised by the higher nervous centers, due partly to insufficient or inappropriate nutrition and partly to faulty development."[3] But the savage knows nothing of the science of neurology. To him the reason for what is now known as hysteria is spirit

[1] Bartels, "Med. Naturvölker," p. 52.
[2] Ellis, "Man and Woman," p. 322.
[3] Ibid.

possession. When an individual is subject to these attacks—performing actions without willing it, or even in spite of his will—it is because a spirit has entered his body, either temporarily or permanently, setting aside his own mind and will, and assuming complete control over the entire man. The desire of the spirits for the one so possessed to devote his life to their service would thereby be indicated. If the devotee is obedient to the divine decision, he will have no trouble in making full proof of his ministry. The native sorcerer of Tasmania is reported by Backhouse to be affected with fits of spasmodic contraction of the muscles of one breast, a malady which sufficed to prove to his people that he was inspired.[1] Among the Amazulu, hysterical symptoms are counted as indications that the *imyanga*, or diviner, is inspired,[2] and possessed "by the 'Amatongo,' or ancestral spirits." [3]

The gods or ancestral spirits make known their will to favorites in dreams. One of the most convincing proofs of spirit intercourse is the ability to dream dreams, and to put upon those dreams the proper interpretation. If a man can do this, he will have no trouble in establishing his right to be called a medicine man. And so we read that among the Dieyerie of South Australia, boys who dream of seeing the devil are regarded as especially fitted to become medicine men.[4] A medicine man among the Pima Indians adopted his profession because of frequent dreams

---

[1] Backhouse, "Australia," p. 103.
[2] Callaway, "Religious Systems of the Amazulu," p. 185.
[3] Ibid., pp. 183—259.
[4] Bartels, "Med. Naturvölker," p. 76.

that he had been visited by some one who endowed him with magic power.[1] The Mincopies believe that the medicine man has communion with the unseen powers through dreams, and in that way is able to look upon the spirits of the ancestors of a sick man.[2] In East Africa, the medicine man dreams his dream, and then gives forth oracles at intervals according to the exigencies of the case; sometimes they are delivered in a frenzied state.[3] Among the Land Dyaks, according to Henry Ling Roth, "there are two descriptions of *manangs*,—the regular and the irregular. The regular are those who have been called to that vocation by dreams, and to whom the spirits have revealed themselves. The irregular are self-created and without a familiar spirit." [4] And Dixon writes of the Chimariko Indians, "The sign that a person was destined to become a shaman was a series of dreams. These were in the case of a man often the result of solitary visits to remote mountain lakes, in which the person would bathe at dusk. In these dreams instructions were given the neophyte by various supernatural beings, and these directions must be followed exactly." [5]

It is not possible for the shaman to inspire confidence unless he produces palpable evidence that the gods are on his side. But it not uncommonly happens that a man

[1] Russell, "Pima Indians," Bur. Eth., XXVI, p. 257.
[2] Bartels, "Med. Naturvölker," p. 51.
[3] MacDonald, "East Central African Customs," J. A. I., XXII, p. 105.
[4] Roth, "Natives of Sarawak and British North Borneo," I, p. 266.
[5] Dixon, "The Chimariko Indians and Language." University of Calif. Publications in American Archeology and Ethnology. V, p. 303.

aspires to office who has no physical or mental peculiarity to indicate that a spirit dwells within him. The
only recourse in such a contingency is simulation. The
savage is not acquainted with such ideas as "suggestion,"
"auto-suggestion," "hypnotism," and "self-hypnotism."
The medicine man nevertheless often unconsciously makes
use of these phenomena in the practice of his profession. He
does not deliberately say, "Go to, I will now proceed to
hypnotize myself, and thereby cause the people to think
that I am possessed," but, in effect, that is frequently
the very thing he unwittingly does, for possessed he must
be or seem to be.

Sometimes the shaman induces auto-suggestion by staring or gazing at an object. In the Fiji Islands, the priest sits
amid complete silence looking at an ornament made of
the tooth of a whale. Tylor describes his actions: "In a
short time he begins to tremble, slight twitchings of the
face and limbs follow; these increase to strong convulsions,
with swelling of the veins, murmurs, and sobs. Now the
god has entered him, and with eyes rolling and protruding,
voice unnatural, face pale, lips livid, perspiration streaming
from every pore, and the whole aspect of a furiously insane
person, he speaks the will of the gods, and then, the
symptoms subsiding, he looks around with a vacant stare
and becomes himself again."[1]

Among other means which the medicine man uses to
induce the hypnotic state may be named the prolonged
hearing of the same note or rhythmic chord, the concen-

[1] Tylor, "Prim. Cult.," II, p. 134.

tration of the mind on one thought, the monotonous repe-
tition of words; silences, darkness, solitude; continuance of
the same motion; association with persons already under
hypnotic influence. Among the Singpho of Southeast Asia,
the medicine man invokes his "nat" or spirit for assistance.[1] In Patagonia, he induces a real or pretended fit
by drumming or rattling.[2] In Guiana, the method of
producing inspiration was somewhat heroic. The
servant of the gods was forced to endure fasting and
flagellations of extreme severity. Then he was compelled
to dance until he fell to the ground, exhausted and
senseless. In order to revive him, a draught of tobacco
juice, which caused violent nausea and vomiting of blood,
was administered. This treatment was kept up day after
day, until the subject dreamed dreams, saw visions, was
seized with convulsions, or gave incontrovertible evidence that the spirits of the heavenly regions had taken
possession of him.[3] It is very perceptible that practices of
this kind act upon the mind in such a manner as entirely
to alter its ordinary habits.

Trance and ecstasy are two aids of the medicine man
to claims of divinity. In ecstasy there is a certain want of
muscular control, and the mind is actively employed in
seeing visions; during trance the countenance expresses
an inspired illumination of a more than earthly character,
and, on waking, the subject is able to recall his visions.

[1] Bastian, "Östl. Asien," II, p. 328.
[2] Falkner, "Patagonians," p. 116.
[3] Meiners, "Geschichten der Religionen," II, p. 162.

An habitual means of inducing the ecstatic state is by drugs. Among all peoples some knowledge of narcotics used to bring about strange and vivid hallucinations is found.[1] The priests of ancient Mexico employed an ointment or a drink made with the seeds of *olloliuhqui* which induced visions and delirium.[2] Among the Commis of Central Africa, the medicine man drinks *mboundou*.[3] The negroes of the Niger had their "fetich-water;" the Creek Indians of Florida had their "black drink;"[4] the *Kalingas* of northern Luzon, Philippine Islands, have their *base*. In some parts of Mexico the natives took the *peyotl*, and the snake plant.[5] The Japanese have their *sake;* the Africans, from Egypt down to Zanzibar, have their *bussa*, which is the well-known hydromel, made from honey and water. The Samoyeds of Siberia, and some tribes of California used the poisonous toadstool. In other parts of California the *chacuaco* was employed for this purpose.[6] Among the Walapai of Arizona, the medicine men drank a "decoction of the leaves, roots, and flowers of the 'datura stramonium' to induce exhilaration."[7] In Brazil, the priests brought on ecstatic states by smoking

[1] Bourke, "Medicine Men of the Apache," Bur. Eth. IX, p. 455 ff.
[2] Brasseur de Bourbourg, "Mexique," III, p. 558.
[3] Wood, "Natural History of Man," I, p. 576.
[4] Brinton, "Religions of Primitive Peoples," p. 67.
[5] Ibid; and Brinton, "Nagualism," pp. 8—9.
[6] Ibid.
[7] Bourke, "Medicine Men of the Apache," Bur. Eth. IX, p. 455.

tobacco;[1] the priestess of Delphi inhaled stupefying vapors from a deep fissure in the ground.[2]

The medicine man often resorts to sleeplessness, seclusion, and obstinate gloating on some morbid fancy in order to bring about hallucinations. He is usually successful, for it is a fact well known to medical science that the more frequently these diseased conditions of the mind are sought, the more readily are they found. The shaman, therefore, tries repeatedly until finally, as in the case of Doctor Jekyll, the nature which he has so assiduously striven to induce by artificial means comes without seeking. Then without effort he possesses hallucinations with all the garb of reality.

Other means for entering into communion with the gods are by gyrations and by flagellations. Among the Dyaks of Borneo, the medicine man, after running many times in a circle, simulates unconciousness, and it is then that he is supposed to possess greatest power.[3] The shaman of the Tshi-speaking peoples, when about to communicate with the deities, pretends to be convulsed, and by hurling his body about and twisting it in contortions, brings himself to such a state of frenzy that his eyes roll madly, and foam falls from his lips.[4] The Malanau medicine man (or medicine woman), with hair disheveled, twirls around until his staring eyes show that he is nearly insane. Then it is thought he is able to commune with the

---

[1] Müller, "Amerikanische Urreligionen," p. 277.
[2] Myers, "Ancient History," pp. 178—179.
[3] Roth, "Natives of Sarawak and British North Borneo," I, p. 282.
[4] Ellis, "Tshi-Speaking Peoples," pp. 125—126.

spirits, and gain from them power to withdraw the daimon from the body of the sick person.[1] In Southern India, the shaman "uses medicated draughts, cuts and lacerates his flesh until the blood flows, lashes himself with a huge whip, presses a burning torch to his breast, drinks the blood which flows from his own wounds, or drinks the blood of the sacrifice, putting the throat of the decapitated animal to his mouth. Then, as if he had acquired new life, he begins to brandish his staff of bells, and to dance with a quick but wild, unsteady step. Suddenly the afflatus descends. There is no mistaking that glare, or those frantic leaps. He snorts, he stares, he gyrates. The daimon has now taken bodily possession of him; and, though he retains the power of utterance and of motion, both sides are under the control of the daimon, and his separate consciousness is in abeyance."[2]

Sexual continence and ecstatic visions stand in close relationship. This connexion, to be sure, is not conceived by the savage in modern scientific terms. But by repeated trials, failures, and successes, the medicine man perceived that when he praticed sexual abstinence he was the better fitted to enter into the ecstatic state. He learned, therefore, unwittingly and no doubt accidentally, that the phenomena of the religious life are to a large extent based on sexual life. Consequently the intelligence that continence was often required throughout the whole novitiate of individuals in training for the holy office is not at all amazing.

[1] Roth, "Natives of Sarawak and British North Borneo," p. 283.
[2] J. A. Society of Bombay, 1886, pp. 101—102.

And visions came, not as heavenly visitants, but because repression of sex impulses is sometimes concomitant with the stimulation of religious auto-intoxication. The medicine man is not always a paragon of virtue and sex morality; he is sometimes the reverse. It is when he wishes to induce theoleptic fits that he practices continence. On his recovery from the theopneustic trance, his repressed emotions sometimes explode with abnormal violence. These emotions having been, as it were, diverted into a foreign channel, and meanwhile increased in force, when the reason for their repression no longer exists, break back into their normal course with intensified vehemence.[1] Says an acute observer: "I know no fact of pathology more striking and even terrifying than the way in which the phenomena of the ecstatic state may be plainly seen to bridge the gulf between the innocent fooleries of ordinary hypnotic patients, and the depraved and repulsive phenomena of nymphomania and satyriasis."[2] By reason of the facility with which the ecstatic state passes into abnormal sexual emotion, it not infrequently happens that after their return to normal consciousness the representatives of the gods are guilty of unspeakable dissoluteness.[3]

The exponent of the gods, after much experimentation, came to know that the ecstatic state can be induced by abstinence from food. Fasting, indeed, is one of the strongest means of interfering with the healthy action of bodily

---

[1] Ellis, "Man and Woman," p. 295.
[2] Anstie, "Lectures on Disorders of the Nervous System," Lancet, Jan. 11th, 1873, p. 40.
[3] Ellis, "Tshi-Speaking Peoples," I, p. 122.

and mental functions, and so of producing visions of de-
light. The primitive interpretation of phenomena of this
kind is that of divine visitation. While fasting and praying,
the medicine man receives much preparation for his work.
Even the name by which he is sometimes known is
significant, the word "shaman" being a corruption of the
Sanscrit term for "ascetic."[1] Schoolcraft says, "Among the
American Indians, the 'jossakeed' or soothsayer prepares
himself by fasting and the use of the sweat bath for the
state of convulsive ecstacy in which he utters the dictates of the familiar spirits."[2] In Zululand, the doctor,
in order to enter into communion with the *amadhlozi*
or ghosts from which he is to obtain direction, limits himself to spare, abstemious diet, and subjects himself to suffering, castigation, and solitary wandering in the forest.[3]
Among the Ojibways, a *wabeno* will sometime in his youth
withdraw from the village and fast for several days, so that
he may be visited by dreams and visions that will be his
guides.[4] Dobrizhoffer says of the Abipones, "Those who
aspire to the office of 'keebet' or juggler are
said to sit on an aged willow overhanging some
lake, to abstain from food for several days, till they
begin to see into futurity."[5] The Boulian of North
Queensland, after starving for three days, is rewarded
by the fancied apparition of a *malkari* or nature-

----

1 Mallery, "Picture Writing of American Indians," Bur. Eth.,
    X, p. 490.
2 Schoolcraft, "Information Respecting the Indian Tribes of
    the United States," III, p. 287.
3 Callaway, "Religious Systems of the Amazulu," p. 387.
4 Hoffman, "The Midewiwin of the Ojibway," Bur. Eth., VII, p. 156.
5 Dobrizhoffer, "Abipones," II, p. 67.

spirit, which proceeds to stick pebbles or bones or quartz-crystals into his body, and thus makes him a medicine man.[1] Of the Greenlanders, Crantz reports that whoever aspires to the office of shaman must retire to a solitary place, and call upon *tormgarsuk* to send him a *tormgak*. After a time, because of abstinence from food and flagellation of the body, his imagination becomes distorted; he sees blended images of men, beasts, and monsters. Irregularities of the body follow, and convulsions, which he endeavors to augment, give the final proof of possession.[2]

But why multiply instances of fasting which have produced their natural effects in ecstatic visions? They have been resorted to by shaman and priest, by heathen and Christian, by Protestant and Catholic, for the same purpose of bringing about communion with the unseen powers. Old men have dreamed dreams because of gorged stomachs. As a result of rigorous fasting young men have seen visions. But, in the words of Dr. Tylor, "Bread and meat would have robbed the ecstatic of many an angel visit; the opening of the refectory door must many a time have closed the gates of heaven to his gaze."[3]

Another expedient, which in the minds of his constituents serves to establish the claims of the medicine man, is the art of jugglery. The majority of the human race are open to this kind of evidence. A successful business man in recent years, upon witnessing an alleged miracle

[1] Roth, "Superstition, Magic, and Medicine," North Queensland Ethnography, Bulletin, Number 5, p. 29.
[2] Crantz, "Historie von Grönland," I, p. 194.
[3] Tylor, "Prim. Cult.," Edition of 1905, II, p. 415.

performed by a charlatan spiritual healer, acknowledged the
religious leadership of that sensationalist. If such gullibility
is possible to a cultured man in an advanced stage
of civilization, what would be the attitude of the savage
toward the doer of strange deeds? He would without
question bow at the feet of the master. When no physical
or mental peculiarity, therefore, differentiates him from the
rest of his kind, the medicine man is under constant
stimulus to execute feats and achievements which exceed
the power of the laity to perform or understand.[1]
Hence he is often cunning, clever, and given to
the practice of trickery. By a process of selection
he attains skill, ingenuity, and ability to do the seemingly
impossible. The aspirant for office who is unable,
either by force of intellect, or by artifice, or by adroitness,
or by craft, or by chicanery, to justify his pretentions
goes down in the struggle, and his inferior qualities perish
with him. His more capable companions, on the other
hand, succeed in overawing and hypnotizing the commonalty, and as a result survive. Their superior qualities
and capacities are transmitted to succeeding generations,
until ultimately the ablest and most clever men in the tribe
or nation form what comes to be known as the priest
class.

Many accounts have been given by travellers of clever
feats performed by medicine men, but a few instances will
serve to illustrate the fact that often by executing an extraordinary performance the shaman succeeds in creating and
maintaining a place for himself.

[1] Spencer, "Principles of Sociology," III, p. 184.

According to Howitt, among Australian tribes, the doctors profess to extract from the human body foreign substances which in the native belief have been placed there by the magic of wizards or other doctors, or by supernatural beings.[1] "The black fellow doctors," Howitt further states, "as a class naturally surround themselves with mystery. Their magical practices are not favored by too open examination, and the more that is left to the active imagination of their tribe, the better their assistances are received."[2] Ratzel writes that "a shaman occasionally pulls out his eye and eats it, sticks a knife into his breast, or lets a bullet be shot through his head without being any the worse for it."[3] A Dakota medicine man, who understood sleight-of-hand, appeared to draw from his side below his ribs a quid of tobacco;[4] while the Eskimo *angakoks* during the Sedna feast thrust harpoons into their bodies, taking precautions, however, beforehand to place under their clothes bladders filled with blood.[5] The *wabeno* of the Ojibways was alleged to grasp and handle red-hot stones, and to bathe his hands in boiling maple syrup without suffering any apparent harm.[6] Howitt reports, that in Australia at initiations "a *gommera* [medicine man] will as chief evidence of his powers 'bring up out of himself' quartz crystals, or pieces of vein quartz, pieces of black stone, white substances, pieces of flesh, bone, and the like."[7] Among some of the

---

[1] Howitt, "Australian Medicine Men," J. A. I., XVI, p. 25. [2] Ibid., p. 57.
[3] Ratzel, "History of Mankind," II, p. 229.
[4] Bourke, "Medicine Men of the Apache," Bur. Eth., IX, p. 456.
[5] Boas, "Central Eskimo," Bur. Eth., VI, pp. 593—594.
[6] Hoffman, "The Midewiwin of the Ojibway," Bur. Eth., VII, p. 157.
[7] Howitt, "Australian Medicine Men," J. A. I., XVI, p. 43.

Indian tribes of North America, the medicine man before
treating a patient produced a magical stick, and demonstrated his supernatural power to the amazed spectators.[1]
Boas writes that many performances of the *angakoks* of
the Eskimos require much skill in ventriloquism. "Thus in
invoking a *tornaq* flying to a distant place they can imitate
a distinct voice by a sort of ventriloquism. In these performances they always have the lamps extinguished, and hide
themselves behind a screen hung up in the back part of
the hut. The *tornaq*, being invoked, is heard approaching and shaking the hut. A favorite trick is to have their
hands tied up, and a thong fastened around their knees and
neck. Then they begin invoking their *tornaq*, and all of a
sudden the body lies motionless while the soul flies to
any place they wish to visit. After returning, the thongs
are found untied, though they had been fastened
by firm knots. The resemblance of this performance to
the experiments of modern spiritualists is striking." [2]
Hoffman, quoting from a paper read by Colonel
Garrick Mallery before the Anthropological Society of
Washington, records an interesting feat performed by an
Ojibway *jessakkid* at Leech Lake, Minnesota, about
1858. The *jessakkid*, securely bound by a rope, with his
knees and wrists together and with his face upon his
knees, was placed alone in a lodge erected for the purpose.
After a few minutes of loud noises and after much sway-
ing of the lodge, the spectators heard him direct another
Ojibway, who had wagered that the *jessakkid* could not

[1] Bartels, "Med. Naturvölker," p. 50.
[2] Boas, "Central Eskimo," Bur. Eth., VI, pp. 593—594.

accomplish this feat, to get the rope from a near-by house. The Ojibway found the rope, still knotted, in the place indicated, and on his return beheld the *jessakkid* sitting unbound within the lodge.[1] The medicine men of both the Zuñis and the Pawnees swallowed knives and arrows, and could apparently kill a man and restore him to life.[2] In 1761, a bloody revolt of the Mayas broke out in a number of villages near Valladolid, Yucatan. "It was headed," Brinton records, "by a full-blooded native, Jacinto Can-Ek. Jacinto boldly announced himself as the high priest of the fraternity of sorcerers, a master teacher of magic, and the lineal descendant of the prophet, Chilain Balam, 'whose words cannot fail.' In a stirring appeal he urged his fellow countrymen to attack the Spaniards without fear of the consequences. To support his pretentions he took a piece of paper, held it up to show that it was blank, folded it perhaps the fraction of a minute, and then spread it out covered with writing. This deft trick convinced his simple-minded hearers of the truth of his claims, and they rushed to arms." [3]

Since nature men are so very susceptible to proofs of this description, it is no wonder that in the course of evolution there should appear among them from time to time members of their race who have sufficient mental acumen to take advantage of the disposition to ascribe power to the apparently miraculous, and who by the exhibition of

---

[1] Hoffman, "The Midewiwin of the Ojibway," Bur. Eth., VII, 1891, pp. 276—277.
[2] Bourke, "Medicine Men of the Apache," Bur. Eth., IX, p. 471.
[3] Brinton, "Nagualism," p. 31.

juggling performances foist in upon uncritical minds the convictions that the religious leaders are possessed of spiritual might, and consequently deserving of a place among the noble company of those chosen for divine honors.

In addition to his physical and mental peculiarities, real or feigned, the medicine man understands how to create between himself and his fellow-men other dissimilarities which are calculated to fortify his position, and to confirm and strengthen the esteem in which he is held by the people. Since, however, he usually directs his attention to such activities after his formal induction into office, the discussion of these dissimilarities is reserved for a later chapter.[1]

Two other elements enter into the making of the medicine man: the preparation and training or the novitiate, and the initiation or the public installation into office.

In all professions a prescribed course of study and instruction is required antecedent to graduation. Among primitive peoples, no person is admitted into the goodly fellowship of the elect until the older shamans are satisfied that he is qualified for the place. If as a result of self-preparation a man is able to stand the test, he is sometimes accorded the privilege. In that case he must fast, and spend much time in solitude and prayer, after which by hallucinations or in dreams, it is thought, the spirits by whose power he does his mighty works are revealed. No further training is in many instances required. But in most cases the novice

[1] Vide Chap. IV, pp. 91—103.

must pass a greater or lesser number of hours under the instruction and supervision of older medicine men, learning their secrets, and benefiting by their experiences, in order to be able to convince the other members of the craft that he can carry on the work of the profession. "One Navaho shaman," writes Matthews, "told me that he had studied six years before he was considered competent to conduct his first ceremony, but that he was not perfect then, and had learned much afterwards." [1]

Sometimes the older medicine men, in their anxiety to secure recruits for "orders," make it their business to enumerate to the youth of the tribe the benefits incident to the sacred calling, and point out the ease with which it is to be entered in order to prevail upon them if possible to devote their lives to the making of medicine. When a young man acquiesces, the promise of an easy entrance must be redeemed lest he turn back. Among the Pima Indians, any man could enter the profession if he was instructed by a medicine man, and "got power," as the Pimas said—or acquired proficiency in a few tricks. The initiatory ceremony was not elaborate. The aspirant rested on all fours before an old medicine man, who threw at him four sticks about eight inches long. If the youth fell to the ground, the instructor as the next step coughed up four or five white balls and rubbed them into the breast of the young man. During the entire time that he was engaged in learning his work the prospective shaman had to stay away from the

---

[1] Matthews, "The Night Chant, A Navaho Ceremony," Memoirs American Museum of Natural History, Preface, p. V.

lodges of women, and keep secret the fact that he was preparing for the priesthood. In all, the period of his novitiate
lasted from two to four years. The usual fee for the
instruction was a piece of calico or a horse.[1]

There are primitive tribes in which the thoroughfare
to shamanistic honors is difficult. A novice among the
Shingu Indians, for example, must for months "drink
only starch extract, eat no salt, no flesh, fruit or fish, and
not sleep. He must bathe much, scratch the arm and
breast until the blood runs, and undergo much physical
suffering. His chief art is to use poisons. With these
he not only kills others, but also kills himself in order to
transform himself into other forms."[2] A Cherokee who
aspired to the priesthood was expected in former times
to remember a formula after it had been repeated to him
but once. If he failed to remember, he was considered
unworthy of the profession.[3] The Navaho "chanter" or
medicine man was obliged to devote so much study to
the mastery of every great ceremony that he seldom knew
more than one well. [4]

The novitate of these candidates is not only
arduous, but also expensive, for as a rule the
neophyte must make heavy payments for instruction.
Hoffman, for example, writes of the Menomini
Indians, "Each remedy must be paid for separately,

[1] Russell, "Pima Indians," Bur. Eth., XXVII, pp. 257—258.
[2] Steinen, "Shingu Tribes." After the Sumnerian Collections.
[3] Mooney, "Sacred Formulas of the Cherokees," Bur. Eth.,
1891, p. 309.
[4] Matthews, "The Night Chant, a Navaho Ceremony," Memoirs
American Museum of Natural History, p. 3.

as no two preparations or roots or other substances
are classed together as one; furthermore, the knowledge relating to different remedies is possessed by
different medicine men, each of whom will dispose of the
properties and uses thereof for a consideration only."[1] Of
the Ojibway Indians Hoffman states: "The male candidates
for the *mide* [one of the classes of medicine men] are
selected usually from among those who in their youth were
chosen for that distinction. This selection was made at the
period of 'giving a name' by a designated *mide* priest, who
thus assumed the office of godfather. From that date
until the age of puberty of the boy, his parents gathered
presents with which to defray the expenses of preliminary
instruction by hired *mide* priests, and of the feasts to be
given to all those who might attend the ceremonies of
initiation, as well as to defray the cost of the personal services of the various medicine men directly assisting in the
initiation. Frequently the collection of skins, peltries,
and other goods that have to be purchased involved a
candidate hopelessly in debt; but so great was the desire
on the part of some Indians to become acknowledged
medicine men that they would assume obligations that
might require years of labor in hunting to liquidate; or, if
they failed, then their relatives were expected to assume
the responsibility thus incurred."[2]

It might be said in passing that like physicians
of the present time in view of the long, difficult, and

[1] Hoffman, "The Menomini Indians," Bur. Eth., 1896, p. 69.
[2] Ibid., p. 67.

expensive period of preparation the medicine man, as will later be shown, does not hesitate to charge high fees for his professional services.[1]

After the course of study and training is over, the postulant is not, however, accepted either by the public or by the brotherhood as duly qualified until he is publicly initiated, and subjected to various tests to prove his efficiency. The initiatory rites among various tribes differ in detail, but underneath all of them is the underlying purpose of publicly inducting the aspirant into the number of the "allied." The particular initiatory ceremony of a given race reflects the mental and moral qualities of that race. The established rites of African tribes, for instance, are not on nearly so high a plane as those of the North American Indians, as the following examples will illustrate. Among the Akikuyu of British East Africa, the form for the initiation of the medicine man is childlike in character. Routledge describes the ceremonies. A he-goat is killed, and its meat, half-cooked, "is partaken of by all the medicine men present. Collars made of the skin of the right leg of the goat are placed around the necks of five gourds, each containing a different drug..... The medicine men present have brought their lot-gourds [a special medicine gourd]. Each empties his lot-gourd on the skin apart from his fellows. The neophyte then comes, and grasps a handful from one pile. His wife follows him, and does likewise. With the two handfuls of counters thus obtained, lots are cast to foretell the professional career of the

[1] Vide pp. 158—164.

novice. Finally, the contents so grasped are added to those already in the lot-gourd of the neophyte. Custom requires that the medicine gourds and lot-gourds of the newly received medicine man shall first be stopped with banana leaves, but the next day or later, he replaces them with the tips of tails of cows. The long hair of these forms brushes for the application of medicines, when it is impossible to obtain the correct plants with which to make brushes. A curse has to be *brushed* off. Each medicine man present receives one skin of a sheep or goat for being there."[1] Among the Dyaks of Borneo, the proceedings at the time of the initiation are more worthy of respect. There are three ceremonies. The first is "Besudi," which seems to mean feeling, touching. The *manangs*, surrounding the candidate as he sits on a veranda as though he were ill, "make medicine" over him the whole night. By this time he is supposed to become endowed with the power of touch to enable him to feel where and what are the maladies of the body, and so to apply the requisite charms. It is the lowest grade, and obtainable by the cheapest fees.[2] Henry Ling Roth further describes the other two ceremonies as follows: "The second is 'Beklite' or opening. After a night of incantation, the *manangs* lead the neophyte into a curtained apartment, where, as they assert, they cut his head open, take out his brains, wash and restore them in order to give him a clean mind for penetrating into the mysteries

---

[1] Routledge, "The Akikuyu of British East Africa," pp. 253—254.
[2] Roth, "Natives of Sarawak and British North Borneo," I, pp. 280—281.

of evil spirits and the intricacies of disease; they insert gold
dust into his eyes to give him keenness and strength of
sight powerful enough to see the soul wherever it may
have wandered; they plant barbed hooks on the tips of
his fingers to enable him to seize the soul and hold it
fast; and lastly they pierce his heart with an arrow to
make him tenderhearted..... In reality, a few symbolic
actions representing these operations are all that is done...
The man is now a fully qualified practitioner, competent to
practice all parts of his deceitful craft. He is now no
longer an 'iban,' a name by which all Dyaks speak of
themselves, he is a *manang*. He is lifted into a different
rank of being. And when engaged in their functions, the
manangs make a point of emphasizing this distinction by
constant use of the two words in contrast to each other.
A third grade of *manang* is obtainable by the ambitious
who have the will and means to make the outlay;
they become *manang bangun, manang enjun, manangs
waved upon, manangs trampled on.*" As in other
cases, this involves a nocturnal programme, "but the spe-
cialties conferring this M. D. of Dyak quackery and imposture are three. At the beginning of the performance,
the *manangs* march round and round the aspirant for
the higher honor, and wave bunches of *pinang* flower
about and over him, an action which all over Borneo, I
believe, is considered of great medicinal and benedictional
value in this and many other similar connexions. This
is the *Bangun*. Then in the middle of the veranda a
tall jar is placed, having a short ladder fastened on either

side of it, and connected at the top. At various intervals during the night the *manangs,* leading the new candidate, march him up one ladder and down the other; but what that action is supposed to symbolize, or what special value it is believed to confer, I have not been able to discover. To wind up this play of mysteries, the man lays himself flat on the floor, and the *manangs* walk over him, and trample upon him to knock into him, perhaps, all the *manang* power which is to be obtained. This is the *Enjun.* It is regarded as a certificate of medical superiority, and the *manang* who has passed the ordeal will on occasions boast that he is no ordinary spirit-controller and soul-catcher, but a *manang bangun, manang enjun.*"[1] Among the Tshi-speaking peoples, the initiatory rites are still more elaborate. The candidate is tested by fire; he must show publicly that he is possessed by a spirit, and make predictions which eventually come to pass. Ellis thus describes an initiation among those people in 1886, held after a novitiate of two years. Amid singing, beating of drums, and a continuous roar of musketry, "the new priests and priestesses were taken down to a spot near the beach...and here a sheep was sacrificed and the blood sprinkled around. Next day...hundreds of people were formed up in a kind of hollow square, all facing inwards. In the inner rank of this square were the new priests and priestesses seated upon stools. The whole surface of their bodies, with the exception of the lips, eyes,

---

[1] Roth, "Natives of Sarawak and British North Borneo," I, pp. 280—281.

eyebrows, and crown of the head, was smeared with some white substance, which, from its being much whiter in color than the ordinary white clay, appeared to be chalk. The effect was ghastly in the extreme... With the exception of the children, all wore long necklaces peculiar to the priesthood, which were composed of black and white beads, with an occasional long bead of red cornelian or a small disk of gold. The men had the skull clean shaven with the exception of two or three small circular patches of hair, and to each patch was attached a gold medallion of the size of a florin...... The women wore gold ornaments in their hair, and all of both sexes wore white cloths. The drums struck up, and a crowd of men and youths behind the drummers raised a song in honor of one of the tutelary deities.... After a time one of the new priests, who was sitting down, began to tremble and roll his eyes. A god was beginning to take possession of him. Two or three men at once went to him and removed the gold ornaments from his head and some bracelets of beads as a precautionary measure to prevent loss, and then bound each wrist with a d d o r. In the meantime the trembling increased, and soon the priest was shuddering as in an ague fit... Next, with open mouth, protruding tongue, and with eyes widely rolling, he worked himself, still seated and quivering violently, into the middle of the arena. There he suddenly leaped in the air, extending his arms over his head and the quivering ceased. His eyes were closed, his tongue hung from his mouth, and with the slow and uncertain gait of a drunken man he walked backwards and forwards. After a short time he directed his steps towards one side of the square and passed out, the spectators making way for him, and returned in a few minutes without his white cloth, but with a short cotton skirt depending from the waist to the knee, and ornamented with two narrow flounces at the waist. Still with closed eyes and appearing half dazed, he walked to and fro; then with a sudden spring he faced the drums, and, throwing his arms in the air, he waved his reed brush. Next, he stooped forward, and placing both hands upon a large drum, hung his head down between his arms, shook it sideways, and uttered a gurgling, choking noise. This was the god preparing to give utterance. Then he sprang upright, and in a hoarse, unnatural voice, said: 'I am come. I am So-and-so;' naming a tutelary deity. The drums at once struck up the rhythm in honor of this deity, the singers commenced singing, and the priest began to dance. After a few movements he stopped, and, putting his head on one side, raised his hand to his ear. This signified that the god who now possessed him could not hear the song in his honor: the singers were not singing loudly enough, or distinctly enough, or the particular rhythm of the drums peculiar to the god was not sufficiently marked. The songs and the drumming stopped. Then after a few seconds a fresh start was made; the priest danced a few steps and again stopped. The expression of acute and rapt attention, as though he were straining every nerve to listen, was exceedingly well assumed. These false starts were repeated several times, until at last the god appeared to hear satisfactorily, for the priest danced furiously, bounding in the air, twisting round and round, turning his body now here, now there, and tossing his arms wildly about, throughout the whole performance keeping perfect time to the rhythm of the drums. The exercise was most violent, and in a few minutes the performer was streaming with perspiration. After some little time he threw his arms over his head, and then waved his brush over the drummers. This signified that the first god had left him and another had entered him. The entire performance was then repeated. It should be said that every now and then he let fall words or sentences, spoken in a croaking or guttural voice. These utterances were the words of the possessing god, and ... referred, some to past events, and some to future. In the latter case they were sufficiently vague and ambiguous, for it is by these that the priest is chiefly tested; and should he make any definite and clear prediction which afterwards should be falsified by events, he would be driven out of the society as an impostor, unless he could give some satisfactory explanation. One such utterance I heard was: 'If the gods do not help, there will be much sickness soon.' Now if sickness ensued, it would be because the gods would not help; if it did not ensue, it would be because they had helped. After the first priest had retired, all of the novices went in turn through the same performances. Their features during possessions were distorted beyond recognition, but when seen in repose they were not of a bad type, and seemed to pro-

mise intelligence above the average. For the novices had
not commenced that career of imposture, vice, and debauchery, which almost invariably, and especially in case
of the priestesses, leaves its impression upon the features
of the priesthood." [1]

The ordeal of fire among the Tshi-speaking peoples,
according to Ellis, was a test of purity; if the priests and
priestesses had refrained from sexual intercourse during the
period of retirement required of candidates for the priesthood, they would, it was believed, receive no injury from
the flames. The priest when thus tested was made to
step into a clear space surrounded by glowing embers
that formed a circle three yards in diameter. Ellis
continues, "Immediately rum, kerosene oil, and other
inflammable liquids are thrown upon the embers, so
that the flames leap high in the air, sometimes as high as
the head of a man. After an interval the process is
repeated a second and a third time, and the ordeal is over.
If the candidate has been able to stay in the circle each
time till the flames have subsided, and has sustained no
injury, it is believed that he is pure, and that the gods
have protected him from the fire. If he has been compelled
by the intense heat to leap out, or if he has sustained a
burn of any kind, he is not pure. This test is not
submitted to while the candidate is naked, and persons
subjected to it always wrap themselves up closely in their
clothes." [2] If an aspirant cannot stand the test of fire,
he must offer sacrifices to the gods, and receive pardon for

[1] Ellis, "Tshi-Speaking Peoples," p. 131—136.   [2] Ibid., p. 138.

his transgression...... Very few priests are able to come from the fire unscathed. Most of the priestesses confess that they have been unchaste, and do not undertake the ordeal, thus through making sacrifices that cost but five or six dollars avoiding much pain.[1] *

Among the Ojibways, there were three classes of medicine men—the *wabeno*, the *jessakkid* and the *mide*. Candidates were initiated into each class with impressive forms and ceremonies. In the Midewiwin, or society of the *mide*, there were four degrees, into each of which the candidate was inducted as he attained suitable proficiency. The initiation into the fourth degree was most elaborate. For several days beforehand, the aspirant, after a sweat bath, went each morning with his preceptor to the four entrances of the Midewigan, and deposited offerings. On the evening of the fourth day, the other priests visited the candidate and the preceptor in the sweat lodge, where they engaged in ceremonial smoking. Such a smoke-offering, in honor of "Ki tshi Man ido" was the first ceremony of the day of initiation, and was followed by an original song sung by the candidate. Then the initiation began. The priests, arranged in line in order of

[1] Ellis, "Tshi-Speaking Peoples," p. 139.

* Note:—It might not be out of place to remark here that the author, in a wide range of ethnographical reading, lighted upon some very interesting magazine articles on "Indian Medicine," and "Curiosities of Therapeutics," in the Popular Science Monthly for September 1886, and The Therapeutic Gazette for April 1887, from the pen of Dr. G. Archie Stockwell. Some of the statements of Dr. Stockwell were striking and even sensational; but the writer could not check them up, and so, after much deliberation and with considerable reluctance, he has excluded this material, which had he been sure of its scientific character would have been most pertinent.

rank, marched toward the eastern entrance of the Mide-wigan, where the first four in turn peeping through the door, viewed six malevolent *manidos* that were supposed to be within,—the panther, turtle, wolverine, fox, wolf, and bear. The candidate, impersonating the good Bear Manido, now crawled on hands and knees toward the main entrance; then impersonating an archer *manido*, took a bow and four arrows, and feigned four times to shoot toward the interior of the lodge. The last time he sent an arrow within, and rushed after it as if pursuing the spirits. He repeated these actions at the other three doors of the wigwam. Then the chief priest said to him, "Now is the time to take the path that hath no end. Now is the time. I shall inform you of that which I was told—the reason I live." The second priest added, "The reason I now advise you is that you may heed him when he speaks to you." After a chant and after the wigwam had been cleared of evil spirits by exorcism, the four chief priests performed the next ceremonies; each of the three inferiors shot his *migis* into the breast of the candidate, and the chief priest shot his into the forehead of the novice. The candidate then spit out a *migis* shell previously concealed in his mouth, and this ended the initiation. After distributing presents, he went in turn to each of his fellows, saying, "Thank you for giving to me life." A curious ceremony ensued in which the priests feigned to shoot their *migis* shells at one another, or to swallow and recover them. A feast, furnished by the newly elected member and prepared by his female relatives, followed the ceremony. Smoking and conversation occupied the remainder of the day until sunset, when every one quietly departed.[1]

The fourth degree of the Midewiwin initiatory rites constituted the most important, as certainly the most spectacular, of all the ceremonies of the Ojibways; and it serves to show the degree of intellectual development which those Indians had attained, possessing as they did the ability of elaborating detailed and striking ceremonials. A comparison between this ritual and that of the Akikuyu, for example, would form an excellent subject for anthropogeographical inquiry.

SUMMARY. In this chapter, the making of the medicine man has been discussed. It has been found that since in the thought of primitive man malicious spirits are responsible for all the ills of life, the chief object of the savage is to bring about a change of relationship between heaven and earth. But because the struggle between mortals and immortals is unequal, the necessity arises of a specialist, who by reason of a spiritual nature is competent to act as intermediary. Qualifications for the office of shaman are recognized in a variety of ways. The easiest explanation of the unusual in nature is that of spirit possession. This assumption saves the labor of reflecting and the anguish of inquiring. The savage, therefore, to whom the thought and act of exertion are never agreeable, refers physical and mental deformity to the imaginary environ-

---

[1] Hoffman, "The Midewiwin of the Ojibway," Bur. Eth., VII, pp. 258—274.

ment, and looks upon the unfortunate person in whom such peculiarities are manifested as being possessed by divinities. So it sometimes happens that the victim of major hysteria, epilepsy, or the like, for example, is regarded as marked out by heaven to represent the gods on earth. In other cases the qualification and office of medicine man are handed down from father to son. When the supply of candidates is too small to meet the demand, the older members of the profession, jealous of the reputation of their order, either by the exertion of their influence on parents or by the appeal to the element of self-interest in the youth of the tribe, often succeed in inducing a goodly number of young men, and not infrequently young women, to allow themselves to be trained in the mysteries of the sacred rites. Among the North American Indians, the most frequent reason for selecting an individual to the office is the obvious wish on his part to acquire knowledge, and his willingness to pay the price. But an aspirant must make full proof of his capabilities. The performance of a feat of dexterity will often have this effect. In some instances these achievements are mere tricks of legerdemain, as among the Pima Indians, whose medicine men cause their people to wonder and admire by holding hot coals of fire in their hands and mouths, always being careful, however, to have a layer of ash or mud next to the skin.[1] The performances of the shaman have been known to impress members of the white race. But in order to leave no possible doubt as to his qualifications the

[1] Russell, "Pima Indians," Bur. Eth., XXVI, pp. 259 ff.

candidate may develop clairvoyant and psychic conditions by means of drugs, gyrations, fasting, and self-inflicted physical tortures. He often blundered upon scientific truth, as is evidenced by the fact of recent observations and investigations showing that some of the methods to which he resorted have the effect of producing anemic disarrangement or disorganization of the great nerve centers, enabling the subject to manifest wonderful powers. According to Spencer, the medicine man was the originator of the professions and sciences.[1] Among our Indians, he is usually the ablest man intellectually speaking in his group,[2] and is frequently the best specimen of physical manhood in his tribe.

---

[1] Spencer, "Principles of Sociology," German Edition of 1897, IV, pp. 223—368.
[2] Harper's Weekly, September 12, 1914.

CHAPTER III

MEDICINE WOMEN.

Hitherto men have been spoken of as shamans. But shamans are not always men; women sometimes are considered superior enough to attain the coveted position. In "Die Medizin der Naturvölker," Doctor Bartels asserts that this is the case among the Ashanti, among the negroes of Loango, in Lubuku, in Zululand, in Borneo, in Australia, in Siberia, and among some of our Indian tribes.[1] In the Ojibway nation, the "Midewiwin," so-called, was the society of the mide or shamans, who might be either men or women, and whose number was not fixed.[2] In Central Australia, "in connexion with medicine men and women alike, restrictions such as those applying to Mura are laid on one side during the actual exercise of their profession."[3] Among the Creeks, women doctors were as numerous as male doctors; among the Dakotas, they were nearly as powerful as the male doctors in each village.[4] Schultze says that in the Dakota nation, "medicine men and medicine women can cause ghosts to appear on occasion."[5] Nansen reports of the Eskimos that *angakoks* might be of

---

[1] Op. cit., p. 53.
[2] Hoffman, "The Midewiwin of the Ojibway," Bur. Eth., VII, p.164.
[3] Spencer and Gillen, "Native Tribes of Central Australia," p. 530. (Note).
[4] Bartels, "Med. Naturvölker," p. 53.
[5] Schultze, "Fetischismus," pp. 148—149.

either sex, though it would seem the weaker sex has never had so many representatives in the profession as the stronger.[1] Bourke, quoting "The Arctic Searching Expedition," by Richardson, says, "'Both medicine men and medicine women are to be found among the Eskimos.'"[2] According to De Groot, in China, the exorcists "were of a certain class of priests or priestesses entirely possessed by spirits of Yang," and engaged in invoking the ancestral spirits, doctoring the sick, and bringing rain.[3] Among the Saoras of Madras, the *kudang* is the medium of communication between the ancestral spirits and the living. Some *kudangs* are women.[4] In Korea, says a writer, "women are not shamanesses by birth, but of late years it has been customary for the girl children of the sorceress to go out with her and learn her arts, which is tending to give the profession an hereditary aspect. It is now recruited partly from hysterical girls, and partly from among women who seek the office for a livelihood, but outside of these sources a daimon may take possession of any woman, wife or widow, rich or poor, plebeian or patrician, and compel her to serve him."[5] Concerning the former customs of the New Hebrides, it is said that wizards were analogous to modern spiritualistic mediums. The "tenues" or spirits controlled them. Women as well as men had communications with

[1] Nansen, "Eskimo Life," p. 284. (Note).
[2] Bourke, "Medicine Men of the Apache," Bur. Eth., IX, p. 469.
[3] De Groot, "Religious System of China," I, pp. 40—41.
[4] J. A. Soc. of Bombay, I, p. 247.
[5] Bishop, "Korea," p. 423.

the spirits.[1] Among the Negritos of Zambales, Philippine Islands, both sexes may belong to the *mediquillos* [native doctors], who are known as "magña-anito," and are called in cases of mild illness to expel the spirit and thus cure the patient.[2] Among the Araucanians, writes Smith, "the office of medicine man, though generally usurped by males, does not appertain to them exclusively, and at the time of our visit the one most extensively known was a black woman, who had acquired the most unbounded influence by shrewdness, joined to a hideous personal appearance, and a certain mystery with which she was invested."[3]

Ancient historians attribute the invention of medicine to the gods. This is due to the anthropomorphic conception of the divinities. The gods were once human beings. The medicine man is often regarded as a god[4] even before death, and after his deification he is believed to be more powerful than ever. When he goes to the spirit world he retains all the powers and attributes which he had on earth. He was a healer while living; since death he is more intensely skilled in the art of healing. He inspires his servants, thereby giving them the knowledge and power to prosecute the work which he began. The worship by the ancients of female deities points back to the existence of the Matriarchy.[5] The fact that to those

[1] Leggatt, "Malekula," Aust. Ass. for Adv. of Science, 1892, p. 707.
[2] Reed, "Negritos of Zambales," pp. 65—66.
[3] Smith, "Araucanians," pp. 238—239.
[4] Vide pp. 135—136.
[5] Lippert, "Kulturgeschichte," II, pp. 76 and 260.

goddesses were attributed important relationships to the
healing art indicates that they were medicine women
when living. In Egypt, peculiar medical skill was assigned
to Isis, the wife and sister of Osiris. Tradition had it
that she gave unequivocal proof of her power by restoring
Horus, her son, to life. She was believed to have discovered several remedies, and the materia medica of the
time of Galen contained drugs that were named in her
honor. In the esoteric language of the priestly physicians
of Egypt, for example, the vervain was called "the tears
of Isis." [1]

Among the Greeks, Hygeia, daughter of Aesculapius,
god of medicine, was worshipped in the temples of Argos
as the goddess of both physical and mental health. Hera,
under the name of Lucina, was held to preside over the
birth of children, and was thought to possess healing
power. Medea and Circe, according to tradition, for the
purpose of counteracting the effects of poisons, made use
of herbs in their enchantments; while Ocyroe, the daughter
of Cheiron, the Centaur, was famed for her skill in
leechcraft. This information, although derived from fabled
story, serves the important purpose of preserving in alle-
goric form facts from which the inference is to be drawn
that in remote antiquity women were engaged in the
practice of medicine. [2]

While the laws and customs of the Romans forbade
women to practice medicine, yet Pliny and others have
handed down the names of a few of the gentler sex

[1] Reference lost. [2] Reference lost.

who engaged with distinction in the curing of diseases. Among the names thus preserved are Salpe, Sotira, and Favilla. Nothing definite is known, however, regarding the work of these female practitioners.[1]

In the Middle Ages, when every kind of knowledge was steeped more or less in superstition, women as well as men yielded to the pressure of their times, and exercised the double vocation of sorceresses and healers of the sick.[2]

The Universities of Cordova, Salamanca, and Alcala conferred the doctorate upon many women in the sixteenth century. In England, during the seventeenth century, Anna Wolly and Elizabeth of Kent engaged in the preparation of drugs, and published books on medical subjects. In Germany, such women as the Duchess of Troppau, Catherine Tissheim, Helena Aldegunde, and Frau Erxleben took up the study of medicine. The latter was one of the most successful women doctors of her time, and was eminent for her skill and erudition.[3]

These instances are mentioned to direct attention to the fact that while the office of medicine man always has been and still is more or less restricted to the sterner sex, yet cases are on record in all stages of the history of the world in which, through force of circumstances, or, more often, through force of character, women have frequently

---

[1] Bolton, "Early Practice of Medicine by Women," Popular Science Monthly, XVIII, p. 192.
[2] Ibid., p. 191.
[3] Ibid., p. 199.

acquired surgical skill, and often have pursued successfully the divine art of healing.

What are the functions of medicine women, and what is their social standing in the group? In comparison with the shamans, the shamanesses sometimes are not so important either in point of numbers, or in point of functions to be performed, or in point of respect accorded. In other cases they are apparently on an equality with men; while in other societies, the ministrations of the "weaker vessel" are so highly regarded that the most powerful and influential healers are women.

The following instances show that numerically women often rank second to men. In Central Australia females occasionally, although rarely, become doctors.[1] Among the Eskimos, as already noted (pp. 72—73 supra), though the *angakoks* might be of either sex, the women apparently have always been in the minority.[2] With the aborigines of both American Continents, fewer women than men attain the sacred office, and in some cases no mention whatever is made of female doctors.[3] Among the Australians and Polynesians, there is a very strong tendency toward the exclusion of females from the class of shamans.[4] In most Land Dyak tribes on the contrary, while there are five or six priests in each district, in some parts of the country half of the female population are included under the name of priestesses,

---

[1] Spencer and Gillen, "Native Tribes of Central Australia," p. 526.
[2] Nansen, "Eskimo Life," p. 469.
[3] Dixon, "Some Aspects of American Shamanism," Jour. Am. Folk Lore, Jan. 1908, p. 2.   [4] Ibid.

but most of them never become skilful enough to practice their profession.[1]

That man has in some instances exercised his dominating disposition and reduced woman to a secondary place in the practice of the priestly art, and that she, true to her nature, has passively accepted what was left her is quite evident. Among the Dakotas, it is stated that the shamanesses were next to the male doctors.[2] Spencer says concerning the Chippeways, "'Women may practice soothsaying, but the higher religious functions are performed only by men.'"[3] Among the Wascow Indians, the medicine women are not feared so much as men, and they are not thought to have such absolute power over life and death.[4] In Vancouver, women doctors were sent for only in cases of less serious sickness. But their standing is above the common women in the tribe.[5] Among the Tapantunnuasu in Central Celebes, shamanesses cannot marry, but they enjoy high standing and are supported by their village associates.[6] In Central America, medicine women of all women are allowed in the bath houses,[7] and in Southern California, though they were not absolutely entitled to material recompense for their services, they expected and generally received presents. Powers thus tells of a medicine woman called to extract an arrow-head from the body of a white man. Fan-

[1] Roth, "Natives of Sarawak and British North Borneo," I, pp. 259—260.
[2] Bartels, "Med. Naturvölker," p. 53.
[3] Bourke, Bur. Eth., IX, p. 469, Quoting Spencer's "Descriptive Sociology."
[4] Bartels, "Med. Naturvölker," p. 53.
[5] Ibid. [6] Ibid. [7] Ibid.

tastically attired, she walked round the patient, chanting
and touching the wound with her wand. "Finally she
stooped down and applied her lips to the wound; and after
a little while she ejected a flint from her mouth (previously placed there of course), and assured the man he
would now speedily recover. For this humbug, so trans-
parent, and yet so insinuatingly and elegantly administered,
she expected no less a present than a gaily-figured ban-
dana handkerchief and five pounds of sugar." [1]

In some tribal groups, there is in existence among the
doctors a division of labor, so to speak, the specialty of the
women lying in a different province from that of the men.
In Korea, the male doctors attend to the duties of exorcism, while it is the work of their female colleagues to
propitiate the spirits. The exercise of these functions
by the woman doctor is occasional as well as periodic. The
periodic exercise is in some instances public and in
other cases private. Both forms are celebrated with
appropriate ceremonies, but the central figure always
is the shamaness, who first discovers which god
must be propitiated, and then offers the proper
oblation to secure the continuance of the goodwill of the
spirit.[2] Among the Karok, according to Powers, there
are two classes of medicine men—the root doctors and the
barking doctors. The barking doctor is generally a woman,
"and it is her office to diagnose the case, which she does
by squatting down on her haunches like a dog and bark-

---

[1] Powers, "Tribes of California," Contribut. to North Am. Ethn.,
  III, p. 131.
[2] Bishop, "Korea," p. 410.

ing for hours together. She is more important than the root doctor. In addition to her diagnostic offices, she doctors 'poisoned' cases, which are very many among these people. They think they often fall victims to witches who cause some noxious reptile or animal to grow through the skin into the viscera. The barking doctor first discovers where the animal or reptile is located, and then sucks the place until the skin is broken and the blood flows. Then she administers an emetic to herself, and vomits up a frog or some other animal, which she pretends was sucked out of the patient."[1] Speaking of a medicine woman of another tribe, Powers says, "This priestess is really only a shamaness, corresponding nearly to the female barking doctor of the Karok. She is supposed to have communication with the devil, and she alone is potent over cases of witch-craft and witch-poisoning."[2] In Sarawak and British North Borneo, the medicine man is summoned in cases of sickness, while the office of the medicine women, as Roth says, "consists chiefly in doctoring the rice paddy by means of their dull, monotonous chants."[3]

From the earliest times women have specialized successfully in the science of gynecology. While it is true that in ancient Egypt the priest physicians sedulously concealed their superior knowledge from an ignorant people, and especially from women, yet the account of the birth of Moses goes to show that female

[1] Powers, "Tribes of California," Contribut. to North Am. Ethn., III, p. 26.
[2] Ibid., pp. 67–68.
[3] Roth, "Natives of Sarawak and British North Borneo," I, pp. 259–260.

gynecologists were not unknown among the Egyptians. Concerning the Apache, Bourke writes, "These medicine women devote their attention principally to obstetrics."[1] The same author, giving Mendieta as authority, says that among the Mexicans the medicine men attended to the sick men and the medicine women to the sick women.[2]

For centuries after the dawn of civilization, the superior strength of the male sex continued to assert itself, and, save in exceptional cases, women were forbidden both the acquirement of an accurate and systematic knowledge of the diseases peculiar to their sex, and the exercise of any branch of the science of medicine. The Athenian Agodice (300 B.C.), one of the first women to receive a medical education, was compelled to pursue her studies in male attire. After studying under Herophilus, she preserved her disguise and practiced medicine with great success in Athens, devoting her attention in particular to gynecology. When her sex was eventually disclosed, and she was brought to trial, the wives of the most influential men in Athens succeeded in having the law that prohibited women from studying medicine revoked.[3]

During the Middle Ages, especially in Mohammedan countries, there arose a class of women who became especially skilled in attending to the requirements of their own sex. Thus Albucasis of Cordova, one of the most able surgeons of the twelfth century, when operating on

---

[1] Bourke, "Medicine Men of the Apache," Bur. Eth., IX, p. 468.
[2] Ibid., p. 469.
[3] Bolton, "Early Practice of Medicine by Women," Popular Science Monthly, XVIII, pp. 192—193.

women, always had women assistants. Avicenna the Great
mentions a collyrium for eye troubles, which he says was
compounded by a woman who had great knowledge of the
science of medicine. Among the adherents of Islam, however, the sentiment against the independence and equality
of women is so strong that female gynecologists among
the Arabs always were and still are few in number.[1]

In some stages of culture the social position of a medicine woman exhibits characteristic features. In Korea, for
example, when a woman enters upon this work, she forsakes
husband, children, parents and friends, and gives herself
wholly to her calling. Although she is looked upon as an indispensable adjunct to society, she is thenceforth regarded
as a pariah.[2] If a man marries such a person, it is only to
gain an easy livelihood from the earnings of his wife,
and his social standing is low. A shamaness of noble origin
is permitted to deal exclusively with the spirits of her
own house. At death, however, she is not buried in the
family hut, but in a hole in the mountain side.[3] Among
the Tshi-speaking peoples, Ellis writes, "the social position
of priestesses is peculiar in that they are not allowed to
marry; they belong it is thought to the god they serve,
and, therefore, cannot belong to any man. Yet custom
allows them to gratify their passion with any man who
may chance to take their fancy..... A priestess who is
favorably impressed by a man sends for him to come to
her house, and this command he is sure to obey, through

[1] Bolton, "Early Practice of Medicine by Women," Popular
Science Monthly, XVIII, pp. 192—193.
[2] Bishop, "Korea," p. 410.   [3] Ibid., p. 425.

fear of the consequences of exciting her anger. She then tells him that the god she serves has directed her to love him, and the man thereupon lives with her until she grows tired of him or a new object takes her fancy. Some priestesses have as many as half-a-dozen men in their train at one time, and may on great occasions be seen walking in state followed by them. Their life is one continual round of debauchery and sensuality, and when excited by the dance they frequently abandon themselves to the wildest excesses. Such a career of profligacy soon leaves its impress upon them, and their countenances are generally remarkable for an expression of the grossest sensuality."[1]

So far as can be seen, it sometimes happens that the medicine woman is the equal of the medicine man in the manner of her making, in her social standing, in her functions, and in all other respects. In China, for example, De Groot says, priestesses "act as mediums for the spirits which have descended into them in consequence of conjuration, eye-opening papers, incense, drumming, cymbals, and music, and which give oracles by their mouths, unintelligible but for interpretation by female experts. In such a state of possession the medium will hop and limp, supported by a woman on either side, since her tightly compressed feet make her liable to tumble. Rattles suspended from her body indicate by increase or decrease of their noise the extent of her possession. So far there is not any essential difference between the work of such a woman and that of a possessed 'Ki Tông' or priest. The spirit

[1] Ellis, "Tshi-Speaking Peoples," pp. 121—122.

which is called into her is mostly that of 'S a m K o,' 'Third
Aunt or Lady,' a mysterious being who is professedly one
'Tsze-Ku,' or 'Lady Tsze,' who, according to a valuable
communication from the pen of Ch'en Kwah, was
called and consulted in China many centuries ago."[1]
Among the natives of Central Australia, the medicine
women, while fewer in number than the shamans, seem
on an equality in other regards. In the matter of initiation, for instance, the method of procedure is precisely
the same in the case of women as in that of men.[2]

According to Powers, a priestess among the Indians of
Southern California, like her male rival, before being consecrated, has great hardships and trials to endure. For she
must lie prostrate on the ground during nine successive
nights, and throughout the entire period can partake of
nothing but water.[3]

In East Central Africa, the medicine woman combines
with her functions of healing and prophecy the
office of witch detective. MacDonald writes at
length of her attributes: "She is the most terrible
character met with in village life. It is to her the
gods of ancestral spirits make known their will. This they
do by direct appearance and in dreams and visions...
When she sees the gods face to face, which always happens
at the dead hour of the night, she begins by raving and
screaming. This she continues till the whole village is astir,

[1] De Groot, "Religious System of China," VI, pp. 1323—1324.
[2] Spencer and Gillen, "Native Tribes of Central Australia," p. 526.
[3] Powers, "Tribes of California," Contribut. North Am. Eth., III,
   pp. 67—68.

and she herself utterly prostrated by her exertions. She then throws herself on the ground and remains in a state of catalepsy for some time, while the villagers gather round her awe-stricken, waiting for her revelations. At last she speaks, and her words are accepted without question as the oracles of God...She may order human sacrifices and no one will deny her victims....As a detective of wizards and witches the prophetess is in constant demand. When travelling on official duty, in this capacity, she goes accompanied by a strong guard, and when she orders a meeting of the clan or tribe, attendance is compulsory on pain of confessed guilt. When all are assembled, our friend, who is clad with a scanty loin-cloth of leopard skin, and literally covered from head to foot with rattles and fantasies, rushes about among the crowd. She shouts, rants, and raves in the most frantic manner, after which, assuming a calm, judicial aspect, she goes from one to another, touching the hand of each person. As she touches the hand of the bewitcher, she starts back with a loud shriek and yells, 'This is he, the murderer; blood is in his hand.' I am not certain if the accused has a right to demand the M w a i [investigation by the elders of the tribe], but it appears this may be allowed. My impression is that the law does not require it, and that the verdict of the prophetess is absolute and final. The condemned man is put to death, witchcraft being a capital crime in all parts of Africa. But the accuser is not content with simply discovering the culprit. She proves his guilt. This she does by 'smelling out,'—finding—'the horns' he used in the prosecution of the unlawful art. Since she herself has secretly buried these, it is easy for her to find them. She follows the bank of a stream, carrying a water vessel and an ordinary hoe. At intervals she lifts water from the stream which she pours upon the ground and then stops to listen. She hears subterranean voices directing her to the hiding place of the wizard at which, when she arrives, she begins to dig with her hoe, muttering incantations the while, and there she finds the horns deposited near the stream to poison the water drunk by the person to be bewitched. As they are dug from the ground, should anyone not a magician touch them even accidentally, the result would be instant death. Now how does the witch detective find the horns? By the art of what devil does she hit upon the spot where they are concealed? The explanation is very simple. Wherever she is employed she must spend a night in the village before commencing operations. She does not retire like the other villagers, but wanders about the live-long night listening to spirit voices. If she sees a poor wight outside his house after the usual hour for retiring, she brings that up against him the next day as evidence of guilty intention, and that, either on his own account, or on account of his friend, the wizard, he meant to steal away and dig up the horns, which the prophetess has taken care to bury in her night wanderings. The dread of such dire consequences keeps the villagers within doors, leaving the sorceress the whole night to arrange for the tableau of the following day." [1] It would seem from the foregoing that in

[1] MacDonald, "East Central African Customs," J. A. I., XXII, pp. 105-107.

East Central Africa, the medicine woman has as much power over life and death, inspires as much fear, and, therefore, has as great a social position as the medicine man of other tribes.

Among civilized nations, there are cases of women attaining notable surgical skill, and pursuing with success the art of healing on an equal footing with men. At Salernum, in the year 1059, for example, women were occupied in the preparation of cosmetics and drugs, and engaged in the practice of medicine among persons of both sexes. Some notable names are Costanza Calenda, the talented and beautiful daughter of a brilliant physician with whom she took studies leading to the doctorate; Abella, author of two medical poems; and Adelmota Maltraversa, Rebecca Guarna, and Marguerite of Naples, all of whom obtained royal authority to practice medicine.[1] Among most peoples, however, man has insisted as a general thing on keeping woman out of the most important and lucrative positions, and it is only in recent years, and in the most advanced stages of civilization, that the "weaker vessel" is given an opportunity to demonstrate her fitness to engage in the practice of the profession on equal terms with her male counterpart.

It is not uninteresting, however, to set forth that in primitive societies medicine women frequently exceed medicine men in importance. This is true of the Carib Tribes and of the Indians of Northern California.[2] The condition no doubt harks back to the Mother Family, when

[1] Bolton, "Early Practice of Medicine by Women," Popular Science Monthly, XVIII, p. 195.
[2] Jour. Am. Folk Lore, Jan. 1908, p. 2.

woman was the dominating factor of both the home and
the society, and the chief reason for the existence of man
was to do her bidding. In Korea, the female idea of the
shamanate prevails to such an extent that the men who take
up the profession wear female clothing while performing
their duties, and the whole shaman class in spoken of as
feminine.[1] This is also the case in Patagonia.[2] In Siberia,
writes Sieroshevski, "The *shamanesses* have greater power
than the *shamans;* in general, the feminine element plays a
very prominent *rôle* in sorcery among the Yakuts. In the
Kolmyck district the *shamans* for want of any special
dress put on the dress of women. They wear their hair
long and comb and braid it as women do. According to
the popular belief, any *shaman* of more than ordinary
power can give birth to children and even to animals and
birds."[3] Among the Dyaks, says Henry Ling Roth, the
"*manang bali* is a most ordinary character; he is a male
in female costume... He is treated in every respect like a
woman and occupies himself with feminine pursuits.... If
he can induce any foolish young man to visit him at night
and sleep with him, his joy is extreme; he sends him away
at daylight with a handsome present, and then openly
before the women boasts of his conquest, as he is pleased
to call it. He takes good care that his husband finds it out.
The husband makes quite a fuss about it, and pays the
fine of the young fellow with pleasure. As episodes of

[1] Bishop, "Korea," p. 409.
[2] Dixon, "Some Aspects of American Shamanism," Jour.
Am. Folk Lore, Jan. 1908, p. 2.
[3] Sumner, "Yakuts," Abridged from the Russian of Sieroshevski,
J. A. I., XXXI, p. 104.

this kind tend to show how successfully the *manang bali* has imitated the character of a woman he is highly gratified, and rises accordingly in the estimation of the tribe as a perfect specimen." [1]

SUMMARY. The position of shaman is not confined to members of the male sex. Women often succeed in attaining that desideratum. In all ages, among all peoples, and in all stages of culture, there have been female specialists in the science of gynecology, many having reached eminence in that branch of the medical profession. The making, the functions, and the consecration of medicine women in general do not differ materially from the making, the functions, and the consecration of medicine men. In particular instances, however, men shamans, on the one hand, exorcise spirits and attend the bedside of male patients; women shamans, on the other hand, propitiate spirits and minister to patients of their own sex. When medicine women combine the function of prophet with that of witch detective, they become objects of tremendous dread and fear to all persons in the tribe. As regards social position, that of the female shaman is sometimes so very low that for a woman to embrace the profession of medicine is tantamount to renouncing honorable marriage, or, if she be already married, to forsaking husband and children, and becoming an outcast from society. In other instances, although they do not enjoy the same social privileges as male doctors, yet

Roth,"Natives of Sarawak and British North Borneo," I, p. 270.

female practitioners move in a wider circle than do others
of their sex, and occupy a place in the social group superior
to that of ordinary women. In still other cases, medicine
men and medicine women meet on terms of social equality;
while it not infrequently happens that the female idea of
the shamanate prevails to such an extent that the most
powerful shamans are women, and in order to render themselves more worthy in the eyes of their constituents
medicine men attire themselves in female habiliments.

CHAPTER IV

ADVENTITIOUS AIDS; CHARLATANS;
THE SOCIAL POSITION OF THE MEDICINE MAN.

In addition to his physical and mental peculiarities, real or feigned, to which attention has been directed,[1] the medicine man understands how to create between himself and his patrons other dissimilarities which enhance his influence and power. These differences are many and varied. He holds himself aloof from the other members of the tribe; he lives in a house different in structure from those of the common people; as a rule he does no laborious work, but is supported by his fellows; he eats a special food; he paints his body, masks his face, and does many things which would be considered "sinful" for an ordinary individual to attempt. He is readily distinguishable from the laity by his taciturnity, his grave and solemn countenance, his dignified step, and his circumspection. All of these peculiarities tend to heighten his influence, and, by rendering his appearance impressive and suggestive of superiority, serve to increase his control over the people.

Specific accounts, taken from reliable sources, of the dress, language, and manner of living of the medicine man will enable the reader to perceive what effect these arti-

[1] Vide pp. 32—55.

ficial divergencies from the normal have upon the savage mind. Among the Andamanese Islanders, the native doctor has an especial diet—he eats no flesh, but partakes of a small plant that has the flavor of fish.[1] The shamans of the Loango Indians are permitted to drink water only at certain places and at certain hours of the day or night. They are not allowed to look at fish and beasts. Their food and drink consists of roots and herbs, and blood of animals.[2] In Victoria, the medicine man eats at unseasonable hours, sleeps while others are awake, and is awake when the other members of the tribe are asleep. He seldom hunts, or fishes, or does any kind of work. He makes strange noises in the night, wanders off in the darkness, seeks to frighten the people, and turns to advantage his peculiar manner of living.[3] In some countries, priestly celibacy is a matter of law; in all it is for many persons a godly practice.[4] Among the Dyaks of Borneo, the medicine man is given at his initiation a new generic name, and is thought to enter into a new rank of being.[5] In ancient Mexico, the shaman was specially trained in such subjects as "hymns and prayers, national traditions, religious doctrine, medicine, exorcism, music and dancing, mixing of colors, painting, drawing and ideographic signs, and phonetic hieroglyphs."[6]

The priest class, furthermore, has developed a separate language. It goes without saying that chants containing

[1] Bartels, "Med. Naturvölker," p. 52.
[2] Ibid.
[3] Ibid.
[4] Ratzel, "History of Mankind," III, p. 528.
[5] Roth, "Natives of Sarawak and British North Borneo," I, p. 283.
[6] Ratzel, "History of Mankind," I, p. 67.

prayers and legends are in this esoteric dialect; frequently, too, the religious rites are conducted in a tongue not known to the worshippers. Thus the songs and incantations of the Eskimo *angakoks* are couched in a special language, which is in part symbolic, and in part merely obsolete.[1] The Cherokee shamans, in order to preserve inviolate the secrecy of their sacred speech, keep their writings from the eyes of laymen and of rival priests, and speak so softly in conducting ceremonies, that even those nearest them cannot distinguish the words.[2] Among the Dakotas, too, there is a sacred as well as a common tongue, and among the Ojibways, a special sacerdotal language is attained through abbreviation of the ordinary speech.[3] Among the Algonquins, the incantations of the priests of Powhatan were not in the vernacular, but in a jargon not understood by the laity.[4] In Sarawak and British North Borneo, according to Henry Ling Roth "the language used by the *manangs* in their incantations is unintelligible even to the Dyaks themselves, and is described by the uninitiated as '*manang*' gibberish... It may be simply some archaic form of the ordinary spoken language interspersed with cabalistic formulas, spells, and charms for different purposes."[5] "Special priests' languages," says Ratzel, "recur among the most different races of the earth."[6] This esoteric use of

[1] Boas, "Central Eskimo," Bur. Eth., VI, p. 594.
[2] Mooney, "Sacred Formulas of the Cherokees," Bur. Eth.,1891,p.310.
[3] Bourke, "Medicine Men of the Apache," Bur. Eth., IX, p. 464. Quoting Henry Youle Hind.
[4] Beverly, "Histoire de la Virginie," p. 266.
[5] Roth, "Natives of Sarawak and British North Borneo," I, p. 270.
[6] Ratzel, "History of Mankind," I, p. 55.

language survives with the priesthood of barbaric and even civilized peoples, as is illustrated in the Egyptian hieroglyphics and the Sanscrit. In both the Roman and Greek Catholic Churches, divine service is always conducted, not in the language of the people, but in an ancient, dignified, and sacred tongue.

Anything that differentiates the medicine man from the commonalty serves to call attention to that individual above other persons in his group, and increases his influence. Among the Klamath Indians of Oregon, the skin of a fox dangles from an obliquely-placed stick on top of the house of the shaman.[1] In Western Borneo, before the house of the medicine man there are commonly heads of serpents fastened on the ends of two small branches of trees.[2] The houses of the medicine men of the Bechuanas in distinction from all others have carpets made from the skin of speckled hyenas. On these they hold their consultations.[3] The priest-doctors of the Annamites have in their houses at least two poorly constructed altars, one consecrated to the ancestors, the other to the superior deities of the tribe. The first altar is made of a dish, over which hangs a tablet with the name of the master of the state, and an inscription which changes with the year of the birth of the chief shaman. Before it are dishes with offerings of flowers and fruit; further off are rattles, a coal-basin, pipes, drums, torches, arrows, and flags. Behind the house is a pit representing hell, where the spirits of which the medicine man is possessed, throw their

Bartels, "Med. Naturvölker," p. 55. [2] Ibid. [3] Ibid.

adversaries.[1] Either in the house of the Persian doctor or in the bazaar next to it was a booth for the receiving of reports. The floor was decked with a felt or a reed mat. Near the wall stood a number of boxes, pitchers, and flasks, filled with electuaries, pills, and elixirs.[2] In the newly-built towns of our great Northwest, the house of the Roman Catholic priest is generally the most attractive dwelling to be seen.

Among some tribes, as for example the natives of Australia and the North American Indians, the medicine bag is indispensable. The medicine man makes this of the skin of his totemic animal with the hair on the outside. He decorates the bag with feathers, beads, and porcupine quills. Inside he places bones, pebbles of quartz, and splinters, together with roots and herbs to which he attaches magical significance.[3] This bag is as inseparable from the medicine man as were the "saddle-bags" from the eighteenth century physician, and it acts as a suggestive influence.

It is in his peculiar dress or professional costume that the medicine man finds his greatest adventitious aid. This is often strange and unaccountable. Among some tribes, every article has been devised and constructed in the wildest fancy imaginable, and is absurd in the highest degree. Vanity is one of the reasons for this unusual apparel. Vanity, in fact, was the primary motive for the adoption of clothing or dress of any kind. A shell or an ornament attached to the most convenient parts of the

[1] Bartels, "Med. Naturvölker," p. 56.   [2] Ibid.
[3] Waddle, Am. Jour. Psychology, XX, p. 229.

body, the waist or the neck, for others to see and admire, constituted the first article of clothing adopted by man. Wearing apparel afterwards came to be put on from a sense of shame (which is akin to vanity), and for protection against the cold.[1] The medicine man, as the idea and practice of dress advances in the "folkways," desires an attire different from the rabble, that he may be envied by those who have it not. Hence his robes of office. In addition to vanity is the striving after effect. What savage would fail to be impressed by the appearance of a man, different from all others in so many respects, in garments the like of which even the wildest imagination of the ordinary individual could not conceive? He would feel that he was in the presence of a superior being whose every movement throbbed with divinity, whose every look could wither, and whose every behest must be obeyed. Such is the hold which his peculiar dress assists the medicine man to acquire and retain upon his people.

Ethnography abounds in descriptions of the regalia of the primitive doctor and his incentive to its adoption. According to Ellis, among the Ewe-speaking peoples, the shamans are distinguished from the commonalty by special dress and privileges. They generally wear articles of clothing forbidden to others, and commit crime with impunity. No shaman in former times was subject to capital punishment.[2] In Dahomey, the priests wear a peculiar dress,

[1] Lippert, "Kulturgeschichte," I, pp. 375 ff.
[2] Ellis, "Ewe-Speaking Peoples," p. 147.

and make their persons appear odd and conspicuous. They
shave one half of the hair from their heads, and allow the
other half to grow in long tufts.[1] The head of the Buddhist
priest is entirely shaven. The priest of Tibet is distinguished by a striking red or yellow robe (varying according to his
sect) and by his yellow helmet.[2] Dress, too, was a
conspicuous feature of the medicine men of our Indians,
the shamans of the Creeks, for example, for all their
sombre looks being garbed in gowns of brilliant shades.[3]
Bartram reported of the same people that their medicine
men dressed in white robes, * and carried on their heads, as
insignias of wisdom and divination, great white owl skins.[4]
In the northern part of the land occupied by the Yakuts, all
of the medicine men wear their hair long enough to fall
down to their shoulders. They usually tie it into a tuft,
or braid it into a queue.[5] Among the Atnatanas of Alaska,
one can always detect a medicine man by his un-
covered and uncut hair.[6] In Africa, the fetich-man in order
to impress the people with his superior powers, dresses
himself in the most astonishing paraphernalia, and when
called upon to officiate on public occasions makes as much
display as possible in order to magnify his office.[7] The
dress of the priestesses of the Land Dyaks, says Henry
Ling Roth, "is very gay; over their heads they throw

[1] Dowd, "The Negro Races," p. 247.
[2] Ratzel, "History of Mankind," III, p. 528.   [3] Ibid., II, p. 155.
[4] Bartram, "Travels in the Carolinas," p. 502.
[5] Sumner, "Yakuts," Abridged from the Russian of Sieroshevski,
J. A. I., XXXI, p. 102.
[6] Smithsonian Reports, 1886, Part One, p. 266.
[7] Dowd, "The Negro Races," p. 248.
* This contradiction may be explained by the difference of
ceremonies in which these shamans officiated.

a red cloth, on the top of which they place a cylindrical
cap, worked in red, white, and black beads, and their short
petticoats are fringed with hundreds of small, tinkling
hawk-bells. Around their neck is hung a heavy bead necklace, consisting of five or six rows of black, red, and
white opaque beads strongly bound together. In addition,
they hang over their shoulders, belt-fashion, a string of
teeth, large hawk-bells, and opaque beads." [1] Bourke describes a medicine hat of an old blind shaman named
Nan-ta-do-tash. It was made of buckskin, and was
dirty from age and use. Upon the body of the hat
were figures in pigment, some brownish yellow,
and some a dingy blue, representing the spirits which
aided the wearer. It was adorned with soft feathers,
eagle plumes, bits of abalone shell and chalchihuitl, and
it was surmounted by the rattle of a snake. The old man believed the hat gave life and strength to him that wore it,
enabling him to peer into the future, to tell who had stolen
ponies from other people, to foresee the approach of an
enemy, and to aid in the cure of the sick. [2] In China, says
De Gioot, the priest is wont to "don a special vestment,
while performing religious work. The principal article of
his attire is a square sheet of silk representing the earth;
for, according to the ancient philosophy, expressed in the
writings of Liu Ngan, 'Heaven is round and earth is
square.' The silk is worn as a gown with a round hole for
the neck, an opening down the front, and no sleeves. The

---

[1] Roth, "Natives of Sarawak and British North Borneo," I, p. 250.
[2] Bourke, "Medicine Men of the Apache," Bur. Eth., IX, p. 589.

back of it is heavily embroidered with gold thread in various designs. On it are shown a continent, towering with mountains and beaten by waves; the sun and moon, personated by a crow and a rabbit, their legendary inhabitants; animals symbolizing felicity, such as elephants, lions, unicorns, tigers, phoenixes, and dragons; and the flaming palaces of the God of Heaven and of the lesser divinities. At the front of the gown are ribbons embroidered with gold to represent the parts of the universe. The garment is called by the priests the 'gown of Tao' or gown of the order of the Universe." The wearer of the gown "is invested by it with the power of the order of the world itself, and this enables him to restore that order whenever by means of sacrifices and magical ceremonies he is averting unseasonable and calamitous events, such as drought, untimely and superabundant rainfall, or eclipses. Besides, since the Tao is the mightiest power against the daimon world, the vestment endows the wearer with irresistible exorcising power." [1] Among the Tshi-speaking peoples, the dress of the representatives of heaven reflects a more primitive stage of culture. Thus Ellis says, "On the Gold Coast... priests and priestesses are readily distinguishable from the rest of the community. They wear their hair long and uncared for, while other people, except the women in the towns on the seaboard, have it cut close to the head. They also wear around the neck a long string of alternate black and white beads, which descends nearly to the waist. They generally

[1] De Groot, "Religious System of China," VI, pp. 1264—1266.

carry with them a stick from three to four feet in length,
to which about the middle are bound parallel to it
....three short sticks from three to four inches long.
These latter and adjacent parts of the long stick are
daubed with the yolk and albumen of eggs, with pieces
of the shell adhering. Very commonly priests wear a
white linen cap which completely covers the hair, and a
similar cap is worn by the priestesses, but only when they
are about to communicate with a god. Frequently both
appear with white circles painted round the eyes, or with
various white devices, marks, or lines painted on the
face, neck, shoulders, or arms. While ordinary people
wear, when their means permit, clothes of the brightest
colors and most tasteful patterns, the priesthood may prop-
erly only wear plain clothes of a dull red-brown color,
and which are so dyed with a preparation called *abbin,*
made from the bark of the mangrove tree *(abbin dwia),*
with which fishermen tan their nets. On holy days and
festivals, however, they appear arrayed in white clothes,
and on special days with their bodies covered from head to
foot with white clay. The costume of a priest or priestess, when professionally engaged in the dance, consists of a
short skirt reaching to the knee, and made in the interior
districts of woven grass of *addor,* on the sea-coast of
cotton print. At such times, too, they always carry in the
hand a short brush made of reeds." [1]

When exercising his function as healer, the medicine
man invests himself with an attire which is calculated to act

[1] Ellis, "Tshi-Speaking Peoples," pp. 123—124.

as a suggestive influence upon the minds of his patients. As will be shown later,[1] suggestion is his most important method in the treatment of disease. The sick man is given the impression that the doctor dresses in such a manner as to frighten away the disease daimon. The patient, believing the words and in the treatment of his physician, often recovers, for "according to your faith so be it unto you."[2] "The head dress of the Zulu witch doctor," as described by Ratzel, "is covered with a tall official cap of plaited straw." In conformity "to his dignity he is adorned with a carefully-tended beard, which reaches from his chin to his breast... Round his neck, as priestly adornment, hang strings of white coral, upon which the fetich" is thought to "descend during incantations. A silken sheet of gay colours, fantastically knotted and covered all over with charms, rolls down over the dress of the priest. In his hand he carries a wisp of rushes, a fetich-whisk. This is here and there exchanged for the tail of a cow or buffalo, and is always regarded among fetich-men as the symbol of the priestly office. His naked feet are adorned with sandals of red leather, and his ankles with chains of coral... A more peculiar impression cannot be conceived than is produced by the unexpected appearance of a *ganga* [shaman], rigged out in this way, dancing, singing, and ventriloquising."[3] The medicine man of the Black Feet Indian tribes, when exercising his art upon a sick person, arrayed himself in the most absurd costume which

[1] Vide, pp. 217—222.
[2] St. Matthew, 9 : 29.
[3] Ratzel, "History of Mankind," pp. 365—366.

the mind of man ever conceived. For a coat he wore the skin of a yellow bear. The skin of the head was formed into a mask, which entirely hid the features of the enchanter. On his person in addition to the skin of the yellow bear—an article exceedingly rare and, therefore, in itself a powerful medicine—were the skins of various wild animals which were also anomalies or deformities and hence, in the savage estimation, medicine. There were also skins of snakes, frogs, field mice, snails, the beaks and tails of birds, hoofs of deer, goats, and antelopes, in a word, the odds and ends, the fag ends and tips, of everything that swims, flies, or runs. In one hand he held a magic wand, in the other a fearful rattle which contained the arcana of his order. On coming into the lodge where a sick man lay, he shook the rattle and brandished the magic wand, to the clatter, din, and discord of which he added wild startling jumps and Indian yells, and the horrid and appalling grunts, growls and snarls of the grizzly bear, calling on the bad daimon to leave the patient. It was necessary to see the dress of that medicine man before a person could form a just conception of his frightful appearance. There are some instances in which the exhausted patient unaccountably recovered under the application of those absurd forms.[1]

In civilized nations the priests and ministers of religion adopt, for the most part, various modes of apparel to typify their office and the function which they perform. Among

---

[1] Catlin, "North American Indians," I, pp. 39—40; Wood, "Natural History of Man," II, p. 680.

A Blackfoot Medicine Man in Full Regalia.
(After Catlin).   See pp. 101—102.

the Hebrews, the high priest had a peculiar dress which was passed on to his successor at his death. In some Christian churches, the stole, the surplice, the cope, the chasuble, and other vestments serve to differentiate priest from people, assist in rendering the service awe-inspiring and impressive, and suggest to the minds of devout worshippers holy, solemn, and sacred things.

In every tribe and nation there is a tendency on the part of medicine men to form among themselves an intimate alliance. Human nature is the same the world over. Shamans desire to learn secrets and methods belonging to others of their class, but at the same time they wish to prevent their secrets from being shared by outsiders. Hence an association is formed for the mutual benefit of the initiated, and for the exclusion of the uninitiated from all rights and privileges. It comes to pass, therefore, that society is made up of two classes— the "Ins" and the "Outs;" [1] the "Wes" and the "Yous;" the profession and the laity. This class distinction makes for the building up of the learned sect. If the priest class is the most favored in the nation, the young men will wish to avail themselves of the benefits and emoluments which issue from membership in the fraternity. The older medicine men, jealous of the credit of their profession, are always busy pointing out those advantages to the youth, and endeavoring to induce them to become members. Individuals, therefore, in whose veins flows the best blood in the nation, being led by the desire to be enrolled

[1] Keller, "Societal Evolution," p. 123.

within the ranks of the "Ins," often enter the sacred profession. Thus it comes about that the shamanic brotherhood includes many members of the superior class.[1]

Of the existence of secret societies made up entirely of medicine men, we have direct evidence. Such are the societies of the Korean *pan-su* [or shamans] who not only form guilds but even provide money for the erection of lodges in which they may meet.[2] Among some American Indian tribes, the *mide* had secret societies, which extended from the southern states to the northern provinces. There were four degrees, each having an especial secret which was kept with great care. Only a few select shamans received the highest degree.[3] Among the Tshi-speaking peoples, says Ellis, "the medicine men study sleight-of-hand, and, it is said, ventriloquism; while they have acquired a knowledge of the medicinal properties of various herbs which materially assist them in the maintenance of their imposture. All being united to deceive the people, they are careful to assist each other and to make known anything that may be generally useful. They send to one another information of what is taking place, what people are likely to come to seek their service, and for what purpose they contemplate coming. Sometimes a priest will inform an applicant that the god he serves refuses to accord the information or assistance required, and will recommend him to go to another priest, to whom in the meantime he has communicated every particular; and on consulting this second priest

---

[1] Vide, p. 51.
[2] Bishop, "Korea," p. 402.
[3] Bartels, "Med. Naturvölker," pp. 63—64.

the applicant is astonished to find that he knows, without being told, the purpose for which he has come."[1]

It might not be out of place at this point to discuss a phase of the subject concerning which frequent inquiry is made, namely, the proportion among primitive medicine men of quacks and frauds to those who are honest and sincere. Investigations indicate the fact that the ratio of the false to the true among the uncivilized is practically the same as among the civilized. There are black sheep in every fold. The condition is inevitable. "It must needs be that offences come."[2] Of the twelve original apostles one was a traitor. There are many insincere clergymen; there are many quack doctors; but in either case the greater number of clergymen and doctors are reliable and trustworthy men. So, too, while medicine men are mistaken in that their major premise is wrong, most of them enter upon their profession in good faith, and, indeed, succeed in achieving ends which on the whole make for the good of their society. The results of a wide range of reading are here given in substantiation of what has been said.

The evidence as to the number of quacks may first be adduced. Among the Tshi-speaking peoples, "the possessors of *ehsuhman*... a sub-order of priests ... are conscious of their own imposture."[3] The same writer states, "There are some medicine men, who though conscious of their own fraud and of the mythical nature of the gods they themselves serve, still implicitly believe in the existence

---

[1] Ellis, "Tshi-Speaking Peoples," p. 128.
[2] St. Matthew, 18:7.
[3] Ellis, "Tshi-Speaking Peoples," p. 192.

and power of other gods who are regarded as greater."[1] An investigator writes concerning her observation of the Head-hunters, "For fever, some of these native doctors have splendid medicine; but on the other hand many of them are awful humbugs, and ascribe every kind of magical power to some absolutely rubbishy concoction, and charge accordingly."[2] In Tibet, "there are undoubtedly devout *lamas,* though the majority are idle and unholy."[3] In Queensland, there are sharp-witted individuals who arrogate to themselves powers similar to those of the publicly-recognized medicine men. An authority states that "to differentiate between the truly qualified practitioners and the quacks is often no easy matter—and the difficulty is only increased when one bears in mind that the effects produced by either class of individuals are for all practical purposes identical."[4]

According to Laflesche, among the Indians of North America, in contradistinction to good shamans "there was another kind of medicine man, who held no office of public trust, for he lacked one of the essential qualifications for such a responsibility, and that was truthfulness; he continually wandered in thought, word, and deed from the straight path of truth. He was shrewd, crafty, and devoid of scruples. The intelligent classes within the tribe held him in contempt, while the ignorant of the community feared him. His pretentions

[1] Ellis, "Tshi-Speaking Peoples," p. 147.
[2] Cator, "Everyday Life Among the Head-Hunters," p. 189.
[3] Bishop, "Among the Tibetans," p. 88.
[4] Roth, "Superstition, Magic, and Medicine," North Queensland Ethnography Bulletin, Number 5, p. 31.

enabled him to carry on successfully his profession of deception upon the simple. He was a 'Healer,' something similar to the healer known to the civilized folk now-a-days as 'divine.' ..... He was a keen observer of nature and human nature, and he used his acumen solely to his own advantage. If he had possessed book learning in addition to what he gleaned from experience, and lived in New York City or Chicago, he would not have failed of many followers. Or, he might have been useful in the Weather Bureau at Washington, for when he said it would rain, it did rain." [1]

In proclaiming oracles the medicine man does not in every instance deliberately set himself to the task of imposing upon the people. He may often be an earnest man, so intensely possessed by the thought of a spirit speaking within him that in good faith he changes the tones of his voice to suit the spirit utterance. But spirit utterance there must be, and if the oracle refuses to speak voluntarily and spontaneously, the medicine man sometimes resorts to trickery and fraud to facilitate such utterance. In illustration of this point attention is directed to Bastian's "Der Mensch in der Geschichte," in which it is said that among the Congo people the medicine man is accustomed to use ventriloquism in proclaiming oracles.[2] Ratzel writes, "Complete masters of this priestcraft are versed in animal magnetism, ventriloquism, and sleight-of-hand." [3] In these instances ventriloquism is not

[1] Laflesche, "Who was the Medicine Man?" Thirty-second Annual Report of the Fairmount Park Art Association, p. 12.
[2] Op. cit., II, p. 200.   [3] Ratzel, "History of Mankind," II, p. 156.

practiced unconsciously and in the belief that the gods
are speaking through their anointed, but by artificial
stimulation and with the premeditated purpose of deceiv-
ing the people, and beguiling them into the belief that
the will of the gods is thus being revealed. Abominable
conduct such as this was no doubt responsible for some
of the strong utterances of Bourke, as for example, "It will
only be after we have thoroughly routed the medicine men
from their intrenchments, and made them the objects
of ridicule, that we can hope to bend and train the minds
of our Indian wards in the direction of civilization. In my
own opinion, the reduction of the medicine men will effect
more for the savages than the giving of land in severalty,
or the instruction in the schools at Carlisle or
Hampton."[1]

There would seem to be conclusive proof, on the
other hand, that the greater number of medicine men are
honest and sincere. Primitive doctors in the majority of cases
are not consciously and utterly impostors. The shamans
believe that they have spoken to the gods face to face,
have heard their voice, and felt their presence. The faith
of the priest is generally real, and cannot be shaken.
And, "as one thinketh in his heart, so is he."[2] Among
the Yakuts, says Sieroshevski, "some shamans are as
passionately devoted to their calling as drunkards to drink.
One had several times been condemned to punishment; his
professional dress and drum had been burned, his hair had

---

[1] Bourke, "Medicine Men of the Apache," Bur. Eth., IX, p. 594.
[2] Proverbs, 23 : 7.

been cut off, and he had been compelled to make a number of obeisances and to fast. He remarked, 'We do not carry on this calling without paying for it. Our masters [the spirits] keep a zealous watch over us, and woe betide us afterwards if we do not satisfy them: but we cannot quit it; we cannot cease to practice shaman rites. Yet we do no evil!'" [1] Of the Eskimos, Boas writes, "Most of the *angakoks* believe in their performance, as by continued shouting and invoking they fall into ecstasy, and really imagine they accomplish flights and see spirits." [2] Concerning the natives of West Africa, it is said, "If you ask me frankly whether I think these African witch doctors believe in themselves, I think I must say, 'Yes;' or perhaps it would be better to say they believe in the theory by which they work, for of that there can be little doubt. I do not fancy they ever claim invincible power over disease; they do their best according to their lights. It would be difficult to see why they should doubt their own methods, because, remember, all their patients do not die; the majority recover ... Africans of the West Coast ... are liable to many nervous disorders. In these nervous cases the bedside manners of the medicine man may be really useful." [3] Hoffman quotes an authority to the effect that the "dreamers" [a class of shamans among the Menomini Indians] "were evidently thoroughly, even fanatically, in earnest." [4] Among the Omahas, four

[1] Sumner, "Yakuts," Abridged from the Russian of Sieroshevski, J. A. I., XXXI, p. 102.
[2] Boas, "Central Eskimo," Bur. Eth., VI, p. 594.
[3] Kingsley, "West African Studies," pp. 217—218.
[4] Hoffman, "The Menomini Indians," Bur. Eth., 1896, p. 160.

demands were made of the one who "was to deal with
the mysteries enshrined in the rites and ceremonies of
the tribe: First and foremost, was the recognition of the
sanctity of human life. The man who was to mediate
between the people and Wa-kon-da must stand before his
tribesmen and the Great Spirit with hands unstained with
the blood of his fellow man. Secondly, he must be a man
whose words never deviate from the path of truth, for
the Great Spirit manifests the value placed upon truth
in the regular and orderly movements of the heavenly
bodies, and in the ever-recurring day and night, summer
and winter. Thirdly, he must be slow to anger, for the
patience of the Great Spirit is shown in his forbearance
with the waywardness of man. Fourthly, he must be
deliberate and prudent of speech, lest by haste he should
profane his trust through thoughtless utterance. The man
thus chosen was true to the sacredness of his office." [1]
Among the Land Dyaks, the shamanesses "are not necessarily impostors; they but practice the ways and recite
the songs which they received from their predecessors,
and the dignity and importance of the office enable them
to enjoy some intervals of pleasurable excitement during
their laborious lives." [2] Nansen, in his "Eskimo Life,"
says, "The influence of these *angakoks* of course depended
upon their adroitness; but they do not seem to have been
mere charlatans. It is probable that they themselves partly
believed in their own arts, and were convinced that they

[1] Laflesche, "Who was the Medicine Man?" Thirty-second
Annual Report of the Fairmount Park Art Association, p. 9.
[2] Roth, "Natives of Sarawak and British North Borneo," p. 259.

sometimes received actual revelations."[1] That medicine men in the capacity of physician generally learn their profession in good faith, and retain their belief until the last, is evidenced by the fact that when they fall ill or are in straits, they solicit assistance of others in the same profession.[2] A case in point is the Dieyerie tribes of South America, whose shamans, when they are themselves sick, call in other medicine men to wait upon them.[3] That would seem to show their sincerity.

The medicine man, adverse criticism to the contrary notwithstanding, is not always and everywhere an unprincipled, unmitigated knave. For though it cannot be denied that many a shaman preys upon the superstitions, gullibilities, and weaknesses of the ignorant, the savage doctor is nevertheless often useful in achieving results which at a primitive stage of culture might not be wrought in any other way. In sickness the people rely absolutely on his healing powers. According to Mooney, the Cherokee Indian trusts his medicine man as a child trusts a more intelligent doctor.[4] In Australia, during sickness "the natives have implicit confidence in their medicine men, and in serious cases, two or three, if they be available, are called in consultation."[5] Throughout the Malay Archipelago, and throughout America and Australia, the people place absolute reliance upon the shamans.[6]

[1] Op. cit., p. 282.
[2] Brinton, "Religion of Primitive Peoples," p. 58.
[3] Bartels, "Med. Naturvölker," p. 92.
[4] Mooney, "Sacred Formulas of the Cherokees," Bur. Eth., VII, p. 323.
[5] Spencer and Gillen, "Native Tribes of Central Australia," p. 530.
[6] Bartels, "Med. Naturvölker," p. 50.

The methods used in the hour of sickness are well calculated to give a feeling of confidence; and the effect produced on the mind of the patient without doubt reacts favorably upon his physical organization. Suggestion is the great stock-in-trade of the savage doctor,[1] and faith is the *sine qua non* on the part of the patient. The divination, magic, prayers, and hocus pocus of the medicine man all tend to inspire in the mind of the sick the greatest hope and expectancy for recovery.

With the thought of shamanic sincerity in mind, instances of remarkable cures effected by aboriginal healers through suggestion or some other means may not be uninteresting. Mrs. Allison says of the Similkameen Indian medicine men, that aside from their mysteries they have "really valuable medicines. People apparently in the last stages of consumption have been cured by them."[2] Bartels, quoting Büttikofer, relates that in Liberia in certain sicknesses even white people have been cured by the medicine man, after the European doctors had confessed their inability to do anything for the patient.[3] Concerning the success of a medicine man among the Head-hunters it is related, "We met a woman lately who had come from Freetown with a dreadful disease in her face, and our doctors could do nothing for her; and so her husband brought her right up here in the interior

---

[1] Vide pp. 217—222.
[2] S. S. Allison, "Similkameen Indians of Brit. Columbia," J. A. I., 1891, p. 311.
[3] Bartels, "Med. Naturvölker," p. 50.

to one of these 'medicine men' to be cured 'country fashion' and she is getting better every day. Her suffering was intense, but now she has absolutely no pain, and is evidently on the high road to recovery."[1] The following account of a striking cure is taken from Hearne's Journal: "During our stay at Anaw'd Lake, as several of the Indians were sickly, the white doctors undertook to adminster relief particularly to one man who had been hauled on a sledge by his brother for two months. His disorder was that of the dead palsy, which affected one side from the crown of his head to the sole of his foot. Besides this dreadful disorder, he had some inward complaints with a total loss of appetite, so that he was reduced to a mere skeleton, and so weak as scarcely to be capable of speaking. In this deplorable condition, he was laid in the center of a large conjuring-house, and that nothing might be wanting towards his recovery, the medicine man swallowed, or feigned to swallow a large piece of board about the size of a barrel stave. Then six of his co-workers, stripped naked, followed him into the conjuring house, where they soon began to blow, suck, sing and dance around the paralytic, and continued to do so for four nights and three days . . . and it was truly wonderful, though the strictest truth, that when the sick man was taken from the conjuring-house he had not only recovered his appetite to an amazing degree, but was able to move all the fingers and toes of the side that had been so long dead. In three weeks he had

[1] Cator, "Every day Life among the Head-Hunters," p. 189.

recovered so far as to be capable of walking, and at the end of six weeks he went hunting with his family." [1] In view of such achievements how could savage doctors do otherwise than believe in the theory by which they work?

One other aspect of the subject remains to be discussed in this chapter, and that is the social position of the medicine man. This depends upon the respect and fear which he is able to inspire by this attitude of aloofness and by the strength of personality, as well as upon the popular belief in his influence and power with the gods. The conviction of his supernatural origin, the effect of his adventitious aids, his superior mental and moral qualities, in addition to the exhibition of truly wonderful powers, cause in the savage mind a feeling of veneration and awe which does not fail to assist in extending the temporal and spiritual sway of the shaman over all classes throughout the land. By many individuals and peoples, therefore, his power is thought to be without limit, extending to the raising of the dead and the control of the laws of nature.[2] The Eskimo medicine men are clever, but they are also crafty. They proclaim their ability in no moderate terms. To speak with spirits, to travel to the underworld or the heavens, to invoke such mighty beings as the *tornarssuk* and obtain information from them—all these tasks are thought to lie within their power to perform.[3] In Victoria, the native doctors maintain that they know all

[1] Hearne, "Voyage à l'Océan Nord," I, pp. 333—336.
[2] Schoolcraft, "Information Respecting the Indian Tribes of the United States," V, p. 423. [3] Nansen, "Eskimo Life," p. 281.

things over and under the earth.[1] Among the Indians of Southern California, it is believed that the shaman can command the elements, read the future, and change himself into whatever form he wishes.[2] In the New Hebrides, the savage doctor was regarded with fear and veneration by the people; he could bring rain or drive it away, he could cause sickness or banish disease. The people believed that he was able to make thunder and lightning and to cause hurricanes. It was also thought that he could make different kinds of food grow, and give or withhold fish from the sea.[3] Among the Mexicans, the medicine man was credited with having the power to transform himself into an animal.[4] The natives of Victoria relate that a medicine man restored the "kidney-fat" of a patient, and so effected a cure after the white doctor had given the man over to die.[5] The priest physicians of the Sea Dyaks try to heighten their prestige among gullible laymen by asserting after every event which takes place, that they knew of it beforehand. Even when a sick person seeks their help, they will say that they foresaw his attack.[6] In Central Queensland, an authority writes, it was believed that "a medicine man could make an individual sick, even when he was miles away, and 'doom him,' so to speak. This 'dooming' meant being cut up into small pieces and put together again; the spear, or other visible cause, was not to blame—

---

[1] Bartels, "Med. Naturvölker," p. 50. [2] Ibid., p. 51.
[3] J. Laurie, "Aneityum," Aust. Ass. for Adv. Science, 1892, p. 711.
[4] Mendieta, "Historia Eclesiástica Indiana," p. 109.
[5] Bartels, "Med. Naturvölker," p. 50.
[6] Roth, "Natives of Sarawak and British North Borneo," I, p. 267. (Note).

it only completed the deed... When [a white man named] Petrie once chaffed the natives about one of their medicine man being locked up in a prison cell, and taunted them about his not being able to get out, he was informed that the prisoner only refrained from escaping through the key-hole, because he did not like to disappoint and insult his European captors; the blacks were quite satisfied that the individual in question could easily have secured his own liberty, if he had wanted to." [1] In Central Australia, it is believed that medicine men can assume the form of eagle-hawks, and when thus disguised, travel long distances during the night, visiting the camps of other tribes, where they are responsible for much suffering and even death by their habit of digging their sharp claws into the sleepers. [2] Among the Tshi-speaking peoples, the shaman is considered able to work miracles. People go to him for information and assistance in almost every concern of life—to expose the thief, the slanderer, and the adulteress, to procure good luck or to avert misfortune, and to detect murderers. In their anxiety to secure his aid, men have been known to enslave themselves in order to obtain the requisite sum for the services of the doctor. [3] The Mi-Wok of Southern California declared that their medicine men could sit on the top of a mountain fifty miles away from the person whom they wished to destroy, and bring about his death by flipping poison towards him with

---

[1] Roth, "Superstition, Magic, and Medicine," North Queensland, Ethnography, Bulletin, No. 5, p. 30.
[2] Spencer and Gillen, "Native Tribes of Central Australia," p. 533.
[3] Ellis, "Tshi-Speaking Peoples," p. 124.

their finger-ends.[1] Miss Kingsley writes that the adherents of the West African Ju-ju priests believe those worthies capable of disguising "a person so that his own mother would not recognize him, this without the assistance of any make-up, but simply by their devilish science; they think that they could cause a tree on the banks of a river to bend its stem and imbibe water through its topmost branches; that they could change themselves into birds and fly away; and that they could make themselves invisible before your eyes and so suddenly that you could not tell when they had done so."[2] In Northwest Queensland, the power of the medicine man is held to be so great that the natives say, without him "the effects of the charm would be harmless, sickness and death would gradually disappear, and there would be a likelihood of the aboriginals living forever."[3] The Algonquin tribes, and the Sacs and Foxes, thought the soul could not leave the body until released at the great annual feast by the efforts of the shaman.[4] According to the belief of some tribal groups, neither death, nor hell, nor the grave offers any escape from the omnipotent power of the medicine man.

It is not difficult to understand that in any community a person wielding a power so enormous in its possibilities as does the shaman, must of necessity occupy a place of great prominence. The position of the medicine man in the society is, therefore, one of tremendous importance. He

[1] Powers, "Tribes of California," Contrib. North Am. Eth., III, p.354.
[2] Kingsley, "West African Studies," p. 499.
[3] Roth, "Superstition, Magic, and Medicine," North Queensland, Ethnography, Bulletin No. 5, p. 30.
[4] J. M. Stanley, Smithsonian Contributions, II, p. 38.

must be treated with reverence, and his wishes consulted, lest in anger he consume the recalcitrants. No individual is honored in any social aggregation unless he commands respect. When a herd of steers receives an additional member, the new comer must at once lock horns with the leader. If he is successful in the conflict, he is treated with such deference that he becomes the corypheus of the herd. If, on the other hand, he is worsted in the combat, he must contest with a less and less able antagonist, until at length the "water finds its level." When a "tenderfoot" arrives at the scene of his future "cow punching," his first task is to meet the bully of the crowd in physical encounter. In case he proves superior to his antagonist, he is respected by the "gang" and his status is assured. But if he goes down in the struggle, he must deal with a successively weaker foe until he finds his stratum. In primitive society the medicine man, even though sometimes a dwarf, is respected because the weapons of his warfare for the most part are not carnal but spiritual. He has a great advantage, therefore, in combat because to the mind of the savage a spirit is the most terrible foe imaginable. It is asserted, for example, that among the tribes of Siberia and the Dyaks of Borneo, the non-sacerdotal physician is far less esteemed than the shaman, who depends upon the possession of mysterious powers which give him control over daimons.[1] Concerning the standing of the shaman in West Africa Miss Kingsley says, "The medicine

---

[1] Roth, "Natives of Sarawak and British North Borneo," I, p. 271.

man is known to possess witch power, and knowledge of how to employ it; but instead of this making him an object of aversion to his fellow men, it secures for him esteem and honor, and the more terrifically powerful his person is known to be, the more respect he gains." [1] According to Bartels, the position of the shaman among all savage tribes is especially honorable and dignified. By the Dakotas he was treated with veneration and provided with the best things in the land. [2] "On the Tully River," says an authority, "the medicine men are respected, and the other blacks will not play any tricks or larks on them, as they often do with others in the camp." [3]

Not only does the mystical influence of the shaman secure for him the respect of his people, but it also inspires them with fear of his dreaded person, of his ill will, and of his anger. Nansen says of the Eskimos, "By reason of their connexion with the supernatural world, the most esteemed *angakoks* have considerable authority over their countrymen, who are afraid of the evil results which may follow any act of disobedience." [4] The dread which the medicine man excites among the Thlinkeets can easily be imagined when it is known that in their land the supreme feat of the power of a conjuror is to throw one of his liege spirits into the body of a person who refuses to believe in his might, "upon which the possessed is taken with

[1] Kingsley, "West African Studies," p. 212.
[2] Bartels, "Med. Naturvölker," p. 49.
[3] Roth, "Superstition, Magic, and Medicine," North Queensland, Ethnography, Bulletin No. 5, p. 30.
[4] Nansen, "Eskimo Life," p. 283.

swooning and fits."[1]   Among the Andamanese the
oko-paiad must be propitiated with frequent, handsome
gifts, lest they visit those at whom they are angry
with disease and even death.[2]

In addition to his alleged intimacy with the gods,
the medicine man of some tribes does not hesitate in
cases of incorrigibility to employ another expedient,
which never fails to smite terror into the heart
of both friend and foe. This may be called his
detective function.[3] Savage peoples cannot conceive of bad
luck, sickness, and death apart from agency.[4] The agents
may be visible or invisible. In either case the question
arises: Who prevailed upon the spirits to despoil the
crops or slay the cattle? Who caused the daimon to enter
into the patient and bring about his sickness and death?
For "proper" answers those questions are always submitted
to the specialist of the imaginary environment. Then woe
unto those unfortunate individuals against whom the
medicine man entertains a grudge; for upon them will
fall the accusation of witchcraft, which is usually followed
by death.[5] This detective function gives the medicine
man an opportunity to gratify his private malice, to punish
the recreant, to whip with perfect safety the disobedient into
line, and at the same time to intensify to a superlative
degree the dread with which popular superstition
enshrouds his own person. In order to show the truth

[1] Spencer, "Principles of Sociology," II, p. 339.
[2] J. A. I., XI, p. 289.
[3] Vide pp. 84—87.
[4] Vide, pp. 4—5; 14; 167.
[5] Kingsley, "Travels in West Africa," p. 463.

of what has just been said the following examples are presented. Spencer and Gillen write concerning the Central Australians, "No such a thing as natural death is realized by the natives. A man who dies has of necessity been killed by some other man or woman, and sooner or later some one will be accused by the medicine man, his life thereby being forfeited." "Sometimes when a man is dying, he will whisper in the ear of the medicine man the name of the culprit, but even if he does not do so, the medicine man will often state as soon as death has taken place, the direction in which the culprit lives and very probably the group to which he belongs. It may be perhaps two or three years before he discovers the actual man, but sooner or later he does so."[1] It is needless to point out what a potent element this custom has been in cowing the masses. In some of parts Africa, the medicine man may "mark" the person who is causing the sickness, and commonly the "marked" individual is put to death as a sacrifice.[2] In Central Africa, a stranger as well as a member of the tribe may be accused of causing a sudden death, and in such cases the medicine man has the right both to judge and to order his victim to speedy execution.[3] Among the Tshi-speaking peoples, the priests "are frequently employed to procure the death of persons who have injured or offended the applicants. It is not supposed, however, that the priests have this power of themselves, but rather that, being

[1] Spencer and Gillen, "Native Tribes of Central Australia," pp. 48 and 533.   [2] J. A. I., XXII, p. 104.
[3] Ibid.

in high favor with the gods, they are able to induce them to adopt their quarrels." [1] The persons against whom the priests exert their powers sometimes really die, and in such coincidences the power of the servants of the gods is greatly enhanced. When the doomed individual does not die from disease or accident, "if the priest be sufficiently interested in the case.... he causes poison to be administered to the man 'pointed out' .. He is careful not to let the applicant know what means he has used to procure the desired end, and the latter attributes the death of his enemy solely to the hocus pocus of the priest... Although a priest who may thus use his influence with a god to destroy life does not appear to be held blameworthy, the applicant who carries out the instructions of the priest, and who is thus believed to have caused the death is, if discovered, himself put to death; and, as it is supposed that the members of his family have been privy to his proceedings, even if they did not instigate the crime, or aid and abet the murderer, they are sold as slaves except in extreme cases, when they are put to death.... How do savage peoples discover the procurer of the death of another? Through the priest. He does not betray a man who has made application to him; such a course would be fatal to his own interests. But if some one has not shown him the proper reverence, that is the individual whom he indicates as the guilty person. Thus many innocent men and women are made to suffer, and the priest can gratify his private malice with impunity." [2]

[1] Ellis, "Tshi-Speaking Peoples," pp. 142—146. [2] Ibid.

It is to the advantage, therefore, of every tribal member to ingratiate himself with the medicine man. If there be a person who can so influence the spirits that they will do his behest, it is obvious that everybody will want to make friends with him. Even if he has no mystical power, if by using his detective function he can throw the blame of evil fortune on the insubordinate, every person in the group will dread him to the extent of showing him respect, reverence, and even worship. All will fear to offend him lest he use the weight of his tremendous power against them. Thus we are told that among the Papuans, the common people live in great terror of the wizard. Remnants of food are carefully collected after a meal and buried or burned lest he get possession of them and so exercise his supposed power of sorcery.[1] The men of Victoria fear to touch the medicine man and, therefore, yield to all his demands; the women quake before him because they believe him able to rob them of their "kidney-fat." A greater reason for these women to fear a shaman is the belief that he is able to make them unfruitful and to kill their children.[2] In some districts "everyone falls down before the medicine man with face to the ground; he commands and all obey in terror lest he should smite them to the earth.... Children have fallen into convulsions, women have dropped dead in the forest from coming upon him unawares."[3] The Sahaptain Indians frequently die

---

[1] S. Ella, "Samoa" Aust. Ass. for Adv. Science, 1892, p. 638.
[2] Bartels, "Med. Naturvölker," p. 51.
[3] Lehmann, "Aberglaube und Zauberei," p. 19; Reclus, "Primitive Folk," p. 235.

from fright on beholding the evil eye of the shaman, and
the Wascow Indians believe that death is certain when he
casts his terrible glance at any person.[1] Among the Yakuts,
says Sieroshevski, shamans and shamanesses are buried
without "ecclesiastical ceremonies in grave or forest. On a
tree near the grave they hang up the paraphernalia of the
deceased. Such persons are buried with great haste by
night, or in the evening, and the places where they are
buried are always carefully avoided."[2] Among some
peoples, when a man becomes obsessed with the idea that
the awful eye of the medicine man has been fixed upon
him, he often sickens, wastes away, refuses food, and dies
of hunger and melancholia.[3]

The special regard and fear aroused by the medicine
man unite in making for him a unique place in the tribal
group. In some instances he enjoys special immunity from
punishment, no matter how great the offence. Connolly
relates an illustrative incident which occured in Fanti-
Land. The account reads as follows: "A certain Kwamina Dorko was at enmity with two friends named
Kújo Atta and Kwéku Dyén, and to take revenge
on them applied to a fetich-priest named Kofi Paka
to inflict some injury on the two friends. At the
inquiry, the fetich-priest...made a very free confession
of his part in the matter and seemed desirous to impress
the natives with a consciousness of his skill. He on
payment of twenty-eight shillings, a present of rum and

---

[1] Bartels, "Med. Naturvölker," pp. 51 and 57.
[2] Sumner, "Yakuts," Abridged from the Russian of Sieroshevski
J. A. I., XXXI, p. 99.
[3] Bartels, "Med. Naturvölker," p. 51.

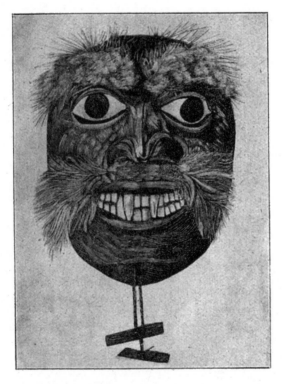

Another Device of the Medicine Man
for Frightening Daimons.

fowls, went with Kwamina Dorko to a path near the town where Kújo Atta and Kwéku Dyén lived, dug a hole in the pathway, and laid therein a large red crab, with cowries tied to it, and sprinkled rum over it. The invocation he made, which he repeated at the inquiry, was, 'O crab-fetich, when Kújo Atta and Kwéku Dyén walk over you, may you take life from them,' that is to say, power, strength, health, or vitality. As soon as this became known, Kújo Atta and Kwéku Dyén dug up the crab-fetich, and in their anger, nearly took the life out of Kwamina Dorko and some of his friends. In their defence, the crab-fetich was produced in court as quite a sufficient provocation for any assault. It is remarkable that no violence was offered to the fetich-priest, and that he came as willingly to give evidence to prove the malice of Kwamina Dorko as he went to gratify that malice by 'making fetich' against the others."[1]

The medicine man is naturally keen in turning to advantage the unusual esteem and privileges which come to him by virtue of his office. Among the Sioux he was the most powerful and influential man in the tribe.[2] The shaman of the Fuegians excels the laymen in cunning and deceit, and, therefore, in influence.[3] In Australia, too, the most influential person in any social group is the medicine man.[4] According to Catlin, among the tribes of his acquaintance, the medicine man had a seat in all the councils of war, he was regularly consulted before any public

[1] Connolly, "Social Life in Fanti-Land," J. A. I., XXVI, p. 151.
[2] Minnesota Historical Collections, Vol. I, p. 269.
[3] Spencer, "Principles of Sociology," p. 339.
[4] Bartels, "Med. Naturvölker," p. 49.

step was taken, and the greatest respect was paid to his opinion.[1] Spencer says that "though the Tasmanians were free from the despotism of rulers, they were swayed by the counsels, governed by the arts, or terrified by the fears of certain wise men or doctors. These could not only mitigate suffering, but inflict it." [2] The medicine man of the Abipones taught his people "'the place, time and manner proper for attacking wild beasts or the enemy. On an approaching combat, he rode round the ranks, striking the air with a palm bough, and with a fierce countenance, threatening eyes, and affected gesticulations, imprecated evil on all enemies.'" [3] Among the primitive Germans, "'the maintenance of discipline in the field as in the council was left in great measure to the priests: they took the auguries and gave the signal for the onset, they alone had power to visit with legal punishment, to bind or to beat.'" [4]

An interesting monograph could be written on "The Parasites of Human Society." Parasites are those who live at the expense of others. They exist among insects. The bee family consists of the queen, the workers, and the drones. The workers are always busy extracting nectar from plant and flower, making it into honey for present use, and storing the manufactured product against the day of need. The drones make no contribution to the common store. They do not even earn their own living, but are sustained by the workers. They are para-

[1] Catlin, "North American Indians," I, p. 41.
[2] Spencer, "Principles of Sociology," II, p. 339.
[3] Ibid., III, p. 111, Quoting Dobrizhoffer's "Account of the Abipones," II, p. 76.   [4] Ibid., III. p. 112, Quoting Stubbs' "Constitutional History of England," I, p. 34.

sites.[1] Human society has always had its parasites. As far back as the reach of knowledge extends, it is found that there have been individuals who lived at the expense of others. The productive class, by labor, intellectual or manual, procure the means of subsistence. The parasitic class have no share in the supplying of material needs, but are furnished by the working class with the means of livelihood. In some regards the medicine man is a human parasite. He and his fellows make up a class which is non-productive of material goods. Their necessities and even luxuries are provided by those who toil. Their non-participation in the competition for life, their superabundance of leisure time, and the wide range of pleasure available to them are made possible at the expense of "the forgotten man." To take a few cases in point, it is said that among the aborigines of Victoria the medicine men do not hunt, fish, or do any kind of labor. They expect gifts from their people, and, in fact, prey on the superstitions of their tribal companions. By their wits and cunning, they preserve an ascendency over their supporters, and live on the profits of their crafty practices.[2] In Dahomey "when a man is once admitted into the ranks of the fetiches, his subsistence is provided for, whether he be one of the 'regulars,' who have no other calling, and who live entirely upon the presents which they obtain from those who consult them, or whether he retains some secular trade and only acts the fetich-man when the fit happens to come on him."[3] Among the Atnatanas of

[1] Maeterlink, "The Life of the Bee," pp. 246 ff. [2] Brough Smith, "Aborigines of Victoria," p. 467. [3] Wood, "Natural Hist. of Man," I, p. 656.

Alaska, the shamans are merely primitive priests and prophets, they produce nothing.[1]

But despite the strong convictions of many persons as to the balefulness of the medicine man, and despite his imposition upon society in the capacity of parasite, his influence has not been wholly for bad. He has, indeed, given to society more than he has received, and has rendered a social service unique in its significance. Even the parasite has its place. Among bees, were it not for the drones, the society would perish. The medicine man and his associates, supplied by other classes with bodily sustenance, constitute a leisure class.[2] Without a leisure class it would seem impossible among savage as well as among civilized peoples for any intellectual progress or culture to be attained. For the leisure class the struggle for existence is eliminated. Their physical wants being supplied by the "toiling millions," they have necessarily a large surplus of mental energy which must be expended, and a large amount of time which must be consumed. That this time and energy has not been wasted we have direct evidence. The priests of New Zealand, for example, turned to account their leisure time by acquiring skill in wood-carving and other arts.[3] Among the Mexicans and Peruvians, the shamans "learned how to mix colors, to paint, to draw hieroglyphics, to practice medicine, music, and also astrology, and the reckoning of time."[4] Under

[1] Smithsonian Report, 1886, Part, I, p. 266.
[2] Spencer, "Principles of Sociology," III, p. 184.
[3] Wood, "Natural History of Man," II. p. 178.
[4] Ratzel, "History of Mankind," II, p. 155.

primitive conditions the intellectual force of the group centers chiefly in the priest class. The medicine men hence become the depositaries of the tribal legends. In many cases they not only are the sole members of the tribe who are acquainted with its history, but are careful to keep this history secret so that they amaze with their knowledge those who come to consult them.[1] Since the medicine men are the preservers of the legends and traditions of the tribe, and of the art of writing, they either actively or passively become teachers of tribal lore and wisdom to the younger generation. In Mexico, in Oceania, and in Central California, the shamans gave long and careful instruction, physical, mental, and moral, to the boys and young men of their respective peoples.[2] The observation of the heavenly bodies, the adjustment of the calendar, and the pseudo-science of astrology are indebted for their beginnings to the regulation by the priest class of religious festivals. From the study and practice of astrology came the real science of astronomy. That the astronomers of ancient Egypt and Chaldea were priests, and that the study of the science of astronomy, in which considerable advance was made by those peoples, was due to the existence of a hierarchy wholly exempt from the struggle for existence, is established by the fact that the results of that study were employed in religious ceremonies. In ancient China a tribunal of mathematicians, which prepared a calendar of eclipses and made calcula-

[1] Ratzel, "History of Mankind," I, p. 55.
[2] Jour. Am. Folk Lore, Jan. 1908, p. 10.

tions of the movements of heavenly bodies, was supervised by the priesthood.[1] Hence, in the last analysis, science had its origin with this parasitic body of men.

SUMMARY. This chapter has served a threefold purpose. It was shown in the first place, that distinctiveness in diet, dwelling, dress, language, and organization has the effect of intensifying the dissimilarities between the medicine man and his people, and so of increasing popular esteem for the representative of the gods. The interesting question of the sincerity of the shaman was next discussed. And while many cases of flagrant imposture were found, yet the conclusion was reached that quackery and charlatanism are no more prevalent in primitive than in civilized societies. The many remarkable cases of healing, indeed, which must be set down to the credit of the medicine man, together with his extraordinary societal[2] control, indicate that it would be difficult for primitive society to survive apart from his activity. This led, in the third place, to a consideration of the social status of the medicine man. Owing to the respect, reverence, awe, and fear inspired by his attitude of superiority, by his so-called detective function, and by his supposed influence and relationship with the divinities, the social standing of the representative of the gods was found to be very high. He is the most influential man of primitive times. As to the use which he makes of his possibilities for good or evil, it was

[1] Dealey and Ward, "Sociology," pp. 280—281.
[2] Societal = of society. Synonymous with "social."

learned to be beyond controversy that the medicine man to some extent has been a reactionary influence in society. But that is not surprising. Since any man or institution possessing capacity for great good possesses also capacity for great evil, it is inevitable that this important personage should at times cast the weight of his influence in the wrong direction. On the whole, the priest class, however, has been of inestimable benefit to mankind, for otherwise societies which harbored the institution must of necessity have given place to other groups not thus trammelled and hindered.

CHAPTER V

THE FUNCTIONS OF THE MEDICINE MAN;
PERILS OF FAILURE; REWARDS OF SUCCESS, INCLUDING FEES.

Having considered the means by which the medicine man attains and retains his position, his belief in his own methods, and his social status, inquiry may next be made into the functions of this most important element of primitive life. From his capacity of mediator between gods and men, those activities are necessarily complex, developing along the various lines in which he may be of service to his social group. Though in barbaric just as in civilized culture there is frequent specialization, as a result of which each function of the medicine man is exercised by a different person, in primitive society the shaman combines in himself the offices of sorcerer, diviner, rain-maker, educator, prophet, priest, and king. In the discussion of the social standing of the exponent of the gods some allusion was made to his professional functions, but for the sake of completeness, this subject must now be taken up in detail.

Among the Indians of this country, says Laflesche, "the entire life of the medicine man, both public and private, was devoted to his calling. His solitary fasts were frequent, and his mind was apt to be occupied in contemplating the supernatural. His public duties were many and often onerous. His services were needed when children were dedicated to the Great Spirit; he must conduct the installation of chiefs; when dangers threatened, he must call these leaders to the council of war; and he was the one to confer upon the warrior military honors; the appointment of officers to enforce order during the buffalo hunt was his duty; and he it was who must designate the time for the planting of 'the maize. Apart from the tribal rites, he officiated at ceremonials which more directly concerned the individual; as on the introduction to the cosmos of a newly born babe."[1]

In view of his social prominence, it is not surprising that this personage makes use of his power to elevate himself to the highest position in the land—that of chief. Why should he not do so? It is characteristic of human nature to acquire all that can be obtained; and the medicine man is no exception to this rule. In Liberia, therefore, he is the leading counsellor and reigning chief in war and peace.[2] Among the Australians, the *gomera* [medicine man] commands and is obeyed. He is master of all the people of the group to which he belongs. He is wizard and headman combined.[3] In Madagascar, the king is the high priest of the realm.[4] The kings of Mangia were the priests of Rongo.[5] The chief in Tauna, according to Turner, was also the high priest of the tribe.[6] Among the Sea Dyaks, the medicine men yielded precedence only to the chiefs, and frequently one man would combine the two offices.

[1] Laflesche, "Who was the Medicine Man?" Thirty-second Annual Report of the Fairmount Park Art Association, p. 10.
[2] Bartels, "Med. Naturvölker," p. 49.
[3] Howitt, "Australian Medicine Men," J. A. I., XVI, p. 43.
[4] Ellis, "History of Madagascar," I, p. 359.
[5] Gill, "Myths and Songs from the South Pacific," pp. 293—294.
[6] Turner, "Nineteen Years in Polynesia," p. 88.

The only requisite for obtaining that dual power was popularity, and the foundation of popularity was skill in interpreting dreams and in expelling spirits.[1] In New Zealand, the priest was generally at the same time chief of his tribe.[2] Among the Amazulu, says Spencer, "a chief practices magic on another chief before fighting with him, and his followers have great confidence in him if he has much repute as a magician."[3] Among the Dakotas, the chief who led the party to war was always a medicine man. It was believed that he had the power to guide the party to success and to save it from defeat.[4] In Humphrey's Island, the king and high priest were one and the same person.[5] Spencer quotes Bishop Colenso to the effect that the sway of Langalibalele, an African ruler, was due to his knowing the composition of the *intelezi* (used for controlling the weather), together with the fact that he was doctor.[6] Among the Incas, the functions of war chief and high priest were blended.[7] The priests of the Chinooks and of the Bolivian Indians were also chiefs.[8] Hitzilopochtil, the founder of the Mexican power, is reputed to have been a great wizard and a sorcerer.[9] Odin, the Scandinavian chief, and Niort and Frey, who succeeded him in power, appear in the Heims-Kringla saga

[1] Roth, "Natives of Sarawak and British North Borneo," I, p. 265.
[2] Thompson, "The Story of New Zealand," I, p. 114.
[3] Spencer, "Principles of Sociology," II, p. 339.
[4] Schoolcraft, "Information Respecting the Indian Tribes of the United States," IV, p. 495.
[5] Turner, "Samoa, A Hundred Years and Long Before," p. 278.
[6] Spencer, "Principles of Sociology," II, p. 339.
[7] Ratzel, "History of Mankind," II, p. 203.
[8] Spencer, "Principles of Sociology," III, p. 56.
[9] Ibid., II, p. 340.

to have been medicine men.[1] "In Peru, the Inca power
was in some degree a theocracy, in which the priest-king,
once presumably elective, had become virtually a hereditary ruler at once head of church and state, claiming
divine origin and receiving divine honors."[2]

The last statement leads to the assertion that
the medicine man in some cases exercises not only
kingly power, but pretends divinity. On the principle of "get all you can," that is to be expected.
The shaman "goes from strength to strength." He
uses his power to make himself greater and greater
in the eyes of the people. According to Bourke, when an
Apache medicine man is in full regalia, he is no longer
a man, but becomes, or tries to become in the eyes of his
followers the power for which he stands.[3] In Loango, the
shaman is also king. The people ascribe to him divinity,
and think that he can control the elements.[4] In Southern
India, the advice of the medicine man is sought on every
occasion, trivial or important, and he is worshipped as
though he were a god.[5] Among the Polynesians, the
priests were called "god-boxes"—usually abbreviated
to "gods,"—that is to say, living embodiments of the
gods.[6] So it is that superstitious dread of his magic power,
of his alliance with the spirits, and of his innate or acquired
capacity for states of ecstasy, augmented by that credulity

[1] Spencer, "Principles of Sociology," II, p. 340.
[2] Jour. Am. Folk Lore, Jan. 1908, p. 11.
[3] Bourke, "Medicine Men of the Apache," Bur. Eth., IX, p. 581.
[4] Astley, "New General Collections of Voyages and Travels,"
    III, p. 223.
[5] J. A. Society of Bombay, I, p. 102.
[6] Gill, "Myths and Songs from the South Pacific," p. 35.

which leads to respect and reverence for the capable individual, raises the medicine man in the eyes of his adherents to heights of might and power which terminate finally in his claims to to be a god.

In all nations and in all ages there have been individuals sensitive to atmospheric changes and, therefore, able to make accurate forecasts of the weather. It is asserted that animals of every kind—pigs, fish, dogs, grouse, sheep and the like,—can perceive these changes. Mr. C. W. G. St. John, who is said to be an accurate observer of animal life, contends that there are few animals which do not afford timely and accurate prognostications of atmospheric disturbances.[1] In man, however, this meteorological sense is not universal. Civilized peoples, indeed, for the most part have become insensible to the electric, barometric, thermometric, hygrometric, and magnetic conditions which announce in advance these atmospheric changes. But at the present stage of culture there are occasionally individuals sensitive especially to the approach of storms. This sensibility may be felt in various ways— through vague pains, a sense of oppression, general discomfort, or heaviness in the head. Thus persons afflicted with rheumatism often before a storm experience pains in the joints with almost barometric certainty. Or a snow storm may be preceded by nervous irritability, derangement of the stomach, and general depression.[2] Among savage peoples this prognosticating ability is regarded as a gift of

[1] St. John, "Short Sketches of the Wild Sports and History of the Highlands," Chapter 33.
[2] Reference lost.

the gods. The medicine man uses the faculty to increase his power. It is not difficult to understand that in primitive societies, the man who has the gift of foretelling the approach of storm and calm, fair weather and foul, comes to be regarded as possessing supernatural power.

Not only can many medicine men make forecasts of the weather, but they have the power of predicting other events with a skill, and accuracy which impress civilized folk. Among the Kelta of Southern California, Powers writes, "the shamans profess to be spiritualists, not merely having visions in dreams, which is common to these Indians, but pretending to hold in their waking hours converse with spirits by clairvoyance. An instance is related of a certain Indian who had murdered Mr. Stockton, an Indian agent, besides three other persons at various times, and was a hunted fugitive. The matter created much excitement and speculation among the tattle-loving Indians, and one day a Kelta shaman cried out suddenly that he saw the murderer at that moment with his spiritual eyes. He described minutely the place where he was concealed, told how long he had been there, and many other details. Subsequent events revealed the fact that the shaman was substantially correct." [1]

The medicine man is not slow in making the most of whatever prophetic powers he may possess. How is the shaman able accurately to predict the place in which game is to be found, to forecast the weather, future events, and other

[1] Powers, "Tribes of California," Contrib. North Am. Eth., III, p. 91.

occurrences? According to primitive belief, by reason of his intimacy with the gods. It is from them that he gains the desired information, be it the location of lost articles, or game, or the advent of bad luck. The prophet, therefore, is a very convenient person for a tribe or community to possess. For, by consulting the aleatory element, he can tell precisely when the ills of life are coming, so that bad luck may be avoided. There is direct evidence that in the lower stages of culture the medicine man and the prophet are one and the same person. Among the Ganguella negroes of Caquingue, the same individual is medicine man, prophet, and magician.[1] Among the Ojibways, says Hoffman, "The *jessakkid* is a seer and prophet.... The Indians define him as a 'revealer of hidden truths.'.....He is said to possess the power to look into futurity; to become acquainted with the affairs and intentions of men; to prognosticate the success or misfortune of hunters and warriors, as well as other affairs of various individuals, and to call from any living human being the soul, or more strictly speaking, the shadow, thus depriving the victim of reason, and even of life." [2]

If Nature has not endowed the medicine man with the gift of prophecy, he often counterfeits it by cultivating the art of divination. As a diviner he learns the signs and the omens which will be auspicious or inauspicious to any undertaking, and specializes in

[1] Bartels, "Med. Naturvölker," p. 49.
[2] Hoffman, "The Midewiwin of the Ojibway," Bur. Eth., VII, p. 157.

the art of augury. Among the Central Eskimos, a curious method of divination applied by the *angakok* is that of head-lifting, described by Boas. "An individual with a thong placed around his head lies down beside a sick person. The thong is fastened to the end of a stick which is held in hand by the *angakok*. The *angakok* then makes interrogations as to the nature and issue of the disease. These questions are supposed to be answered by the soul of a dead person, in such a manner as to make it impossible for the head to be lifted if the answer is affirmative, while the head is raised easily if the answer is negative. It is thought that as soon as the soul of the departed leaves, the head can be moved without difficulty." [1] In East Central Africa, when exercising his art, the diviner rattles his gourd (medicine bag), and examines the pebbles, teeth, and claws inside it. From these he receives his oracles, and gives his answers according to their position. Generally the advice given is shrewd in spite of the fact that it is somewhat ambiguous. [2]

The preparation of love charms and hunting charms, the control of the supply of game, the regulation of the weather, especially the bringing of rain necessary to the growth of crops, constitute other features of the employment of the medicine man. The chief *raison d'être* of the specialist of the imaginary environment is the warding off of bad luck and the bringing of good luck. [3]

[1] Boas, "Central Eskimo," Popular Science Monthly, LVII, p. 631.
[2] J. A. I., XXII, p. 105.
[3] Bartels, "Med. Naturvölker," p. 48.

The worst luck possible to an agricultural people is a
season of drought; the best luck imaginable an abundance
of rain. In the one case there is famine; in the other,
food in plenty. When vegetation is dying, when animals
have no nourishment, and when there is no water to
drink,[1] the man who can make the heavens open and give
forth rain is an important member of society. Rain-making
is one of the great methods by which the medicine man
seeks to establish his reputation as a superior being. If his
power stands the test here, he can rest assured of going
through life with fame untarnished and place secure. But if
he fails in this important particular, he might better hang
his harp upon the willows. In many cases, indeed,
after failure, both harp and player are destroyed.

The identity of shaman and rainmaker is established
by authoritative evidence. Among the Amazulus, for
example, at a time of great drought, a celebrated
medicine man said, "Let the people look at the heavens
at such a time; [then] it will rain." When rain came
the people said, "Truly, he is a doctor." [2] Of Hap-od-no,
a famous shaman of the Indians of California, Powers
writes: Hap-od-no, "by his personal presence, his elo-
quence and his cunning jugglery, has made his fame and
authority recognized for two hundred miles north of his
home...In 1870, the first of two successive years of
drought, he made a pilgrimage,...and at every centrally-
located village he made a pause, and...would...promise

---

[1] Lehmann, "Aberglaube und Zauberei," p. 18.
[2] Callaway, "The Religous System of the Amazulu," p. 391.

the people to bring rain on the dried-up earth, if they contributed liberally of their substance. But he was yet an unknown prophet. They were incredulous, and mostly laughed him to scorn, whereupon he would leave the village in high dudgeon, ... threatening them with a continuance of drought another year far worse than before. Sure enough, the enraged Hap-od-no brought drought a second year, and ... when next year he made a second pilgrimage, offerings were showered upon him in abundance, and men heard him with trembling. He compelled them to pay fifty cents apiece, American money, and many gladly gave more. And he made rain." [1] The assertion that the power of opening the heavens is committed into the hands of the medicine man finds further confirmation. Ratzel says, "The shaman of northern Asia, the African rain-maker, the American medicine man, and the Australian sorcerer are alike in their nature, their aims, and to some extent in their expedients." [2] The priests and exorcists of China possess in themselves, it is thought, the so-called "Yang power" of good, through which they are expected to avert droughts and other troubles by rendering harmless the evil force of darkness or "Yin." [3] In the New Hebrides, the medicine men were wont to use their power for good or evil, but in most cases for such good ends as the causing of rain.[4] The prophet Samuel is alluded to as a

[1] Powers, "Tribes of California," Contrib. to North Am. Eth., III, pp. 372—373.
[2] Ratzel, "History of Mankind," I, p. 58.
[3] De Groot, "Religious System of China," I, p. 41.
[4] Leggatt, "Malekula," Aust. Ass. for Adv. of Science," 1892, p. 700.

rain-maker.[1] Among the Menomini Indians, the shaman
juggler might become a rain-maker if he showed the
requisite power, and it would be his double function to
bring rains, when crops or streams required it, or to
cause it to cease, when the storm grew too heavy.[2] It is
averred that the Huns believed their shamans possessed
power to bring down wind, snow, hail, and rain.[3]

The rain-maker often pretends to make rain by the use
of sympathetic magic. One of the principles of this so-
called sympathetic magic is that any effect may be
produced by imitation. Thus, along the Bloomfield
River, Queensland, the rain-maker dives into the
water, and stirs up and squeezes the leaves deposited at the bottom, so as to cause bubbles to rise to
the surface. Rain can also be produced, according to
popular belief in that country, when one of the "initiated"
dips into the stream his "wommers."[4] Among the North
American Indians, it was the custom of the medicine man
to mount to the roof of his hut, to rattle vigorously a dried
gourd containing pebbles in representation of thunder, and
to scatter water through a reed on the ground in order to
prevail upon the gods to send rain.[5] Among the Pima
Indians, "during the rain making ceremonies,.....one
of the most impressive acts was to pour dry earth
out of a reed until it was half empty, and it would be

---

[1] I. Sam. 12:17, 18.
[2] Hoffman, "The Menomini Indians," Bur. Eth., 1896 p. 150.
[3] Max Müller, "Science of Religion," p. 88.
[4] Roth, "Superstition, Magic, and Medicine," North Queensland
Ethnography, Bulletin No. 5, p. 9.
[5] Brinton, "Myths of the New World," p. 17.

seen that the remainder was filled with water. 'Then it rained right away.' If the *makai* [rain-maker] put one of the magic slates in a cup of water at the time the rain songs were being sung, and also dug a shallow trench to show the rivulets how they should cut their way, it would rain in four days. Another device of the *makai* was to conceal reeds filled with water and then, while standing on a house-top to direct the singers to form a close circle below him. Exhibiting a handful of eagle down or eagle tail feathers, and throwing dust on them to show how dry they were, he would sweep his hand about and scatter water over the spectators and singers, apparently from feathers but in reality from the reeds." [1] Howitt writes that the rain-makers of Australia were said to obtain their powers during dreams. One of the well-remembered *rain-doctors* of the Bratava clan "used to call up storms of wind and rain by filling his mouth with water, and squirting it towards the west. This he did to aid the charms which he sang." [2] The Shuli medicine man takes the horn of an antelope and by a method of hocus pocus makes it into a charm which he asserts never fails to bring rain.[3] When the medicine man of the Lemnig-Lennape wished to break up a season of drought, he was accustomed to retire to a secluded place, and draw upon the earth the figure of a cross. He would place upon the cross a piece of tobacco, a gourd, and a bit of some red material, and

---

[1] Russel, "Pima Indians," Bur. Eth., XXVI, p. 259.
[2] Howitt, "Australian Medicine Men," J. A. I., XVI, p. 35.
[3] Ratzel, "History of Mankind," III, p. 42.

then cry aloud to the spirits of the rains.[1] In the
Caucasian province of Georgia, when the drought has
lasted long, the priests yoke marriageable girls in couples
with an ox-yoke on their shoulders, and drive them through
puddles, marshes, and rivers, both drivers and driven in the
meanwhile screaming, weeping, laughing and praying.[2] In
the Tully River regions, North Queensland, rain
is personified, and it is thought that men and
women named in his honor can always prevail on
him to come. This is usually attempted by hanging
a "whirler" into pools of water. Even if rain does not
follow for several weeks, when it does come it is always
considered to be due to the efforts of the rainmaker.[3] At
Boulia, according to the same authority, the rain-makers
dance around a secluded water-hole, singing and stamping
their feet. This over, the central man dives into the
water and fixes into a hollow log, previously placed there,
the *kumurando* or "rain-stick," an instrument strangely
compounded of wood, gum, quartz-crystals or rain stones,
hair, and string. The men then go back to camp, singing
and scratching their heads and shins with twigs. On their
arrival, they paint themselves with gypsum, and continue
singing and scratching. When the rain finally comes,
the *kumurando* is removed.[4] Continuing, Roth says, "At
Boulia, during the heavy floods and rains in January and
February 1895, I was assured on native authority that

---

[1] Brinton, "Myths of the New World," Edition 1896, p. 115.
[2] Reinegg, "Beschreibung des Kaukasus," II, p. 114. After
Frazer, "Golden Bough," I, p. 524.
[3] Roth, "Superstition, Magic, and Medicine," North Queensland
Ethnography, Bulletin No. 5, pp. 9 ff.   [4] Ibid.

all the rain and water had as usual been produced by the *mai-orli* men; when I begged them to stay proceedings immediately, the reply came that as the flood had risen too quickly to allow of the removal of the rain-stick from out of its submerged position, the rain would have to run its course."[1]

Another function of the medicine man is that of healer. It was established in another chapter that the primitive theory of disease is one of ghost possession.[2] Since sickness is due to spirit agency, the proper means of cure is manifestly the eviction of the spirits. But the ordinary individual is unacquainted with the spirit world, and, therefore, has no knowledge of how to deal with the daimons. The shaman, however, gives unquestionable proof of theurgic power. He himself is possessed by spirits. Consequently nothing is more fitting than that he should be summoned in times of sickness to deal with the daimon in such a manner as to bring about the recovery of the patient. There is abundant evidence that among savage tribes shamans act as physicians. In Guiana, the priests are called "Pe-i-men." In addition to their services at the altar, they act in the capacity of conjurors, judges, and doctors.[3] In the Hawaiian Islands, according to Ellis, priests, sorcerers, and doctors were for the most part identical persons.[4] Among the Saoras of Madras, the *kudang* first learns what particular daimon or ancestral

---

[1] Roth, "Superstition, Magic, and Medicine," North Queensland Ethnography, Bulletin No. 5, pp. 9—10. [2] Vide Chapter I, pp. 7—17. [3] Dalton, "History of British Guiana," I, p. 87. [4] Ellis, "Polynesian Researches," IV, p. 334.

spirit is responsible for sickness, and then directs what
sacrifice is necessary to compel the spirit to take its
departure.[1] In Patagonia, the priests and magicians are
also doctors.[2] "The *piais* [medicine men] of South
America are in the first place magic-doctors who charm
away illnesses with incantations and convulsive movements,
or cure them with infusions of herbs. The Pima priests shoot
painted arrows into the air from painted bows to kill
sickness."[3] Allen and Thomson say that in the interior
of Africa the same man is at once priest, witch-finder, and
doctor.[4] Mollien makes the same assertion.[5] According to
MacCurdy, "the *angakoks* are or rather were the national
priests and doctors of the Eskimos. These two callings
are indissoluble, inasmuch as the people of Ammassalik
look upon sickness as a defect of the soul; their notion is
that in every part, in every member of the human body, there
is a soul which under certain circumstances may be lost;
that part of the body from which it has been lost falls ill,
and only the *angakok* is able by the aid of his spirits
to restore the soul and thereby health to the sick body."[6]
Boas writes of the same people, "The principal office of the
angakok is to find out the reason of sickness and death, or
of any other misfortune visiting the natives. The Eskimo
believes that he is obliged to answer the questions of the

[1] J. A. Soc. Bombay, I, p. 247.
[2] Fitzroy, "Narrative of the Expedition and Surveying Voyage
of the Beagle," II, p. 152.
[3] Ratzel, "History of Mankind," II, p. 155.
[4] Allen and Thomson, "Narrative of the Expedition to the River
Niger," I, p. 327.
[5] Mollien, "Travels in the Interior of Africa," p. 52.
[6] MacCurdy, Sixteenth International Congress of Americanists,
p. 652. After Sumner's Notes.

angakok truthfully. The lamps being lowered, the *angakok* sits down in the back part of the hut facing the wall. He claps his hands, and shaking his whole body, utters sounds which one would hardly recognize as human... Thus he invokes his *tornaq*, singing and shouting alternately, the listeners, who sit on the edge of the bed, joining the chorus and answering the questions. Then he asks the sick person: 'Did you work when it was forbidden? Did you eat when you were not allowed to eat?' And if the poor fellow happens to remember any transgression of such laws, he cries, 'Yes, I have worked! Yes, I have eaten!' And the *angakok* rejoins, 'I thought so,' and issues his commands as to the manner of atonement." [1] Among the Samoans, an old man is regarded as the incarnation of the god Taisumalie, and acts as medicine man. He anoints his patients with oil, pronounces the word "Taisumalie" five times at the top of his voice, and expects the sick to recover. [2] In Southern India, among the Badagas, the same functionaries—the *kurumbas*—heal the sick and officiate at marriages and funerals. [3] The Tahitian doctors, according to Ellis, almost invariably belonged to the sacerdotal class. [4] The doctors among the Tupis of Brazil were called *"payes."* In addition to their healing function, they served as jugglers, quacks, and priests. [5] The Yakut *shamans,* accord-

[1] Boas, "Central Eskimo," Bur. Eth., VI, p. 692.
[2] Bartels, "Med. Naturvölker," pp. 49—50.
[3] Shortt, "Hill Ranges of Southern India," Part I, p. 51. Cited from Spencer's "Principles of Sociology," III, p. 185.
[4] Ellis, "Polynesian Researches," IV, p. 295.
[5] Southey, "History of Brazil," I, p. 237.

ing to Sieroshevski, pretend to cure many ailments, including mental derangement, sterility, diseases of the internal organs, wounds, and broken bones. They look upon consumption, however, as incurable, and, "refuse to treat diarrhoea, scarlet fever, measles, small-pox, syphilis, scrofula, and leprosy, which they call the 'great disease.' They are especially afraid of small-pox, and take care not to perform their rites in a house where a case of it has recently occurred."[1] Catlin says of our Indians, that the same persons practiced conjury, magic, soothsaying, and performed the function of priest.[2] It is remarked of the Carriers that their knowledge of medicinal roots and herbs was very limited, and that their doctors were also priests.[3] Similarly the Dakota priest, prophet, and doctor were one.[4] Mooney writes of the American Indians, "The doctor is always a priest, and the priest is always a doctor," and "the professions of medicine and religion are inseparable."[5]

While it is true that the function of the medicine man as healer is seen most clearly in those societies whose culture is lowest and least differentiated, yet it is found that in civilization down to comparatively recent times the connexion between the priest class and the treatment of the sick has always been very intimate. In ancient Egypt,

[1] Sumner, "Yakuts," Abridged from the Russian of Sieroshevski, J. A. I., XXXI, pp. 104—105.
[2] Catlin, "North American Indians," I, p. 41.
[3] Bancroft, "Native Races of the Pacific States of North America," I, p. 124
[4] Schoolcraft, "History of the Indian Tribes of the United States," II, p. 198.
[5] Mooney, "Ghost-Dance Religion," Bur. Eth., 1896, p. 980.

says Maspero, "the cure workers were divided into several categories. Some inclined towards sorcery, and had faith only in formulas and talismans; others extolled the use of drugs; they studied the qualities of plants and minerals, and settled the exact time when [spells] must be pronounced and remedies applied. The best doctors carefully avoided binding themselves exclusively to either method, their treatment was a mixture of remedies and exorcism which varied from patient to patient. They were usually priests and derived their knowledge from the source of all sciences — the works of Thoth and Imhoptou, composed on this subject soon after the Creation."[1] In ancient Chaldea, according to the same author, "consultations and medical treatment were religious offices in which were involved purifications, offerings, and the whole ritual of mysterious words and gestures.[2] From the national worship of ancient India, there sprang the sciences of medicine and astronomy.[3] Spencer, quoting Gauthier, says "'Among the Hebrews medicine was for a long time sacerdotal, as among other ancient peoples: the Levites were the only doctors.'"[4] In the early history of Greece, medicine was believed to have been initiated by the gods, and those who practiced it desired to be accounted the offspring of Aesculapius.[5] Among the Chinese, according to De Groot, "exorcists were of a certain class of priests or priestesses, entirely possessed

[1] Maspero, "Life in Egypt and Assyria." pp. 119—120.
[2] Maspero, "The Dawn of Civilization in Egypt and Assyria," p. 780.
[3] Hunter, "Indian Empire," p. 148.
[4] Spencer, "Principles of Sociology," III, p. 189.
[5] Grote, "History of Greece," I, pp. 249—250.

by the spirits of Yang, and as such, were deemed especially fitted to perform chiefly three functions," one of which was to "expel diseases and evil in general."[1] The Druids were both priests and doctors, and were accustomed to cut the mistletoe, which was considered an antidote for poisons, with a golden knife.[2] A like connexion between religion and medicine continued throughout the Middle Ages, and in England, as late as 1858, the Archbishop of Canterbury granted medical diplomas.[3]

It is thus seen that medicine men, despite their selfish aims and ambitions, despite their oppression of the the masses, and despite the multitudinous faults and even crimes that have been laid to their charge, must be credited with initiating, fathering, fostering, and for centuries, with preserving the art of healing.

The advantages accruing to the occupant of the sacerdotal office have so far received attention. Those benefits have been found to be many. Under normal circumstances the shaman is feared, reverenced, and even worshipped. As representative of the gods, he is not amenable to the laws which bind other members of the society, but is a law unto himself. He feeds upon the fat of the land, and occupies more commodious and more comfortable quarters than any other member of the tribe. He is the most important person of primitive times, and often attains the office of secular as well as spiritual ruler. He, moreover, is sometimes regarded as the embodi-

---

[1] De Groot, "Religious System of China," I, pp. 40—41.
[2] Pliny, "Natural History," B. XVI, C. 95.
[3] Spencer, "Principles of Sociology," III, p. 193.

ment of the power which he represents, and divine honors are accorded to him.

All of this is most desirable, but there is another side to the question. No path is continually strewn with roses; it is impossible under conditions of the survival of the fitter for any man to be "carried to the skies on flowery beds of ease." The life of the medicine man is not altogether one of sunshine. In some cases the practice of his profession is attended with great dangers. Russell, for example, in his account of the Pima Indians writes, "A plague, which killed many victims in a single day, once prevailed throughout the villages. Three medicine men who were suspected of causing the disease by their magic were killed, and nobody was sick any more." [1] And again from the same author are the words, "An epidemic during this year, (1884), among the Kwahadks, caused the execution of two medicine men who were suspected of bringing the visitation upon the tribe." [2]

It is needless to say that as long as the medicine man succeeds as rain-maker all is well, and he receives great honors. As a matter of fact, he must succeed part of the time by mere chance, but it is impossible to be successful in every instance. What happens in case of failure? Sometimes it means not only the ruin of reputation, but execution to the shaman. Callaway states that in Zululand, when it rained according to the word of a medicine man, the people said, "Truly he is a doctor." But the next

[1] Russell, "Pima Indians," Bur., Eth., XXVI, p. 48.
[2] Ibid., p. 59.

year, when he predicted rain, the heavens refused to open.
The people then persecuted him beyond measure, and it
is even said that they put him to death.[1] Among the Bari
people, the doctor who does not succeed in bringing rain
when it is needed, loses not only his reputation and
practice, but also his head. In 1859, the people experienced a terrible famine, and they demanded of the
rain doctor that he bring rain at once. He exerted all his
powers but in vain. The drought continued. Thereupon
the indignant people killed him.[2]

Not only failures in rain-making, but frequently other
failures are punishable by death. Ellis says of the
Tshi-speaking peoples, "If the priests fail to perform the wonders for which they have been paid,
they are put to death. For example, during the
British-Ashanti war of 1873—1874, a priest was
required to inform the public on which day the British
gunboat lying at anchor would put out to sea. After the
proper conjuration, he announced that it would depart
on the next day. At sunrise the next morning, however,
instead of the departure of the gunboat, two others hove
ominously upon the horizon. The result was that the priest
was beheaded."[3]

Failure to effect cures in cases of sickness may result
in loss of life to the primitive healer. In Patagonia,
the wizards were sometimes killed when unsuccessful in

[1] Callaway, "Religious Systems of the Amazulu," p. 391.
[2] Ratzel, "History of Mankind," III, p. 26.
[3] Ellis, "Tshi-Speaking Peoples," p. 124.

the treatment of disease.[1] Among the Mohave, the relatives
of a dead man consult a spirit doctor, and ascertain whether
their kinsman died from ignorance or neglect on the part
of his physician. If the physician was to blame, he must
either flee for his liberty and life, or throw the blame upon
some witch.[2] A native healer among the Apache, according
to Bourke, was in danger, if he let even one patient die,
provided the spirit doctor gave out that he was culpably
negligent or ignorant. In such a case the unsuccessful
healer could escape destruction at the hands of the relatives
of the dead man only by flight, or by proving to their satisfaction that the death was due to witchcraft.[3] Among the
Mi-Wok of Southern California, the patient must pay
well for the service of a medicine man. But if he dies,
his friends may kill the doctor.[4] Although the Negritos
of Zambales, Philippine Islands, treat their *mediquillos* with
respect and awe, the profession is not popular, since, if the
efforts of a medicine man toward curing a patient prove
unsuccessful, he is held blameworthy, and even runs the risk
of being killed for his failure.[5] It is not merely among the
Tshi-speaking peoples that in the event of failure the
populace sometimes proclaims the priest an impostor,
and frequently puts him to death. Roth says of the
Dyaks, "On the Lingga once, a Dyak doctor was engaged
to attend a sick man, and in the event of his remaining

---

[1] Falkner, "Description of Patagonia," p. 117.
[2] Bourke, "Medicine Men of the Apache," Bur. Eth., IX, p. 454.
[3] Ibid., p. 466.
[4] Powers,"Tribes of California," Contrib. to North Am. Eth., III, p. 354.
[5] Reed, "Negritos of Zambales," p. 66.

alive three days, a payment in jars was to be made as a
fee. The three days expired, and the payment was made,
when the patient died; upon which the son of the dead
man, an impetuous young lad, demanded the restoration of
the jars—a request the doctor refused to accede to. The
son drew his parang, and exclaiming, 'My name may
return to the skies!' cut down the doctor, and severely
wounded his son."…. "Spencer St. John," continues
Roth, "mentions the case of a Bukar father who on the
death of his child accused the medicine man of wilfully
causing its death, and killed him on the spot."[1] Among
the Persians, when a patient dies under treatment,
the doctor not only loses his fee, but incurs blame, for the
opinion prevails that sick persons would not die but for
the influence of the physician. As soon as it is
evident that the end is at hand, the doctor is accustomed
to withdraw, and by this means the patient and his family
are officially notified, so to speak, that there is no hope.
If a doctor unwittingly visits a sick chamber where the
patient has passed away, he is subjected to shameful
treatment by the women and servants. For this reason the
doctor usually sends out scouts, who inform him of the
houses where disease has been fatal, and by this means
he knows which places to avoid.[2] By the Indians of
Oregon, all homicides were attributed to medicine men,
who were put to death when any one was murdered.
Among that people, therefore, while the position of

---

[1] Roth, "Natives of Sarawak and British North Borneo," I, p. 285.
[2] Bartels, "Med. Naturvölker," pp. 59—60.

doctor was honorable and fraught with great power, novices, realizing the dangers attendant upon it, sometimes forsook that vocation for the military profession.[1] With all his special prerogatives, therefore, it is evident that in case of non-success the status of the medicine man is at times far from enviable.

As a means of self-protection, however, it is the business of the shaman to keep his failures from counting, and no one is better able than he to explain away his ill-success. Among the Tshi-speaking peoples, when predicting the future, the priests speak in ambiguous phrases, so that whatever may happen they may claim to have prophesied correctly. When their predictions are falsified by future events, they usually succeed in exculpating themselves by asserting that the spirits were angry because of some offence on the part of the people, and consequently in order to punish the recalcitrants led their servants to predict falsely. Another kind of excuse given is that gods more powerful than the one consulted have been propitiated by the adversary, and that these have nullified all the efforts of the priest first engaged. When on account of a false prophecy the people become suspicious of the genuineness of one priest, and seek out another, they are at a disadvantage, for the priests are in league against them, and in order that no two priests may make contradictory statements, they generally inform one another of every prediction.[2] Among the Apache, in nearly every boast of

[1] Bartels, "Med. Naturvölker," pp. 59—60.
[2] Ellis, "Tshi-Speaking Peoples," pp. 126—127.

power which the medicine man makes, there is "usually a saving clause to the effect that no witchcraft must be made or the spell will not work, no women shall be near in a delicate state," there must be no neglect or disobedience on the part of the patient, and there must be no other medicine man at work with counter-charms.[1] Among sundry Australian tribes, if the medicine man fails, the failure is due to the power of some hostile wizard.[2] The following description by Howitt of the failure of a rain-making performance in Australia is given in order to illustrate the facility with which the rain-maker sometimes gets himself out of an uncomfortable situation. "Far removed from the camp and without any assistance the rain-maker collected a number of nests of the white ant which he......shaped into an oblong mound.....He next made a trench,...continually repeating the word 'do-re' throughout the whole precedure which he finally brought to a close by sprinkling some water in all directions of the compass. Before going away he took two sticks about eighteen inches long, rolled them up in reeds, and fixed them into either end of the mound, upon which, as he walked away, he threw some water behind him. No one was allowed to go near the spot where rain-making was practiced. So much so that when rain did not subsequently fall, on this present occasion (a white man having promised him in the presence of the whole camp a bag of flour if rain came within twenty four hours),

---

[1] Bourke, "Medicine Men of the Apache," Bur. Eth., IX, p. 459.
[2] Howitt, "Australian Medicine Men," J. A. I., XVI., p. 25.

the rain-maker explained his non-success to the other
natives as due to the presence of a white missionary. On
other occasions when rain does not fall, failure is explained
by some one having visited the forbidden spot." [1]

If his patient dies, or if the heavens remain cloudless
in spite of his efforts to bring rain, the medicine man is
usually clever enough to assure the people that had
it not been for his efforts, conditions would have been
much worse, and that for a larger fee he will put forth
greater exertions on behalf of his clients. Thus Spencer
says that in Obbo, when the country needs rain, the rain-
maker explains to his clients "how much he regrets that
their conduct has compelled him to afflict them with unfavorable weather, but that it is their own fault.... He
must have goats and corn. 'No goats, no rain; that's our
contract, my friends,' says Katchiba... Should his people
complain of too much rain, he threatens to pour storms
of lightning upon them forever, unless they bring him so
many hundred baskets of corn," and other presents....
"His subjects have the most thorough confidence in his
power." [2]

The primitive medicine man, furthermore, is fortunate
that his constituents are at the stage of intellectual development in which they cannot appreciate negative evidence, and,
therefore, allow one success to outweigh many failures. Of
the inability to estimate the worth of negative evidence, Lord
Bacon writes, "The human understanding, when it has once

---

[1] Roth, "Superstition, Magic, and Medicine," North Qeensland
Ethnography, Bulletin No. 5, p. 9.
[2] Spencer, "Principles of Sociology," II, pp. 339—340.

adopted an opinion, (either as being the received opinion
or as being agreeable to itself), draws all things to support
and agree with it. And though there be a greater number
and weight of instances to be found on the other side, yet
these it either neglects and despises, or else by some
distinction sets aside and rejects; in order that by this great
and pernicious pre-determination the authority of its former
conclusions may remain inviolate. And, therefore, it was
a good answer that was made by one, who, when they
showed him hanging in the temple a picture of those who
had paid their vows as having escaped shipwreck, and
would have him say whether he did not now acknowledge
the power of the gods, 'Aye,' asked he again, 'but where
are they painted that were drowned after their vows?'" [1]

As to the actual fees which the medicine man expects
and receives for his services, while in some instance they
are small,[2] in the greater number of cases they are
handsome. Thus in the New Hebrides, the native doctor
used to prepare and eat the greater portion of food given
by the natives to propitiate the spirits.[3] Among the Mi-
Wok of Southern California, the shaman had to be paid in
advance. Hence, a person desirous of his services always
brought an offering, and flung it down on the ground,
without saying a word, thereby indicating that he wished
its equivalent in medical treatment.[4] Thurston writes that

[1] Bacon, "Novum Organum," Modern Classical Philosophers by
Rand, p. 33.
[2] Bartels, "Med. Naturvölker," pp. 56 ff.
[3] J. Laurie, "Aneityum," Aust. Ass. for Adv. Science, 1892, p. 711.
[4] Powers, "Tribes of California," Contrib. North Am. Eth., III,
p. 354.

the people of South India, on recovering from illness, bring to the priest thanksgiving offerings of silver and gold. These are deposited in a vessel kept for that purpose in the temple. Children in addition to the silver articles have to place in the vessels one or two handfuls of coins for the benefit of the priests.[1] Henry Ling Roth says of the inhabitants of Sarawak, "For getting back the soul of a man, the medicine man receives six gallons of uncleaned rice; for extracting a spirit from a human body, the same fee, and for getting the soul of the rice at harvest feasts, he receives three cups from every family in whose apartment he obtains it. The value of six gallons of uncleaned rice is the sixtieth part of the amount obtained by an able bodied man for his annual farm labor."[2] Of the Indians of Southern California, Powers relates that when a man is sick he is "wrapped tight in skins and blankets, deposited with his feet to the fire, a stake driven down near his head, and strings of shell-beads stretched from it to his ankles, knees, wrists, and elbows. These strings of money exercise the same magical effect on the valetudinary savage that a gold 'twenty,' placed in the hand of the doctor, does upon the dyspeptic pale-face. The cunning Aesculapian adjusts the distance to the stake, and the consequent length of the strings according to the wealth of the invalid. If he is rich, then by the best divining and scrutiny of his art, the stake ought to be planted about five feet distant; if poor, only one or two. After

[1] Thurston, "Ethnographic Notes on South India," p. 353.
[2] Roth, "Natives of Sarawak and British North Borneo," p. 267.

he has 'powwowed' sufficiently around the unfortunate
person to make a sound man sick or deaf at least, he
appropriates the money." [1] According to Hoffman, a successful Ojibway hunter will, if he ascribes his good luck to
the *wabeno,* give him out of gratitude a portion of the
game. [2] Concerning the Peruvians, Balboa says that the
medicine men refused to help persons who were not
able to pay the fee which they demanded. [3] A Yakut
shaman, if successful, is paid a sum varying from one
ruble to twenty-five rubles or more, besides being entitled
to his entertainment and to a portion of the sacrificial
animal. If the shaman be unsuccessful, however, he
receives nothing. [4] It would seem that those unable to
pay the medicine man are in a bad way in Guiana, for
it is said that those unfortunates have no names. [5] In
East Central Africa, the headman gets his income chiefly
from voluntary offerings, but the medicine man levies his
fees rigidly. [6] In West Africa, says Miss Kingsley, "If
you want a favor from the medicine man you must give
him a present—a fowl, a goat, a blanket, or a basket
of vegetables. If you want a big thing, and want it badly,
you had better give him a slave, because the slave is
alike more intrinsically valuable and more useful." [7] When

---

[1] Powers, "Tribes of California," Contribut. to North Am. Eth.,
   III, p. 217.
[2] Hoffman, "The Midewiwin of the Ojibway," Bur. Eth., VII, p. 157.
[3] Balboa, "History of Peru." After Bourke, Bur. Eth., IX, p. 467.
[4] Sumner, "Yakuts," Abridged from the Russian of Sieroshevski,
   J. A. I., XXXI. p. 102.
[5] Bourke, "Medicine Men of the Apache," Bur. Eth., IX, p. 468.
[6] J. A. I., XXII, p. 105.
[7] Kingsley, "West African Studies," p. 176.

the Dyaks are questioned as to their belief in the easily-exposed deceits of their priests, they say they have no faith either in the men or in their pretensions; but the custom has descended to them from father to son, and they still pay those priests heavy sums to perform the ancient rites.[1] "As the services of the *manang bali*," [medicine man dressed in female attire] Henry Ling Roth goes on to say, "are in great demand, and he is well paid for his trouble, he soon grows rich, and when he is able to afford it, he takes to himself a husband.... But as long as he is poor he cannot even dream of marriage, as nothing but the prospect of inheriting his wealth would ever induce a man to become his husband, and thus incur the ridicule of the whole tribe... The only pleasure of the husband must be in seeing his *quasi* wife accumulate wealth, and wishing her a speedy demise, so that he may inherit the property." [2] In Nubra, Tibet, the rewards of the *lamas* consist of fees, tips *(chang)*, and in general the best that the land affords.[3] Among the Saoras of Madras, the fees of the medicine man are fixed, and include parts of the animal sacrificed, such as the head and a leg, and portions of the food and drink, tobacco and goods, presented to the gods as offerings.[4] The efficacy of the arts of the Eskimo *angakok* is supposed to depend on the amount of his recompense.[5] Bourke quotes Spencer to the effect that the Eskimo priest receives his fee

[1] Roth, "Natives of Sarawak and British North Borneo," I, p. 266.
[2] Ibid., I, p. 270.
[3] Bishop, "Among the Tibetans," p. 91.
[4] J. A. Soc. Bombay, I, p. 247.
[5] Nansen, "Eskimo Life," p. 283.

beforehand,[1] and Boas says, that the *angakok* who cures his patient is paid immediately and liberally.[2] Among the Pima Indians, the fee may consist of a basket, some wheat, a cow, a horse, or some similar gift. If the medicine man sings three nights he will get a horse. If the sick man dies, however, after the native doctor has sung two nights he will receive some compensation, though not a horse.[3] Among the Land Dyaks, Henry Ling Roth writes, "whether the patient lives or dies the *manang* is rewarded for his pains; he makes sure of that before he undertakes the case, for he is put to considerable inconvenience, being fetched away from his own home, and obliged to take up his abode with the patient; he can therefore undertake only one case at a time, but to it he devotes his whole attention. He takes his meals with the family, and in other ways makes himself quite at home. If a cure be effected, he receives a valuable present in addition to his ordinary expenses."[4] Among the Karok, if a patient dies, the medicine man loses his fee. If he refuses to visit a sick person and that individual dies, the medicine man must pay the relatives a sum equivalent to the fee offered him. A famous medicine man, when summoned to go twenty or thirty miles, is well paid—sometimes receiving a horse and often, if the patient is rich, two horses.[5] The Ventura Indian tribes had the following custom, as reported by Yates: "When people were desirous of obtaining favor

[1] Bourke, "Medicine Men of the Apache," Bur. Eth., IX, p. 467.
[2] Boas, "Central Eskimo," Bur. Eth., VI, p. 594.
[3] Russell, "Pima Indians," Bur. Eth., XXVI, p. 261.
[4] Roth, "Natives of Sarawak and British North Borneo," I, p. 266.
[5] Powers, "Tribes of California," Contrib. North Am. Eth., III, p. 27.

from the spirits, they went to the house of the medicine man, where an idol was kept in a basket or other receptacle, and threw offerings into the receptacle until the idol was covered up. The gifts were appropiated by the medicine man."[1] In British Victoria, the medicine man does not share in the work, but is supported by the gifts of the other members of the tribe.[2] Hoffman quotes Marquette to the effect that the Miami, Mascotin, and Kickapoo Indians were very liberal towards their physicians, on the assumption that the more they paid, the more potent would the remedies prove.[3] Among the Kirghiz, the shaman receives as a reward the best part of the sacrificial offering, and the carcasses of the slain animals. Rich people make extra gifts, a live sheep or a new gown.[4] The Navaho medicine man may own property, but his living comes largely from practicing his ceremonies, since for these his fees are excellent.[5] Of the Omahas, it is related that after a company of medicine men had succeeded in effecting a cure, "the fees were distributed. These were horses, robes, bear-claw necklaces, eagle feathers, embroidered leggings, and other articles of value."[6] In Nias, sickness is so costly a thing that one often meets people who have sold themselves into slavery in order to get the necessary funds with which to purchase the services of the medicine

[1] Yates, "Notes on the Plummets or Sinkers," Smithsonian Report, 1886, p. 305.
[2] Bartels, "Med. Naturvölker," p. 56.
[3] Hoffman, "The Midewiwin of the Ojibway," Bur. Eth., 1891, p. 152.
[4] Bartels, "Med. Naturvölker," p. 57.
[5] Matthews, "The Night Chant, A Navaho Ceremony," Memoirs Am. Museum of Nat. Hist., p. 3.
[6] Fletcher-Laflesche, "The Omaha Tribe," Bur. Eth., 1911, p. 489.

man.[1] The same is true of the Tshi-speaking peoples, whose priests require recompense before the first consultation, and make such extortionate demands afterwards that people, in order to secure their valuable aid, have been reduced to poverty and in some cases to slavery.[2] The missionaries Ramseyer and Kühne, Ellis goes on to say, have left on record "that a fee was paid by Kwoffi Kari-Kari to the priests, for consulting the gods concerning the probable result of a contemplated expedition to the Gold Coast. This fee consisted of four hundred dollars in gold dust, twenty loads of salt, twenty goats, twenty sheep, seventy bottles of rum, and fifty slaves. If the gods granted victory, one thousand additional slaves were promised." [3] A medicine man of the negroes of the Loango coast first has to determine what nail has caused the sickness, and for this he receives pay Then the nail must be drawn out. For this he receives more pay. When he turns his attention to the patient, he receives additional pay.[4] The Dakota Indians often gave a horse for the service of the medicine man, and were ready to give all they possessed and even to go into debt, in order to procure the aid of the servant of the gods.[5] In Korea, the sums demanded by the shamans are so great that they are estimated to aggregate annually two million five hundred thousand dollars.[6]

[1] Bartels, "Med. Naturvölker," p. 59.
[2] Ellis, "Tshi-Speaking Peoples," pp. 124—125.
[3] Ibid.
[4] Bartels, "Med. Naturvölker," p. 58.
[5] Ibid.
[6] Bishop, "Korea," p. 403.

SUMMARY. It has been shown that while in well-developed societies there is specialization, as a result of which different activities are exercised by different persons, in the lowest stages of culture the medicine man sums up in himself the various functions of prophet, priest, king, rain-maker, and healer. A person, therefore, of such importance is certain to occupy a position of great dignity. And yet the man who is successful in attaining the much coveted place often does so at his own peril. Sometimes the people will brook no such thing as failure. The attitude of man in religious matters is strangely inconsistent. He sometimes regards the gods as powerful enough to give him any material blessing he asks; but when they fail to grant his requests, he considers them so weak that he destroys them and takes unto himself other gods. The medicine man goes up and down in popular estimation with his gods. He sometimes is feared to such an extent that people upon seeing him occasionally die from fright. But when he fails to make a true prophecy, or when he fails in rain-making, or in healing the sick, he is often subjected to violent abuse, and is sometimes put to death. The shaman, however, is generally shrewd enough to have no failures, or if he has them, not to allow them to count. In rain-making, for example, he prolongs his operations until rain comes, which sooner or later is inevitable. He then takes the credit to himself. The people are so grateful for the rain that they readily attribute it to the powers of the rain-maker, and accord him magnificent material rewards. For foretelling the future, for acting as mediator with the spirits, and for exercising his powers as healer, the recompense likewise is often great—so great that the recipient, by means of wealth thus attained, sometimes becomes chief of the tribe or head of the nation.

CHAPTER VI

THE METHODS OF THE MEDICINE MAN.

Since the methods of the medicine man in dealing with spirits are substantially the same in every case, regardless of the function he is exercising, an example of his efforts in the celestial sphere on behalf of men is to be found in the behavior of the primitive doctor in the chamber of sickness. To this end the daimonistic theory of disease, and the savage conception of other-worldliness must be recalled. The reader will remember that among primitive peoples ignorant of the actual cause of sickness, there is no notion of such a thing as death apart from agency.[1] They attribute the results of what a civilized man would call accident to the baleful influence of evil spirits. Many cases of death by violence come under the observation of nature folk, but even in these they believe, as among the tribal groups about Maryborough, Queensland, that when a warrior is speared in a ceremonial fight his skill in warding off or evading thrusts has been lost because of the malignance of an ill-disposed daimon.[2] It is not difficult, therefore, to see, as has been abundantly shown,[3] that the innumerable cases of sickness and death from invisible causes are ascribed by man at this undeveloped stage of culture to the evil doing of unseen adversaries.

[1] Vide pp. 4—5, 14, 120.
[2] Howitt, "Native Tribes of Southeastern Australia," p. 357.
[3] Vide pp. 7—19.

If it be borne in mind that in primitive belief the other world repeats this world,[1] and that its inhabitants repeat the thoughts, sensations, emotions, and ideals of their originals, it will readily be perceived that, according to savage notions, the ghosts and spirits may be dealt with in the same way as men, and may, therefore, either by threats and coercion or by bribes and praise, be induced to grant blessings or to desist from inflicting evils. Hence the methods of the individual set apart for the special purpose of dealing with the invisible powers are broadly contrasted as antagonistic and sympathetic. In other words, in his treatment of disease, the medicine man employs a positive and a negative method—depending on the notion entertained as to the character of the god, whether he is benevolent and only temporarily angry, or malevolent and venting his spite. In the former case, the method is that of propitiation; in the latter that of avoidance, coercion, or exorcism. According to Lippert, man first conceives the attitude of the deities to be unfriendly,[2] and not until much later does he think of them as entertaining beneficent thoughts towards the children of earth.[3] For the sake of convenience, the two methods will be considered in the inverse order to that stated above, first, the positive and secondly, the negative method.

The medicine man, like the practitioner of today, when called to the bedside of a sufferer, first makes his diagnosis. The twentieth century physician, however,

---

[1] Vide, pp. 6 ff; pp. 22 ff.   [2] Vide p. 23.   [3] Lippert, "Kulturgeschichte," I, pp. 108 ff.

would say that his predecessor in practice does not conduct his diagnosis along scientific lines. For the primitive doctor first makes an effort to discover whether the sickness is due to the anger of an enraged daimon, the loss of the "kidney fat," the absence of the soul, or to the presence of bones, quartz, crystals, or other foreign substances, introduced into the body of the patient by the magical power of some adverse wizard or medicine man. In the second place, the shaman must discover how to restore the lost part, or how to break the evil spell under which the sick man is suffering; or how to extract the extraneous substance, or by what means he can expel the evil spirit from the body of the person whom it is afflicting.[1] As long as ghosts and spirits are thought of as inimical, the medicine man resorts to avoidance or exorcism.

As time goes on, however, the manner of thinking on the part of man advances. He ceases to regard the gods as antagonistic to his welfare, aims, and ambitions, and comes to think of them as friendly powers, concerned in his happiness and well-being, and sympathetic when he comes into collision with the aleatory element.[2] With this change in thought as to the attitude of the superior powers, the method of the medicine man in dealing with them experiences a change. He no longer opposes, antagonizes, or strives to compel the disease daimon to take its flight, but begins to flatter, to coddle, to wheedle, and to bribe the inhabitants of the imaginary environment in order to enlist their support in his efforts on behalf of his patient.[3] For since

[1] Lippert, "Kulturgeschichte," II, p. 412.
[2] Ibid., I, p. 220.   [3] Ibid., II, p. 413.

the gods are anthropomorphic [1] beings, possessing the same characteristics which they had while living, only in an intensified degree, they can be flattered, coaxed, and cajoled into doing what no amount of violent and abusive treatment could compel them to do. Attention is, therefore, directed to the way in which the positive method works itself out and to the results.

It would seem that desire on the part of the weak to propitiate the strong is to be traced among the higher animals. As Spencer says, "On the approach of a formidable Newfoundland or mastiff, a small spaniel in the extremity of its terror will throw itself on its back with legs in air. Instead of threatening resistance by growls and showing of teeth, as it might have done had not resistance been hopeless, it spontaneously assumes the attitude that would result from its defeat in battle; tacitly saying, 'I am conquered and at your mercy.'" [2] The efforts of the dog at propitiation are especially shown after he has come to regard his master as entertaining towards him feelings not unmixed with kindness. When beaten, instead of showing retaliation by sinking his teeth into the calf of the leg, the dog will lick the hand of his master, or put up a paw, clearly manifesting a wish to conciliate the one possessed of the power to work him further ill.

It is to be observed from the foregoing that the act of propitiation is made up of two parts. First, there is a manifestation of submission to a superior, and secondly,

[1] Keller, "Societal Evolution," pp. 60 and 260.
[2] Spencer, "Principles of Sociology," II, pp. 3—4.

there is the performance of some act implying a liking on the part of the weak for the strong, and indicating a desire to please. It is interesting to remark that in dealings as between man and man, these two elements of propitiation are in evidence. The slave expresses submission to his master, and the subject to his lord, by falling on his face, putting the foot of the chief on his neck, crawling on all fours, and by raising his body to a simple kneeling position.[1]

The means of propitiating the gods are the same as those used for getting into the good graces of the mighty of the earth—the manifestation of submission on the part of man, the exaltation of the gods, and the expression of a desire of man to render himself pleasing in the sight of the deities by attitudes, actions, and words signifying attachment. For when alive the gods were pleased by such a display, and now (though they are invisible to man, man is not invisible to them) they will be pleased as gods with the same things that pleased them on earth as men.

If, for example, before their apotheosis the spirits were gratified by applause and expressions of subordination rendered them by their servants, the divinities are still susceptible to the same flattery. This is evidently the interpretation to be placed upon the actions of the Amazulu, who, according to Callaway, praise the dead in order to gain favors and escape punishment.[2] In all religions the

---

[1] Spencer "Principles of Sociology," II, pp. 117 ff.
[2] Callaway, "Religious Systems of the Amazulu," pp. 145—147.

prevailing custom is to preface petitions to the higher powers with propitiatory utterances.

This form of propitiation suggests a remedy for sickness to which resort has been made from the earliest to the latest times, and often with startling effects. That is prayer. The idea in this connexion is to flatter the deity by expressions of submission and terms of endearment, in order if possible to secure his assistance. Thus among the Amazulu, if sickness breaks out in a village, the eldest son of the patient will offer eulogies to all the Amatongo, especially to the ancestral spirit, whom he will praise with the epithets of honor gained by that ancestor in battle.[1] In the Book of Ecclesiasticus this direction is given, "My son, in thy sickness be not negligent; but pray unto the Lord, and he will make thee whole."[2] After the sixth century of the Christian era, the practice of medicine was almost exclusively in the hands of the monks. Their cures were performed by holy water, by relics of the martyrs, and by prayers.[3]

There is much evidence that prayer is still regarded, and with good results, as mightily potent in cases of sickness. As one of many examples in support of this statement, attention is directed to the devotion of worshippers at the shrine of Sainte Anne de Beaupré, near the city of Quebec, Canada. It is said that many years ago, a small company of Breton sailors, during a violent storm at sea, made a vow to Sainte Anne de Beaupré that if she would

---

[1] Callaway, "Religious Systems of the Amazulu," p. 145.
[2] Ecclesiasticus, chapter 38, v. 9.
[3] Sprengle, "Histoire de la Medicine," II, p. 345.

save them from the waves, they would build, and dedicate
to her service, a chapel on the spot where their vessel
touched land. They were delivered and kept their promise.
About 1670, a relic of Sainte Anne was brought from
Carcassonne.[1] Monsignore de Laval, of the cathedral of
Carcassonne, asserts that this relic came indeed from
a finger of Sainte Anne.[2] Pilgrimages are made throughout
the year to the shrine, the sick and those who have received
benefits going by trainloads either to be cured or to give
thanks, and the words, "Sainte Anne, Mère de la Vierge-
Marie, priez pour nous," are breathed by every soul.[3]
Often the sick are cured in absentia in answer to their own
prayers, or to those of their friends. The shrine is now
in charge of the Redemptorist Fathers, who issue a monthly
publication, "Annales de la Bonne Sainte Anne de
Beaupré," in which the various cures of the last few
months are recorded. In order to show that it is not
necessary to go to the old world, and to the Middle Ages,
for instances of cures by prayer, quotations are here made
from several copies of the "Annales" of a comparatively
recent date.

"Ironwood, Mich., July 28 th., 1911. — For nearly two
years I had suffered from ataxia and the doctors had pro-
nounced my case incurable. But on my first visit to the shrine,
July 24th., I was partly cured and left one crutch; and on
July 25th., I ceased to use the other. Heartfelt thanks to Ste.
Anne. Mrs. A. McMillen."

[1] Waddle, "Miracles of Healing," Am. Jour. of Psych., XX, pp.
232—253.
[2] Catholic World, XXXVI., p. 87.
[3] Waddle, "Miracles of Healing," Am. Jour. Psych., XX, pp.
252—253.

"Fort Wayne, Ind., May 18th, 1912. — In compliance with a promise, I hereby state that, through the intercession of Ste. Anne, I was greatly benefited and have practically regained my health after an unfavorable prognosis by all my professional colleagues. I hereby give you permission to publish the above in the Annals. Doctor Geo. J. Studer."

"Halifax, N. S., June 4th., 1912. — Eight years ago, I developed a 'varicose' ulcer just above my left ankle through a broken vein. I was treated at intervals for four years by two doctors; but could not get any relief. About two years ago, they told me they could do no more for me. I then made a pilgrimage to the shrine of Ste. Anne de Beaupré and promised, if my ankle were cured, to go to monthly communion for the rest of my life; to make another pilgrimage, even if I were not cured, but if I were cured to make a pilgrimage in thanksgiving. After coming home, I put aside the ointments of the doctor and used nothing but Ste. Anne oil. For two months, the pain in my ankle was intense whenever I set my feet upon the floor. Just when the pain was almost unbearable there appeared to be an improvement in the sore and it began to heal steadily. Just a month before I made my second pilgrimage the cure was perfect. Now, out of gratitude to Good Ste. Anne, I am pleased to publish my cure, and inclose the certificate of my doctor. Mrs. E. P. Condon." "Halifax, N. S., June 4th., 1912. — This is to certify that, in July and August 1909, and subsequently at intervals, Mrs. E. P. Condon was under my care, suffering from a varicose ulcer situated just above the left ankle; and that from June 1911, up to the present date a healthy scar has occupied the site of the ulcer. J. P. Corston, M. D."

"Houston, Texas, March 22, 1913. — My son was afflicted with a malady that affected his mind. He was in this condition for eighteen months, and did not seem to improve under medical treatment. I made a promise to Ste. Anne that, if he was cured, I would publish his recovery in the Annals. He has entirely recovered and I now publish this with many thanks to dear Ste. Anne. Mrs. Lama DeFrance Fraser."

"Detroit, Mich., Feb. 18th, 1913. — Last October, a child of nine years was taken down with typhoid, was sick for about a month, when he got spinal meningitis. For eighteen days he was unconscious, received the rites of the Church, and the priest prayed over him. The doctors had given him up, and had said that nothing could save him but a miracle. For a week he lay like a hoop, head and heels meeting; he moaned and groaned so that passers-by were attracted. We all prayed to Ste. Anne for him; he held the little statue in his hand, and the little rosary of Ste. Anne around his wrist like a bracelet, when we did not pray on it for him. He also had the little paper pictures of Ste. Anne put on him, and the spring water of Ste. Anne was used. The doctors said he would lose his hearing and sight and perhaps his mind, if he ever should get over it. But now we are happy to say that Ste. Anne has made him well. He is just as he used to be. His hearing, mind, and sight are just as good as ever. We are very thankful to Good Ste. Anne. Miss Theresa Gebhard."

In former times, many cures as results of prayer were thought to be miraculous because the laws under which they were effected were not well understood. Science now explains such recoveries from sickness not by intervention of spirits, but by reflex action according to the law of suggestion.[1]

Since the divinities are conceived to be as sensitive as the living to cold, hunger, thirst, and pain, it is supposed that they can be propitiated by gifts of food, drink, clothing, and similar gifts. Turner writes that among the New Caledonians a chief says to the ghosts of his fathers, "Compassionate fathers! here is some food for you; eat it;

[1] Lippert, "Kulturgeschichte," II, p. 413.

be kind to us on account of it." [1] The Veddah says to a
deceased relative, as the food offering is presented, "Come
and partake of this. Give us maintenance as you did
when living." [2] Shooter says that the Kaffirs attribute
every unlucky event to the ghost of a dead person, and
slay an animal to gain his favor. [3] Among the Karens, when
a person is ill, the medicine man, if he is well paid,
will tell what spirit has produced the sickness, and by what
offering it is to be propitiated. [4] The Yakuts believe that all
diseases are due to spirit possession. Methods of cure
consist in propitiating or exorcising the uninvited guest. [5]

When the supernatural being becomes more developed
in human thought, both the gifts and the motives for
offering them become more worthy of respect. The gifts
and the motives are the same, but the name of the gifts is
changed to oblation. The reason for presenting oblations
to the divinities is shown in an old Greek Proverb which
says, "Gifts determine the acts of gods and kings." [6]
When the ideas of men concerning the deity become
more exalted, offerings, which before were propitiatory
from their intrinsic value, are regarded as making the
giver acceptable in the sight of heaven because they imply
loyalty and obedience.

In order to understand the employment of the positive
method of the shaman in his capacity of healer, it is

[1] Turner, "Nineteen Years in Polynesia," p. 88.
[2] Transactions of the Ethnological Society, New Series, II, p. 302.
[3] Shooter, "The Kaffirs of Natal and the Zulu Country," pp.163—164.
[4] Mason, J. A. Soc. Bengal, XXXIV, p. 230.
[5] Sumner, "Yakuts," Abridged from the Russian of Sieroshevski, J. A. I., XXXI, p. 105.
[6] Guhl and Koner, "Life of the Greeks and Romans," p. 283.

necessary to keep constantly in mind the anthropomorphic
conception of the savage regarding the divinities—that
they have the same likes and dislikes, wants, needs,
pleasures, disappointments as when in the body, and are
therefore to be flattered, bribed, coaxed, in the same way
as before their deification. In Tartary, for example, illness
is believed to be due to the visitation of a *tchutgour*, or
daimon. If the sick man is poor, it is evident that the
tchutgour visiting him is an inferior *tchutgour*, and requires nothing but a short, extemporaneous prayer, or at
most an interjectional exorcism. If the sick person is
very poor, the *lama* will have nothing to do with the case,
but advises the friends to possess themselves in patience
until the patient improves or dies, according to the decrees
of the gods. But if the sick man is rich, the *lama* takes
more notice of his misfortune. Since it is reasonable
to suppose that a daimon who would deign to visit
a person of such consequence must be a powerful daimon,
it would not be becoming for a great *tchutgour* to travel
like an inferior daimon. The friends of the patient, accordingly, must prepare for the *tchutgour* many fine clothes,
and, in case of extreme riches, many fine horses, for the
daimon may be a very great prince, attended by a retinue
of courtiers, all of whom must be provided with means of
conveyance.[1] The daimon here is evidently thought to be
bribed by offerings, which, consisting of clothing and
horses, of course materially benefit the *lama*, but the spirits
of which, he persuades the patient and his friends, are

[1] Huc, "Travels in Tartary," I. chapter 3.

required by the daimon as the price of the recovery of the sick man.

The gods are propitiated, likewise, by offerings of food, the spirit of which, the savage thinks, contributes to the sustenance of the inhabitants of the unseen world. Thus among the Tahitians, if a man is taken violently ill, the fruits of entire plantain fields or over one hundred pigs, are taken to the medicine man; it frequently happens that human victims are presented to the idol in the hope that the sight of them might appease his anger.[1] Among the Northern Chins, a sick man, believing his bad luck due to the agency of an angry deity, offers a young fowl or small dog in sacrifice. If he recovers, it is a sign that the divinities are propitiated.[2] In L'ien-chow, in the province of Kwang-si, China, if a man stumbles over a stone, and afterwards is taken ill, his sickness is believed to be due to the fact that there was a daimon in the stone. His friends, therefore, go to the spot where the misfortune took place, and make an effort to propitiate the daimon by offerings of rice, wine, incense, and worship. Then it is thought that the sick man will get well.[3] The offerings made for propitiating the gods, it is here repeated, contribute to the maintenance of the sacerdotal class; as, for example, among the Koskis, the priest, to appease the angry divinity who has made some person sick, takes perhaps a fowl, which he tells the people the deity requires, and pours out its blood on the ground as an offering.

[1] Farrer, "Primitive Manners and Customs," p. 61.
[2] Hutchinson, "Living Races of Mankind," I, p. 114.
[3] Dennys, "Folklore of China," p. 96.

Then he proceeds to roast and eat the fowl, and, after throwing away the bones, goes back to his home.[1]

The following instances, among many others, illustrate the fact that when man comes to regard the gods as beneficent beings, the method of the medicine man of dealing with them changes from compulsion to propitiation. According to Bancroft, the Nootka Sound People think that pains and maladies are due to the absence or irregular conduct of the soul (which must be recalled by the arts of the medicine man), or to the malignance of spirits, which must be placated.[2] The Dyaks of Borneo believe that every sort of trouble is caused by spirits; their entire medical science consequently consists of a knowledge of charms, which may avert evil, and of a knowledge of the offering of sacrifices, which may appease the wrath of the spirit that has caused the harm.[3] McCullock writes of the Konpooee, "'Whilst the Konpooee enjoys good health, he has little anxiety, but if struck by sickness for any length of time, the chances are he is ruined. To medicine he does not look for a cure of disease, but to sacrifices offered as directed by the priests to certain deities. All his goods and chattels may be expended unavailingly, and when nothing more is left for the inexorable gods, I have seen wives and children sold as slaves to provide means of propitiating the deities.'"[4]

---

[1] J. As. Soc. Bengal, XXIV, p. 631.

[2] Bancroft, "The Native Races of the Pacific States of North America," I, p. 204.

[3] Tylor, Art. "Demonology," Encyc. Brit., Ninth Edition, IV, p. 58.

[4] McCullock, "Selections from the Records of the Government of India," p. 87. Quoted by Spencer in "Principles of Sociology," III, p. 470.

Among all primitive peoples, the most unfailing means of securing the favor of the gods, or of appeasing them when angry, is thought to be the offering of blood. Here, too, it is impossible to understand the original motive for this practice unless the anthropomorphic conception of the savage concerning the divinities be borne in mind. If the deities relished the taste of blood when living, they have not changed since their apotheosis. Burton says that the blood offerings which the inhabitants of Dahomey present to the dead are drink for the deceased.[1] Odysseus describes the ghosts in the Greek Hades as drinking the sacrificial blood which he offers them, and as being reinvigorated by it.[2] Among the ancient Mexicans, the ruling houses descended from conquering cannibals. Their gods were cannibals. Their idols were fed with human hearts. When the priests represented to the kings that the idols were starving, war was waged, prisoners taken, "because the gods demanded something to eat," and for that reason many human lives were sacrificed every year.[3] Herrera says further that the coast-people of Peru offered blood to idols, and that the Indians gave the idols blood to drink, while the priests and dignified persons abstracted blood from their legs and smeared it on their temples.[4]

If the gods are pleased at the sight of blood, why not, when divine wrath is indicated by sickness, make an offering of that precious fluid to appease the dreaded ghosts,

[1] Burton, "Mission to Gelele King of Dahomey," II, p. 164.
[2] "Odyssey," Book XI, line 35 ff.
[3] Herrera, "General History of the Continent and Isles of America," III, p. 207.
[4] Ibid., pp. 210—213.

or to enlist their aid in thwarting the malicious attacks of
the spirits of darkness? This is precisely what man in the
state of savagery often does. For it is said that in British
Nigeria, if misfortune or disease fall upon the people, their
chief divinity must be conciliated by a sacrifice of slaves.[1]
A woman living in the Madras Presidency was barren. This
was said to be due to daimon possession. Her father
consulted an exorciser, who declared a human sacrifice
necessary. One night her father, the exorcist, and six
companions met at an appointed place, and after religious
exercises sent for the victim. Without suspecting any
danger he came, and was given so much alcoholic drink
that he became intoxicated. His head was then cut off,
and his blood mingled with rice was offered to the gods
as a sacrifice.[2]

It is not necessary that an individual be killed in order
to obtain blood to offer to the spirits. Sometimes the skin
of the head is cut with the shell of a snail, and the blood
caught in rags and laid beside a corpse as a substitute for
a victim. The ears and shoulders are sometimes pierced,
and the blood gathered with a sponge, and squeezed out
above a sacrificial vessel. The Aztecs used to sprinkle
their altars with blood drawn from their own bodies.
The Inca-Peruvians bled young boys, and mixed the
blood with bread. Where such blood-bread left a
mark behind, there was thought to be protection from the
spirits.[3]

[1] Mockler-Ferryman, "British Nigeria," p. 259.
[2] Strack, "The Jew and Human Sacrifice," p. 422.
[3] Lippert, "Kulturgeschichte," II, p. 328.

The special method of blood-letting in various local-
ities, especially in Polynesia, Africa, and Central America,
has led in one place to circumcision, in another to
lopping, or piercing the ears, and in a third, to maiming the
fingers by removing one or two joints.[1] In the Tonga
Islands, the natives, in case of illness, cut off a portion
of the little finger with a view to recovery.[2]

The case of ear-boring, referred to above, is interesting. In the house of the Incas all children had to pass
through a ceremony before they were really sons of the
Incas. Along with the usual fasting a sort of test of
ability to carry arms was made; then the king pierced the
ears of those who were found worthy.[3] As an initiation
into life and arm-bearing, the Mohammedans observe
the practice of baptism, cutting of the hair, and
ear-boring, or circumcision in the narrow sense.[4]
Nearly all the forms that distinguish the real Arab are
to be found among the Jews. Among the latter, however, circumcision is used to mark officially the compact
with the state god, while ear-boring has fallen to the use
of binding the slave to his master. The Jewish servant,
if he was to belong to the house forever, was bound over
to the household gods by means of ear-boring, and, therefore, by blood-sacrifice.[5] That was the older law. The
newer law, in repeating the same reference, has weeded out
all connexion with religious ceremonial, has even left out

[1] Lippert, "Kulturgeschichte," II, p. 329.
[2] Mariner, "Account of the Natives of the Tonga Islands," II, p.222.
[3] Lippert, "Kulturgeschichte," II, p. 343.
[4] Ibid., II, p. 345.
[5] Exodus, 21 : 6.

mention of the household gods, and has given the ear-piercing the significance of symbolically fastening the servant to the house: "Take an awl, and stick it into his ear, and into the door: then he is thy servant forever." [1] Here it is evident that ear-piercing was still used as a sign of compact.[2] The old religious compact, with the sign of the ear-boring, survived in Christianity, despite the efforts of some of the Church Fathers against the introduction of heathen customs into its system. Even in the nineteenth century, people were accustomed, for certain illnesses, to make vows to a saint, and, as a sign of their vows, to wear an ear-ring.[3] Before the custom entirely disappeared, it was rationalized. Then it came to be believed that piercing the ear was a remedy for trouble with the eyes.[4] This remedy for eye-trouble has been resorted to within the memory of persons living at the present time. These good people are not aware, however, that it had its beginning in the efforts of the medicine man to propitiate disease daimons by means of blood-letting.

Pliny says that the hippopotamus, having become fat and unwieldy through over-eating, bled himself with a sharp-pointed reed, and when he had abstracted sufficient blood, closed the wound with clay. Men, he asserts, have imitated the operation,[5] and hence the origin of the practice of venesection. How much more simple, satisfactory, and credible an explanation of the beginning of this expedient is made by referring it to the blind efforts of the

---

[1] Deuteronomy, 15:17.
[2] Lippert, "Kulturgeschichte," II, p. 345.   [3] Ibid. II, p. 346.   [4] Ibid.
[5] Pliny, "Natural History," B. VIII, C. 26.

medicine man in casting about for sacrifices with which to appease the angry spirits! Not to any medical beast story, but to childish notions of the shaman as to the cause of disease and the proper means of cure is to be traced the initiation of venesection—the panacea of the seventeenth century physician, and the well-recognized therapeutic agent in the practice of the medical profession of the present time. All animal stories purporting to account for the origin of treatment of sickness are to be relegated to the realm of fable and myth, rather than regarded as affording a basis for scientific explanation.

A more rational ground for blood-letting followed the first rude experience. In the course of evolution, some individual with more intelligence than his companions observed that the abstraction of blood was often followed by beneficial results. He applied it in certain cases. His action was imitated. The practice was transmitted to later generations, and, therefore, instances are on record in which savages and barbaric peoples resorted to blood-letting for well-defined reasons.[1] The Omahas, for example, who advocated bleeding in treating disease, used flint knives with which to gash the flesh between the eyebrows.[2] "The Apache scouts when tired were in the habit," Bourke writes, "of sitting down and lashing their legs with branches of nettles until the blood flowed. This, according to their belief, relieved exhaustion."[3] (It is interesting to note in passing that a form of transfusion

[1] Lippert, "Kulturgeschichte," II, p. 327.
[2] Fletcher-Laflesche, "The Omaha Tribe," Bur. Eth., 1911, p. 582.
[3] Bourke, "Medicine Men of the Apache," Bur. Eth., IX, p. 471.

of blood was known more than three centuries ago. "In the age of Queen Elizabeth," says Southey, "there was a new invention whereof some princes had very great esteem, and used it for to remain thereby in this force, and, as they thought, to live long. They chose a strong young man of twenty-five, dieted him for a month on the best of meats, wines, and spices, and at the end of the month they bled him in both arms as much as he could tolerate and abide. They added a handful of salt to six pounds of this blood, and distilled it seven times, pouring water upon the residuum after every distillation. An ounce of this was to be taken three or four times a year. As the life was thought to be in the blood, it was believed that it could be thus transferred").[1] In cases of dropsy, it is said that Asclepiades practiced scarification of the ankles.[2] Hippocrates is reputed to have been the first medical writer to speak of bleeding. He advised that blood be abstracted from the arm, from the temporal vessels, from the leg, and from other parts of the body in some instances to the point of fainting.[3] Among the nature people of the River Darling, New South Wales, the very sick and weak patients are fed upon blood abstracted from the bodies of their male friends. As a general thing it is taken as soon as it is drawn. But sometimes hot ashes are put into the blood, thus cooking it to a slight extent.[4] Granted that this practice is disgusting, it is scarcely more so than that of nineteenth century physicians who pre-

[1] Southey, "The Doctor," p. 59. [2] Baas, "History of Medicine," p. 137.
[3] Le Clerc, "Histoire de la Medicine," Part I, Book I, Chap. 18.
[4] J. A. I., 1884, p. 132.

scribed fresh animal blood for tubercular and anemic patients.

The striking thing about sacrificial blood-letting is that the medicine man, in his efforts to propitiate the angry spirits by offering up the blood of the patient, unconsciously initiated a therapeutic agency which has never been abandoned—that of venesection. In the seventeenth and early part of the eighteenth centuries, it was applied in every form of sickness. In cases of over-indulgence, the strong and healthy resorted to it for relief with much the same freedom and confidence as in these days they resort to epsom salts. During the last half of the eighteenth century, however, there was a reaction against the excessive use of blood-letting, and the practice to a great extent was discontinued. Within the last few years there has been a revival in its favor.[1] Among its generally recognized advantages, it may be noted that venesection "acts by diminishing the force of the action of the heart, and by diminishing the quantity of blood in the body. It is useful in cases of pneumonia, where from the amount of lung inflamed there is great impediment to the flow of blood, and the veins of the head and neck become turgid from over-distress of the right cavities of the heart. It is useful in apoplexy where the veins are distended, or where there is a full, hard pulse. Local blood-letting is seldom wrong in inflammation of external parts, or of the pleura, or peritoneum."[2] Another authority states that, "during the first years of this century, Roux demonstrated that the

[1] New Sydenham Society Lexicon of Medicine, Art., "Blood-letting." [2] Ibid.

abstraction of blood from animals produced a rapid formation and increase of antitoxins, and where a condition existed that caused a decline of these bodies, bleeding at once checked" [this decline], "and there followed a re-formation" [of antitoxins]. "A few years later, Schröder of Copenhagen published observations on typhoid and allied fevers in man, showing that bleeding up to twenty ounces also here increased the specific agglutinating properties of serum, and, as in animals, under certain conditions where the agglutinating properties had begun to decline, blood-letting checked such a decline and produced a marked increase in this power."[1] It is remarkable, indeed, that a therapeutic measure, employed with beneficial results by twentieth century physicians, should have had its origin in cultural blood-letting. Good out of evil! Saul among the prophets, and Herbert Spencer among the mystics! And this despite the teachings of Zeno.

So much for the method of propitiation. As to the negative method of the medicine man, perhaps the best way of approach is by the imagination. Putting oneself in the place of the savage, and thinking his thoughts, how evident it is to one that, since the entrance of malicious spirits into the body of the patient is the cause of sickness, expulsion of those spirits is the only remedy! Exorcism is, therefore, a part of the stock in trade of the medicine man, and, among the Goras of Northwestern India, any person can become a medicine man who will learn the

[1] Reference Handbook of Medical Sciences, II, p. 199.

formulas which compel the daimons to obey.[1] Of the Mishmis it is said that when a man is sick a priest is summoned to banish the evil spirit.[2] Miss Kingsley says that sickness and death in West Africa are believed to be caused by the body-soul of a deceased person before it has taken its final departure for dead-land, or by various agencies, differing according to the locality. But of all the spirits the "sisa" is perhaps the most annoying. Sometimes it wanders about, and, taking advantage of an open mouth and the absence of a "kra" or dream-soul, enters into a person and causes rheumatism, colic, or other painful ailments. The medicine man has to be summoned at once to get it out. The methods employed to meet this are characteristic of men incapable of the most advanced thinking. All the people in the village, particularly babies and old people—persons whose souls are delicate—must be kept away during the operation, having a piece of cloth over the nose and mouth, and everyone must be howling so as to scare the "sisa" off them if by any chance it should escape from the witch doctor. An efficient practitioner thinks it a disgrace to allow a "sisa" to get away from him; such an accident would be a blow to his practice, for the people would not care to call a man who could allow this to happen.[3] The Chippeways, in treating disease, concerned themselves more about the spells they used to banish the spirits than about the remedies they applied.[4] Among the

---

[1] Dalton, "Ethnology of Bengal," p. 60.
[2] Rowlatt, "Mishmis," Journal of As. Soc. Bengal, XIV, Part. 2, p.487.
[3] Kingsley, "West African Studies," p. 172.
[4] Keating, "Expedition to the Source of St. Peter's River," II, p. 158.

New Zealanders, when any person falls ill, the medicine man resorts to incantations, either to propitiate the angry spirit or, through threats and abuse, to drive it away.[1] The native doctors of the Visayans, with whom the author became acquainted while living in the Philippine Islands, used to place a light under the nipa house in which a child was being born for the purpose, as they averred, of frightning away the "asuangs" [spirits] which otherwise would devour the infant as soon as it was delivered.

One method of exorcism is that of causing the body of the patient to become such a disagreeable habitat that the disease spirit will not remain in it. In some instances this is accomplished in a very heroic manner. The natives of Sumatra, for example, try to banish the daimon from an insane person by putting the patient into a hut and setting fire to the building, leaving the wretch to escape if he can.[2] The sick person, among various savage tribes, is fumigated, made to swallow horrible things, drenched with foul concoctions which only the savage imagination could conceive—all for the distinct purpose of disgusting the unseen intruder.

The savage doctor often tries to expel the evil spirit by physical force. Among the Columbian Indians, he attempts to compel the disease daimon to leave a patient by pressing his clenched fists with all his might in the pit of the stomach of the unfortunate man.[3] Many

[1] Lubbock, "Origin of Civilization," p. 132.
[2] Marsden, "History of Sumatra," p. 191.
[3] Bancroft, "Native Races of the Pacific States of North America," I, p. 286.

innocent old men and old women of the Tagalog people,
Philippine Islands, when thought to be possessed by
vicious spirits, are known to have been cruelly beaten and
otherwise maltreated because the pagan shamans believed
that in this maner the daimons could be exorcised. Herrera
writes of the Indians of Cumana, "If the disease increased,"
[the medicine men] "said the patient was possessed with
spirits, stroked the body all over, used words of enchant-
ment, licked some joints, and sucked, saying they drew out
the spirit; took a twig of a certain root, the virtue
whereof none but the physicians knew, tickled their own
throats with it till they vomited, and bled, sighed, roared,
quaked, stamped, made a thousand faces, sweated for two
hours, and at last brought up a sort of thick phlegm, with
a little hard black ball in the middle of it, which the relations of the sick person carried to the field, saying —
'Go thy way, Devil.'" [1]

The medicine men of the Algonkin, the Ojibways, the Sioux, and other Indian tribes had a
method of exorcism known as the sucking method.
They sucked that part of the body where the pain was
most intense, thinking by so doing to extract the daimon.
Among the Florida Indians, the shamans sucked and
blew on the sick man, and put hot stones on his abdomen
to remove the pain. The medicine men of the Navaho and
Chippeway Indians had a bony tube similar to a stetho-
scope, which they placed over the diseased spot and sucked
in order to give relief.[2] In Australia, says Howitt,

[1] Herrera, "General History of the Continent and Islands of
America," III, p. 310.   [2] Bartels, "Med. Naturvölker," p. 270.

"cures are effected by sucking the afflicted part and exhibiting, as having been extracted therefrom, some foreign body which has caused the ill, or by sucking the place, and expelling the evil influence, or by various manipulations, pinchings, squeezings, to allay the pain. In some cases the 'poison,' as they call it now, is supposed to be extracted through a string, or a stick, from the patient to the doctor, who spits it out in the form of blood."[1] Howitt likewise speaks of the Kernai and relates that one of these, being ill, consulted a Murring doctor, who, after manipulating the patient, sucked the afflicted place, and exhibited a quartz crystal as being the cause of the illness. He also told the patient that it had been thrown at him by another Murring doctor. The man got well, and the reputation of the medicine man was greater than ever.[2] Bourke says that the Apache shaman, in the case of deep-seated pains, sucked the place affected, putting so much energy into his work that he raised blisters.[3] Among the California Indians, the medicine men had a tube called the "chacuaco," made from a very hard, black stone, which they used in sucking such parts of the body of the patient as were subject to great pain.[4] The medicine man of the Shingu Indians wafts clouds of tobacco smoke over his patient, and kneads him vigorously, groaning meanwhile as if he were his own victim, although the sick man

---

[1] Howitt, "Australian Medicine Men," J. A. I., XVI, p. 39.
[2] Howitt, "Australian Medicine Men," J. A. I., XVI, p. 57.
[3] Bourke, "Medicine Men of the Apache," Bur. Eth., IX, p. 471.
[4] Venigas, "History of California," I, p. 126.

remains quiet. After resorting to suction, he appears to spit out the source of the trouble.[1]

To modern man both the ghost theory of disease and suction as a means of exorcism are alike absurd. But the therapeutical expedient so much in vogue today, especially in country districts, known as "cupping," had its beginning in the sucking method of the medicine man. In Alaska, the native doctor used for a sucking instrument the bone of the wing of an eagle. The transition from sucking with the mouth to a real cupping instrument is here seen.[2] By use of a cupping glass in the case of a boil, for example, the blood is drawn to the surface of the body where the boil is located. The phagocytes combat and destroy the cocci bacilli that have gained access to the tissue spaces, and the patient is relieved. What is of interest here is the fact that the procedure of cupping, which is today recognized as a scientific measure, was discovered unwittingly and unawares by the medicine man, whose intention was not to bring blood to the periphery, but to abstract an evil spirit.[3] In many cases he, of necessity, succeeded in effecting a cure. As Bartels says, "At bottom the idea of this procedure [suction] was to draw out the evil spirit that was responsible for the disease or pain, but this process really worked as dry cupping and in some cases was beneficial."[4] The method was passed on to succeeding generations until at length the principles of scientific cupping were grasped.

[1] Steinen, "Shingu Tribes," p. 345.   After Sumner's Notes.
[2] Bartels, "Med. Naturvölker," p. 270.   [3] Mason, "Origins of Invention," p. 203.   [4] Bartels, "Med. Naturvölker," p. 266.

Another method of exorcism is by kneading and massaging the body. Spencer and Gillan describe as follows the process as practiced in Central Australia: "A middle aged man fell ill. His illness was at once attributed to the fact that he had deliberately done what he perfectly well knew was contrary to the custom, and no one was in the least surprised. Among the men in the camp were five doctors, and, as the case was evidently a serious one, they were called into consultation. One of them—a celebrated medicine man from a neighbouring tribe—gave it as his opinion that the bone of a dead man, attracted by the camp fire, or through the influence of a wizard, had entered the body of the patient and was causing the trouble. The others agreed with this opinion, but, not to be outdone by a stranger, the oldest doctor of the tribe in question decided that, in addition to the bone, an arabillia, or wart of a gum tree, had somehow got inside the body of the man. The three less experienced men looked very grave, but said nothing beyond the fact that they fully concurred in the diagnosis of their older colleagues. At all events it was decided that both the bone and the wart must be removed, and under cover of darkness, they were in part supposed to be removed after much sucking and rubbing of the body of the patient."[1] Howitt thus writes of the treatment of an Australian doctor: "His method of cure was to stroke the affected part with his hands until, as he said, he could 'feel the thing under the skin.' Then, covering the place with a piece of cloth, he

[1] Spencer and Gillan, "Native Tribes of Central Australia," p. 516.

drew it together with one hand, and unfolding it he exhibited within its folds a piece of quartz, bone, bark, charcoal, even in one case a glass marble, placed there, as he said, by a wizard, as the cause of the disease."[1] Matthews describes the method of a medicine man of the Navahoes in his treatment of a sick woman. She "was lifted by two other women and laid on her side, ... with her face to the east. While she lay there, the medicine man, amid much singing, walked around her, inscribed on the earth at her feet a straight line with his finger, and erased it with his foot, inscribed at her head a cross, and rubbed it out in the same manner, traced radiating lines in all directions from her body, and obliterated them, gave her a light massage, whistled over her from head to foot and all around her, and whistled towards the smoke hole, as if whistling something away. These acts were performed in the order in which they are recorded. His last operation was a severe massage, in which he kneaded every part of her body forcibly, and pulled her joints hard, whereat she groaned and made demonstrations of suffering."[2] Among the Omahas, the treatment of sickness was especially painful, since it consisted not only of bleeding, sucking, and of kneading the body, but of pulling the flesh below the ribs.[3]

A survival of the rubbing or massaging process is to be observed in the practice of osteopathy. The osteopath, be it

[1] Howitt, "Australian Medicine Men," J. A. I., XVI, p. 39.
[2] Matthews, "The Mountain Chant," Bur. Eth., 1888, p. 423.
[3] Fletcher-Laflesche, "The Omaha Tribe," Bur. Eth., 1911, p. 567.

understood, does not pretend to remove a spirit or any other disturbing object by his operations. His idea is to restore healthy action in a dormant organ. Massaging is recognized by the best physicians as a therapeutic agency in case of sprains, bruises, indigestion, and many other ailments. There is no doubt that both the medicine man and the osteopath produce results; although no evil spirit or foreign object is cast out, as the savage thinks, neither does disease have its origin in the spine, according to the theory of the osteopath and the chiropractor. In both instances cures are effected in spite of an illusory major premise. The reason for the success of the application of massage is that bodily organs are often stimulated to renewed activity by friction through which the blood is brought to those organs, in addition to the fact that certain patients are particularly amenable to suggestion.

In what is conceived to be the more difficult form of exorcism, one daimon is employed to expel another. The medicine man pretends to subdue the daimon in the patient by virtue of the spirit with which he himself is possessed; or he creates the impression that he is able to enlist the aid of friendly supernatural powers. This method of exorcism known as "dualism" continues among civilized peoples. An ancient Egyptian inscription relates that Princess Bint-resh, sister of Queen Noferu-ra, recovered from a serious sickness when the image of the god Khon-su was brought to her bedside. Although the "learned expert" Thutenhit was unable to do her any good, her recovery was immediate when the god appeared in the sick chamber of the princess, the evil spirit of the disease acknowledging the superior power of Khon-su, and leaving at once his usurped abode.[1]

Fire is regarded as a powerful means of spirit expulsion. Whence came fire? How in the beginning did man obtain possession of it? In volcanic regions its discovery is easily explained. It was belched up from the bowels of the earth. To the savage there is but one explanation of volcanic eruption—it is mysterious, and, therefore, due to spirit activity. Hence the resulting fire either contains a spirit or is itself a spirit. But while fire is ubiquitous, crater disturbances are not found in many parts of the earth. In the light of this knowledge, how is the presence of fire to be explained? Electrical storms have always occurred all over the world. Fire, then, must have come from bolts of lightning[2] which ignited trees of the forests and grass of the stepps. But since the lightning comes out of the skies it must in savage thought have been sent by the spirits who abide in the heavenly regions. The fire, therefore, enkindled by the lightning must be possessed by, or be one or more of those celestial inhabitants. Fire crackles, sputters, and inflicts pain when one comes too near it. The savage ascribes these properties to spirit possession. Since fire itself is a spirit, or contains a spirit, may it not be instrumental in frightening away spirits? This the savage believes. He finds fire serviceable in ridding himself of his mundane foes. Insects fear it; if

[1] Brugsch-Bey, "Egypt under the Pharaohs," II, pp. 192—193.
[2] Lippert, "Kulturgeschichte," I, p. 253 ff.

they chance to come within its reach they are destroyed. The most savage and ferocious animals will not approach it; the blaze dazzles their eyes, the heat burns them. They are easily subdued or put to flight by the brandishing of a burning stick or lighted torch. Since fire is an effective means of vanquishing earthly enemies, it follows that it will be equally advantageous in driving off invisible and spiritual foes. Concerning the Yakuts Sieroshevski says, "The most trustworthy agency to drive out daimons which torment people in sleep is fire, placed between the victim and his tormentor. An expiring fire-brand cast down by the threshold of the house-door is often used by the Yakuts to prevent evil spirits from getting into the house. Often when they first bring into the stable beasts which they have newly obtained, they lead them through fire." [1] A Yakut "boy," he continues, "whose finger became inflamed came to the conclusion, which the bystanders shared, that a 'yor' [spirit] had established itself in the finger. Desiring to drive it out the boy took a burning coal and began to apply it around the place while blowing upon it. When the burned flesh began to blister, and then burst with a little crackle, the curious group which had crowded around him flew back with a cry of terror, and the wounded boy, with a smile of self-satisfaction, said: 'You saw how he jumped out!'" [2] "A man who had the rheumatism," he again says, "had his body marked all over with deep burnings. As soon as he had any pain, he applied fire to the seat of it." [3] In ancient Chaldea, the

[1] Sumner, "Yakuts," Abridged from the Russian of Sieroshevski, J. A. I., XXXI, p. 105.   [2] Ibid.   [3] Ibid.

exorcists were expert in expelling daimons which caused disease. The priests sometimes made a fire of herbs, the flame of which was thought to frighten away the daimons, and the evils for which they were responsible.[1] Leland gives a Russian gypsy incantation by which fire was invoked to cure illness. It is as follows: "'Great Fire, my defender and protector, son of the celestial fire, equal of the sun who cleanses the earth of foulness, deliver this man from the evil sickness that torments him day and night!'" [2]

It is striking to note in this connexion that unconsciously, accidentally, unintentionally, and in spite of himself, the medicine man by his use of fire initiated a scientific method of procedure. Fire is the only infallible germicide known to the scientific world. By it water is purified, surgical instruments are sterilized, and by the cooking of food, germs of disease have been destroyed, thus preventing many a period of sickness. And the therapeutic use of fire had its beginning in the efforts of the medicine man, searching for ghost-banning influences. One may read that among the Araucanians a cautery of burning pitch was used [3]; while Grinnell declares that among the Indians of his acquaintance "cauterizing with red hot irons was not infrequently employed." [4] In Gilbert Island cauterization is accomplished by means of small pieces of hot cocoanut shell.[5] The California Indians for the initial stage of syphilis applied a hot coal to the indurated chancre.[6]

---

[1] Maspero, "Dawn of Civilization in Egypt and Chaldea," p. 780.
[2] Leland, "Gypsy Sorcery," p. 40. [3] Smith, "Araucanians," p. 233.
[4] Grinnell, "The Healing Art as practised by the Indians of the Plains," Cincinnati Lancet and Observer, VII, 1874, pp. 145—147.
[5] Bartels, "Med. Naturvölker," p. 287. [6] Ibid.

Among primitive peoples water is considered a powerful means of influencing the spirits. The sea rolls, the
breakers roar, the waves lash the shore. Rivers flow
ceaselessly, the currents now slow, now swift, now falling
over cataracts, eroding earth and stones, causing rapids
to wear gulches—all this calls for explanation. After heavy
rains freshets are formed, fields are overflowed, trees and
rocks are washed away, and often men and beasts are victims of the flood. An ill-fated canoe, laden with human
freight, is sometimes lost in a whirlpool; springs bubble
up out of the ground; water veins are struck underneath
the surface of the earth. It is impossible to project
developed ideas of civilized man back into the undeveloped mind of the savage, and say that the latter
attributes those phenomena to natural causes. The best
he can do with his untrained intellect and limited
fund of knowledge, is to ascribe those extraordinary
occurences to spirit influences. One hears, therefore, of
the "God of storm and calm, the vexed sea and the quiet
harbor," of water sprites, fairies, and elves. Since water
manifests such convincing proof of spirit possession,
why should it not be useful as a means of banishing
spirits? Primitive man believes in its ghost compelling
power. The savage is not slow to observe that water can
be made to cleanse material substances. With it he removes
the dirt from his bow and arrow, cleanses his garments,
and renders his person more attractive. Since water is a
means of purifying visible and tangible things, the primitive
man reasons that it can banish those invisible and intangible

influences that inflict both corporeal and spiritual evil. It is stated, for example, that the "Malagasy, considering all diseases as inflicted by an evil spirit, consult a medicine man whose method is to remove the daimon by means of a little grass, or the water with which the patient has rinsed his mouth." [1] Animals fear water. By it dogs can be made to stop fighting, a mad dog can be swerved from his course, a mad bull can be put to flight. If to the savage mind this element has the power, by virtue of indwelling spirits, to drive away animals, it can surely keep at a distance the invisible enemies of the spirit world, some of which are metamorphosed animals. In the Jewish Hades, therefore, it will be remembered, a great gulf separated the spirits of the unjust from the spirits of the just[2] ; and in the Greek belief the soul had to cross the river Styx before it could reach the spirit world. In this connexion, it is told that the Omahas believed ghosts would never cross a stream, and, therefore, if pursued by these unwelcome apparitions, a man would go post-haste to the nearest rivulet and cross it. The extent of the barrier made no difference to the ghost; it was unable to cross any running water.[3]

Tylor writes: "With all the obscurity and intricacy due to age-long modification, the primitive thought that overrules water ceremonies in vogue among many civilized peoples is still open to view. There has been a transition from practical to symbolic cleansing, from the removal of

[1] Ellis, "Madagascar," I, pp. 221—232.
[2] St. Luke, 16 : 26.
[3] Fletcher-Laflesche, "The Omaha Tribe," Bur. Eth., 1911, p. 591.

bodily impurity to deliverance from moral and spiritual impurity. But there is a survival in all water rites of the savage idea of spirit-banning. Holy water is in full use in the Greek and Roman Churches. It bathes the worshipper as he enters the temple, it cures diseases, it averts sorcery from men and animals, it drives daimons from the possessed, it stops the pen of the spirit-writer, it drives the spirit-moved table as it is sprinkled upon it to dash itself against the wall; at least these are among the powers attributed to it and vouched for by ecclesiastical authority."[1] Why does all this power reside in water? The reason may not have been expressed, but the explanation goes back to the savage idea of spirit possession.

In the use of water to expel the disease daimon, the medicine man unconsciously, accidentally, and without purpose, hit upon a remedy, the therapeutic value of which, although not comprehended either by himself or by anybody in his class, is now generally recognized. In 1702, Sir John Floyer referred the water cure system to baptism, and assigned as a reason for rachitis the fact that "children in baptism were no longer plunged in water in pious England, but simply had their heads wet."[2] In 1829, Vincenz Priessnitz, of Gräfenherd, Austria, inaugurated hydrotherapy as a system.[3] Hydrotherapy was introduced into England by Captain Claridge, and to John Smedley is given the credit for popularizing the system among English-speaking peoples. In this century hydrotherapy is advocated

[1] Tylor, "Prim. Cult.," II, pp. 440—441.
[2] Baas, "History of Medicine," p. 722.
[3] R. Metcalf, "Life of Vincenz Priessnitz," pp. 77 ff.

by reputable physicians as a rational method of procedure in certain cases of sickness. In the treatment of hyper-pyrexia the cooling bath holds a recognized position; in certain diseases all physicians recommend the wet sheet pack; the Turkish bath, it would seem, has come to stay; the morning "dip," "shower," "tub," or "sponge,"—these are only a few ways in which hydrotherapy has contributed to public health. And hydrotherapy harks back to the efforts of the shaman to banish spirits by means of water.

In pointing out the methods of the medicine man in ministering to the sick, mention should be made of amulets and charms. An amulet is something hung around the neck, or otherwise attached to the body, and worn in order to ward off the attacks of spirits. A charm is used for the same purpose, but it is not always suspended from the body. Amulets and charms are supposed to have spirits residing in the materials out of which they are made. Hence they are fetiches. Since to the savage mind, charms and amulets are the abodes of spirits, it is thought that they are efficacious in vanquishing evil spirits. But the material object is not responsible for the cures referred to the healing agency of amulets and charms. The spirit residing in the outward form has driven out the 'daimon of disease—that is the reason assigned for the recovery of the patient. Sometimes a charm is made of an herb or root and taken internally. The primitive man, however, never looks for the physiological effect of what would now be called the medicine. The shaman thinks that the spirit, which dwells in the root or herb, enters into the body of the

patient, and, searching through the vitals, discovers and
drives out the disease daimon, which is the cause of the
sickness.[1] Among modern Egyptians, when a man is sick,
he is made to swallow pieces of paper on which are written
texts from the Koran.[2] It is not difficult to perceive
that the notion here is that the spirit dwelling in the
inspired words is supposed to expel the spirit of disease.
Another reason for this method of exorcism is the fact
that the materials out of which charms and amulets are
fashioned are often portions of the bodies of dead animals
and dead men. The ghosts and spirits have the same fears
and sensibilities as when in the flesh. The savage thinks
that the possession of a part of a living man gives power
over him because by some mysterious means the soul of
the man is identified with that part. Reasoning from
analogy, it is clearly seen that the possession of a portion
of a dead man will likewise give power over him. Some
peoples believe that a dead man, even as a live man, has
need of every part of his body. Of the Israelites we read
that "Joseph gave commandment concerning his bones,"[3]
that is, that they might be preserved against the day of
resurrection. The Peruvians and the inland negroes of
Ardra preserve the hair and nails of their dead, apparently
for the same reason.[4] The inference, then, would seem
justified that in the belief of these peoples, if one
possesses the relics of a dead man or dead animal, he has

[1] Nassau, "Fetichism in West Africa," pp. 97 ff.
[2] Ebers, "Egypt," II, p. 61.
[3] Hebrews, 11 : 22.   [4] Garcilasso de la Vega, "The Royal Commentaries of the Incas," I, p. 127; Bastian, "Der Mensch," II, p. 357.

a means of hurting the dead owner. In order, therefore, to drive away the spirits which cause sickness, the medicine man has only to obtain some part, real or supposed, of the body of a dead man or animal. In other words, since the ghosts of the dead are responsible for sickness, and since they have need of all their parts, the shaman, by means of amulets and charms made of those parts, can coerce the spirits into doing his bidding. Disease being sometimes believed to be due to an animal, or to the spirit of an animal, amulets and charms are often made from relics of animals. Among the Dyaks of Borneo, the charms belonging to a medicine man consist of some teeth of alligators and honey-bears, several tusks of boars, chips of deer horn, and claws of animals.[1] In Afghanistan, it was believed that the graves of the dead had power to cure disease.[2] The inhabitants of North Hants, England, used to wear a tooth taken from a dead body suspended from the neck, as a cure for toothache.[3] According to the same authority, bones taken from graveyards, from time immemorial, have been used as charms against disease.[4] Often a root or herb, which really has medicinal value, is used for a charm. Some one of the predecessors of the medicine man, in casting about for a means to exorcise disease daimons, happened to blunder upon a leaf, bark, or root, which, when given internally, proved efficient. Not knowing the "modus operandi" of the drug,

[1] Boyle, "Adventures Among the Dyaks of Borneo," p. 207.
[2] Simpson, "Ancient or Buddhist Remains in Afghanistan," Frazer's Magazine, Feb., 1880, pp. 197—198.
[3] Black, "Folk Medicine," pp. 98—99. [4] Ibid.

the savage doctor jumped to the conclusion that he had discovered either a fetich more powerful than the spirit of the sickness, or a herb by means of which the malicious spirit finally was propitiated. This root or herb was passed on to later generations, until some individual arose who possessed sufficient intelligence to observe that it had a physiological rather than a magical effect,[1] and in that manner a valuable medicinal agent was discovered.

In the use of amulets and charms for the purpose of exorcism, the medicine man practices what is known among primitive peoples as the "white art." The "white art" is distinguished from the "black art" in the fact that while the former is passively defensive, the latter is actively offensive. The "black art" exists for the purpose of injuring or killing somebody; the "white art" exists for the reason that one by its use can defend himself from adversaries. To the savage manner of thinking, the defensive use of "white magic" is analogous to the defensive use of a gun. If a thief breaks into a house, the natural thing is to drive him out by the firing of a pistol, and even, in case of necessity, to kill him. If, in like manner, a malignant spirit gets into the body of a primitive man and makes him sick, the medicine man by the use of a charm, which contains an exceedingly potent spirit, pretends to compel the ill-disposed daimon to take its departure. "White magic" to the savage mind is very powerful. It is able to suspend the law of destiny, it can defend against the withering glance of the "evil eye," it can render the spell of

[1] Nassau, "Fetichism in West Africa," pp. 106 ff.

the magician of no effect.[1] Thus in Borneo, the Dyak
medicine man waves and jingles charms over the affected
part of the sick man, and pretends to remove the
spirits.[2] The shaman of Sumatra practices medicine chiefly
by charms; when called to treat a patient, he usually asks
for "something on account" with which to purchase the
appropriate charms.[3] The medicine of the Abyssinians
to a large extent consists of the use of amulets and charms.
That is the method of treating even leprosy and syphilis.[4]
The Magi recommended that a species of beetle, taken up
with the left hand, be worn as a charm against quartan
fevers.[5] For tertian fever the Magi and the Pythagoreans
prescribed the gathering of the "pseudo-anchusa," during
which the one who plucked it was to utter the name
of the individual to be cured, after which the plant was to
be fastened to the patient.[6] In ancient Egypt, both men
and, as averred, gods wore amulets and charms for
protection, and used magical formulas to coerce each
other.[7] The Bezoar stone in former times was used against
melancholia. It was reputed to remove sadness, and to
make him merry who resorted to it.[8] The Fumaria
Capreolata, it is said, derives its name from the Latin
fumus, smoke, because the smoke of this plant was claimed
by exorcists to possess the power of banishing spirits.[9]

[1] Nassau, "Fetichism in West Africa," pp. 100—112.
[2] St. John, "Life in the Forests of the Far East," I, p. 201.
[3] Marsden, "History of Sumatra," p. 189.
[4] Baas, "History of Medicine," p. 68.
[5] Pliny, "Natural History," B. XXII, C. 24; B. XXX, C. 30.
[6] Ibid.
[7] Erman, "Life in Ancient Egypt," p. 353.
[8] Burton, "Anatomy of Melancholy," II, p. 131.
[9] C. A. John, "Flowers of the Field," p. 32.

Sometimes knots are used as charms. The following example is taken from Cockayne's "Saxon Leechdoms": "As soon as a man gets pain in his eyes, tie in unwrought flax as many knots as there are letters in his name, pronouncing them as you go, and tie it around his neck."[1] A common cure for warts is to tie as many knots of hair as there are warts and throw the hair-knots away.[2] In the Popular Antiquities of Brand is this remedy: "If in the month of October, a little before the full of the moon, you pluck a sprig of elder, and cut the case that is betwixt two of its knots into nine pieces, and these pieces be bound in a piece of linen, and by a thread so hung about the neck that they touch the spoon of the heart or the sword-form cartilage, you have a sovereign cure for epilepsy."[3] Brand records also a Devonshire cure for warts: "Take a piece of twine, tie it in as many knots as you have warts, touch each wart with a knot, and throw the twine behind your back in some place where it will soon decay—but tell no one what you have done. When the twine is decayed, your warts will disappear without any pain or trouble, being in fact charmed away."[4] In Lancashire, England, people commonly wear charmed belts for the cure of rheumatism.[5] In some parts of England a cord is worn about the waist to ward off toothache.[6] Black gives a New England charm for an obstinate ague: "The

[1] Cockayne, "Saxon Leechdoms," I, Preface, p. XXIX.
[2] Black, "Folk Medicine," p. 185.
[3] Brand, "Popular Antiquities," III, p. 285.
[4] Ibid., p. 276.
[5] Black, "Folk Medicine," p. 176.
[6] Ibid., p. 177.

patient must take a string made of woolen yarn, and go by himself to an apple tree; there he must tie his left hand loosely with the right to the tree by a tri-colored string. Then he must slip his hand out of the knot, and run into the house without looking behind him."[1] A popular folk remedy for fever in the time of Pliny was to take the dust in which a hawk had bathed herself, tie it up in a linen cloth, and attach it to the body with a red string.[2] Pliny gives another remedy for the same disease: "Some put a caterpillar in a piece of linen, and pass a thread three times around it, and then tie three knots, repeating at each knot why it is that the operation is performed."[3]

It not infrequently happens that individuals sufficiently protected by amulets and charms believe themselves to be invulnerable to diseases, mishaps, plagues, and pestilences. Thus "the Badaga folk," says Reclus, "mountaineers of the Neilgherries, insure their children against accident and sickness by talismans made of the earth and ashes of funeral pyres."[4] "At Christmas tide, in Christian countries," as Nassau remarks, "decorations with the holly bush are made without the thought that the December festival was originally a heathen feast, and that superstitious forefathers spread the holly as a guard against evil fairies. The superstitious African negro does the same thing today. As the holly bush does not grow in his tropical air, he has substituted the cayenne pepper bush. The spirits which he

[1] Black, "Folk Medicine," p. 38.
[2] Pliny, "Natural History," B. XXX, C. 30.
[3] Ibid.
[4] Reclus, "Primitive Folk," p. 232.

A Kaffir Medicine Man Prescribing.
(Courtesy of Miss Janet Cummings and "Travel").

fears can no more pass over that pepper leaf with its red pods than the Irish fairy can dare to pass the holly leaf with its red berries."[1] The ancient Egyptians were buried with their amulets in order that the spirits of those amulets might protect their owners against the evil spirits of the other world. A great number of charms were found on the body of Horuta, at the time of excavations at the pyramid of Hawara. They were the most magnificent series of amulets that have ever been seen.[2] For a protection against epilepsy, Alexander Trallianus prescribed bits of sail cloth taken from a ship-wrecked vessel. These were to be tied to the right arm and worn for seven weeks.[3] According to Brand, if a boy were beaten with an elder stick his growth would be hindered; but an elder-bush on which the sun never shone was esteemed a protection against erysipelas.[4] Cornelius Agrippa used to say that the "cinquefoil," or five-leafed grass, resists poison, and expels evil spirits by virtue of the number five.[5] The Negritos of Zambales, Philippine Islands, believe in the efficacy of certain kinds of wood. Worn on the limbs, those pieces of wood are supposed to cure rheumatism; worn around the neck, they are thought to be remedies for colds and sore throat.[6] It is a common occurrence to meet men who carry in their pockets horse-chestnuts as a protection against rheumatism.

[1] Nassau, "Fetichism in West Africa," p. 101.
[2] Petrie, "Ten Years' Digging in Egypt," p. 94.
[3] Smith, "Dictionary of Greek and Roman Antiquities," Articles, "Therapeutics," and "Amulets," p. 91.
[4] Brand, "Observations," III, p. 284.
[5] Morley, "Life of Cornelius Agrippa," I, p. 165.
[6] Reed, "Negritos of Zambales," p. 66.

It must not be omitted, in passing, to remark upon the use of some dangling or fluttering object, which by attracting the "evil eye" is believed to protect the wearer from its malignant influence. Everybody is cognizant of the strange power which one mind has of working on another through the eye. If the eye of man can have this strange, mysterious power over an individual with weaker will, how much greater will be the effect of the eyes of spirits! So came about the notion that the "evil eye" lies in wait for the fortunate and prosperous to work them harm. One reason, therefore, for bad luck is the fact that spirits, jealous of the good fortune and happiness of man, trip him up, and send loss, pain, and calamity.[1] Whatever dangles or flutters, however, will attract the attention of the "evil eye" to itself and away from the individual who is to be protected.[2] Among the Semites, therefore, rags or dirty clothing used to be hung on children to protect them from the "evil eye."[3] For the same reason, the Moslems decorated themselves and their horses with shining, waving articles, and adorned their houses with streamers on which were printed texts of the Koran."[4] The Anodyne necklace, which consisted of beads turned out of the root of the white Bryony, and which was hung around the necks of infants in order to assist their teething, and to ward off convulsions, was placed there to distract the attention of the "evil eye."[5] Quartz, coral, and precious stones are

---

[1] Bartels, "Med. Naturvölker," pp. 43 ff.
[2] Monier-Williams, "Brahmanism and Hindooism," p. 254.
[3] W. R. Smith, "Religion of the Semites," p. 448.
[4] Sumner, "Folkways," p. 517.
[5] Salverte, "Philosophy of Magic," I, p. 195.

much in use as charms and amulets, because it is thought that those minerals are effective in warding off the glance of "evil eye."

Among the many notions entertained by the savage concerning the soul is the identification of the name with its possessor.[1] From this identification arises the idea that possession of the name of a person is equivalent to getting hold of his throat. The possessor thus has the possessed at such a disadvantage that he can coerce him into doing his will. Bancroft says of the native races of the Pacific States of North America, "With them the name assumes a personality; it is the shadow or spirit, or other self of the flesh and blood person."[2] Mooney writes: "The Indian regards his name not as a mere label, but as a distinct part of his personality, just as much as his eyes or his teeth, and believes that injury will result as surely from the malicious handling of his name as from a wound inflicted on any part of his physical organism."[3] This may account for the manifestation, on the part of primitive man, of a desire to keep his name a secret. For it is said of the Land Dyaks, that they "often change the names of their children, especially if they are sickly, there being an idea that they will deceive the inimical spirits by following this practice."[4] It may be for the same reason "that both Powhatan and Pocahontas are known in history under assumed appellations, their true names having been concealed from the whites until the pseudonyms were too

[1] Vide p. 16. [2] Bancroft, "The Native Races of the Pacific States of North America," I, p. 245. [3] Mooney, "Sacred Formulas of the Cherokees," Bur. Eth., 1891, p. 343. [4] St. John, "Life in the Forests of the Far East," I, p. 197.

firmly established to be supplanted." [1] Since to the mind
of primitive man there is little difference between the dead
and the living, pronouncing the names of ghosts and
spirits gives power over those most dreaded enemies.
This explains why nature people dislike to utter
the names of the gods, for by so doing it is
believed their anger is kindled. Thus the Chinese,
thinking it wrong to use the name of their supreme Ruler
on ordinary occasions, use instead the name of his
home, 'Tien,' Heaven.[2] According to Exodus, the third
chapter, Javeh is not to be spoken of by his true name.[3]
Again it is written, "Thou shalt not take the name of
Javeh thy God in vain," [4] that is, thou shalt not use the
name, thou art *permitted* to mention, in a light or frivolous
manner. The savage identification of the name with the soul,
together with the derivative idea that calling the names
of the ghosts and spirits gives power over them, and
may kindle their anger, is responsible for the practice
of the necromancer when he makes his invocations.
In I Samuel, 28:15, the shadow of the prophet asks
why he has been disturbed by the calling of his
name. Spencer notes that "an Icelandic saga describes
ghosts severally summoned by name as answering
to the summons;....and the alleged effect of calling the
name is implied in the still-extant, though now jocose saying,—'Talk of the devil, and he is sure to appear.'" [5]
Thus the savage idea of other-worldliness, implying

[1] Mooney, "Sacred Formulas of the Cherokees," Bur. Eth., 1891, p. 343.
[2] Edkins, "Religon in China," p. 71. [3] Exodus, 3 : 13 - 15.
[4] Ibid., 20 : 7. [5] Spencer, "Principles of Sociology," I, p. 249.

that the spirit world repeats this world, fosters the notion
that the spirits can be acted on by arts similar to those
which act on the living—that possession of the name gives
over the gods an influence and power like that which it is
supposed to give over ancestors and rulers before their
apotheosis.

It is not surprising, therefore, to find the medicine
man directing his activities along lines suggested by
these notions. Since to possess the name of a god is to have
power over him, why not make use of this advantage to
exorcise the daimon of sickness? Why not enlist the aid
of other spirits, more powerful than those responsible for
the mischief, to assist in driving away the daimon of
darkness? This method, already refered to as dualism,[1]
is resorted to by the medicine man, as well as by his
successors in practice, the priest-doctors. Thus among
the Indians of Acadia, it was the custom of the
medicine man to work himself up into an ecstatic
condition, at the same time invoking the names
of his gods. When fully inspired by what modern
spiritualists would call his "control" he, appearing more
like a devil than like a heavenly being, would assert in
firm tones what the condition of the patient was, and
sometimes make a fairly accurate guess.[2] The Homeric
Greeks held to the savage notion of the inherent
connexion between the name or word, and the soul.
Odysseus, for example, after depriving the Cyclops

[1] Vide pp. 195 ff.
[2] Hoffmann, Quoting Charlevoix "Journal of a Voyage to North
America," II, p. 177, Bur. Eth., 1896, p. 139.

of his sight, refused to tell his name, lest the giant
should curse him. Shortly afterwards the Cyclops learned
the name of the wily Ithacan, and, therefore, was able
to call down upon him a powerful imprecation.[1] The inference is plain that getting possession of the name in this
case was regarded as equivalent to getting possession of
the soul, and, consequently, of being able to invoke male-
dictions. Even the cultured among the Greeks never wholly
rid themselves of this idea.[2]

Since the name of a man is identical with his soul or
spirit, it readily follows that the written name or word is a
spirit, or contains a spirit, and, therefore, is a fetich. In his
treatment of disease, consequently, the medicine man often
pretends to subsidize the spirit dwelling in the written
or spoken word, and by the means of this more powerful
being to ward off, or expel, the malignant spirits of disease.
Survivals of this practice have continued throughout the
ages. Sir John Lubbock says that "the use of writing as
medicine prevails largely in Africa, where the priests or
wizards write a prayer on a piece of board, wash it off,
and make the patient drink it." [3] Of the Kirghiz, Atkinson
says that the *mullas* [shamans] sell amulets at the rate of a
sheep for each piece of written paper.[4] According to
Erman, the belief that there are words and actions by
which men could produce an effect upon the powers of
nature, upon every living being, upon animals, and even

---

[1] Odyssey, Book IX, II. 425 ff.
[2] Spencer, "Principles of Sociology," I, p. 245.
[3] Lubbock, "Origin of Civilization," p. 16.
[4] Atkinson, "Siberia," p. 310.

upon gods, was indissolubly connected with all the actions
of the Egyptians. The formulas used by the magicians
were believed to be revelations from the gods themselves.
They were made up wholly or in part from some foreign
tongue or a meaningless jargon, and the more mysterious
and difficult of understanding they were, the greater
their power was thought to be.[1] Cockayne, in his preface
to "Saxon Leechdoms," gives one of the charms
of Marcellus against inflamed eyes. It is as follows: "Write
on a clean sheet of paper ουβαιχ, and hang this round the
neck of the patient with a thread from the loom. In a
state of purity and chastity write on a clean sheet of paper
φυρφαραν, and hang it round the neck of the man. The
following will stop inflammation coming on, written on a
clean sheet of paper: ρουβος, ρνονειρας, ρηελιος, ως, χαντεφορα,
χαι παντες ηαχοτει; it must be hung to the neck by a
thread; and if both the patient and operator are in a state
of chastity, it will stop inveterate inflammation..... Blood
may be staunched by the words *sicycuma, cucuma, ucuma,
cuma, uma, ma, a.*"[2] Alexander Trallianus gave the
following prescription for quotidian ague: "Gather an
olive leaf before sunrise, write on it in common ink χα, ροι,
α, and hang it round the neck." "For gout, write on a
thin plate of gold, during the waning of the moon, μεί,
θρεύ, μόρ, φόρ, τεύξ, ζά, ζών, θέ, λού, χρί, γέ, ζέ, ων, and
wear it round the ankles; pronouncing also ιαζ, αζύφ, ζύων,
θρεύξ, βάιν, χωώχ."[3] Morley, in his "Life of Cornelius

---

[1] Erman, "Life in Ancient Egypt," pp. 352—353. [2] Cockayne, "Saxon
Leechdoms," I, Preface, pp. XXIX—XXX. [3] Smith, "Dictionary of Greek and Roman Biography and Mythology," I, p. 127.

Agrippa," records that rabbi Hama used to give his people a sacred seal with divine names written in Hebrew, which he declared would cure not only all kinds of sickness, but heal all kinds of grief.[1] The same writer says that the first Psalm, when written on doeskin, was regarded by certain persons of that time as a help to women in childbirth.[2] After the death of Pascal, a billet of writing was found sewed to his clothing. This was a "profession of faith," which he always wore as a charm or amulet. It was thought that Pascal attached the "profession of faith" to every new garment he bought.[3]

It is said that some of the Jews believed Jesus had learned the Mirific Word (true pronounciation of the name of God), and by the use of that fetich wrought his wonderful cures. In Jewish belief, this word stirred all the angels and ruled all creatures.[4] In the Book of Acts, St. Paul is represented as casting out daimons and healing disease in the name of Jesus. Some Jewish exorcists, stimulated by the success of St. Paul, took upon themselves to name the name of Jesus, saying, "ὁρκίζω ὑμᾶς τὸν Ἰησοῦν ὃν Παῦλος κηρύσσει." And the evil spirit answered, "τὸν Ἰησοῦν γιγνώσκω καὶ Παῦλον ἐπίσταμαι, ὑμεῖς δὲ τίνες ἐστέ;" and the man having the unclean spirit drove them from the house.[5]

---

[1] Op. cit., I, p. 191.
[2] Ibid., I, p. 81.
[3] "Thoughts of Blaise Pascal," Wright's Translation p. 2.
[4] Berdoe, "Healing Art," p. 265.
[5] Acts, 19 : 13 - 16. Translation: "I adjure thee by Jesus whom Paul preaches. And the spirit answered, Jesus I know and Paul I have believed, but who art thou?"

Here the belief in dualism is plainly indicated. St. Paul succeeded by the help of the mightier spirit; the exorcists, lacking that spirit, failed. Alexander Trallianus is said to have used this formula for exorcising gout: "I adjure thee by the great name Ἰαὼ Σαβαώθ': that is צְבָאוֹת יְהוָה; and again, 'I adjure thee by the holy names Ἰαὼ Σαβαώθ 'Ἀδωναί 'Ἐλωί': that is יְהוָה צְבָאוֹת אֲדֹנָי אֱלֹהָי "[1] Here the survival of the primitive idea of exorcism by means of the spirit-filled word is too obvious to require comment.

This chapter cannot fittingly be brought to a close without fuller discussion of one therapeutic agency which was initiated by the medicine man, and is applied at the present day by successful practitioners in all parts of the world. The power of suggestion is as old as humanity. All nervous tissue is characterized by amenability to its laws. But Mr. Samuel L. Clemens shot wide of the mark when he said, "The Christian Scientist has taken a force which has been lying idle in every member of the race since the world began."[2] That force was discovered long before the time of Mary Baker Eddy. The medicine man, in his capacity of intermediary between gods and men, lighted upon it, and far from lying idle, it has been active in tepee, at shrine and tomb, in temples and churches, for thousands of years.

[1] Smith, "Dictionary of Greek and Roman Biography and Mythology," I, p. 127. Translation: Ἰαὼ Σαβαώθ = Jehovah of Sabbath; יְהוָה צְבָאוֹת = Jehova of Sabbath. Ἰαὼ Σαβαώθ, 'Ἀδωναί 'Ἐλωί = Jehovah of Sabbath, Lord, God. יְהוָה צְבָאוֹת אֲדֹנָי אֱלֹהָי = Jehovah of Sabbath, Lord, God.

[2] Mark Twain, "Christian Science," p. 86.

To take the method of propitiation, by way of illustration, there is no doubt that the primitive patient acquires ease of mind and conscience by the assurance that the angry gods have been appeased, that he need no longer worry, his recovery being most certain; that even if he dies, that will be still greater proof that the gods are no longer angry, for not only will the daimon of disease have been expelled, but the sick man will have been taken to a far better place than the one in which he is at present.[1] His mind thus being soothed and calmed by the infusion of hope and comfort, it is useless to deny that the mental state of the patient is far more conducive to recovery than if he were beset with doubts and fears about the present and future. There is an old aphorism that happiness is the best of tonics. This is just as true for primitive as for civilized man; and physicians are aware that the presence of hope in cases of sickness is as influential for the good of the patient as despair is influential for harm. It is not intended to assert that the medicine man consciously acts on the principle of suggestion, and so induces a mental attitude that leads to recovery. It has already been said, on the contrary, that he is unacquainted with such ideas as this word expresses.[2] But it is maintained that the savage doctor, whether consciously or unconsciously, initiated a method of healing which charlatans have applied from time immemorial, and which every progressive present day practitioner legitimately uses as an adjunct to his profession. When a physician of

[1] Lippert, "Kulturgeschichte," II, p. 413.
[2] Vide p. 43.

former times was summoned to the bedside of a patient, he entered the room with a serious expression on his countenance, told the sick man that he was indeed very ill, and often spoke of death and of the judgment to come, thus having the effect of lowering the spirits of the individual, and of rendering less efficacious the measures and remedies applied. A modern physician comes with a cheerful mien, and with a note of confidence, positively assures the sick man that he will get well. There is no reason to doubt that under such conditions the power of the mind over the body asserts itself with the result of raising the morale of the patient. And when the morale of a sick person is raised, that in itself is no small contribution towards his recovery. It cannot be denied that Christian Science, working on the same principle, brightens the passing moments of some persons who have no object in life, and who have no other occupation than that of evoking pains and ailments by thinking about themselves. Neither can it be gainsaid that the cult of Mrs. Eddy, by forbidding its adherents to speak, or even think, of symptoms, "nerves," sickness, or pain, conduces to a healthy mental attitude, the possession of which is a priceless boon to any man or women.

With regard to exorcism, it is related that among the Araucanians, the medicine man, having brought on a state of trance, real or pretended, during which he is supposed to have been in communication with the spirits, declares, on his recovery, the nature and seat of the malady, and proceeds to dose the patient; and he also manipulates the part affected until he succeeds in extracting the cause of the sickness, which he exhibits in triumph. This is generally a spider, a toad, or some reptile, which he had carefully concealed about his person.[1] It is not surprising that the superior mind of the healer often constrains the more obtuse mind of the patient to believe that the daimon has been expelled from him, and, according to his faith so be it unto him. Nearly every doctor of medicine has witnessed the effect of a hypodermic injection of water in soothing a restless patient to sleep.[2] The story has it that Mary Baker Eddy, in early life, attended a typhoid patient. Near the crisis, the medicine, a saline solution of high potency, ran short, and in order to make it last until the doctor came, the solution was diluted from time to time with water, until no perceptible taste remained. This continuously weakened solution was given in teaspoonful doses, frequently repeated, and the patient continued to improve. The patient, in other words, was benefited by taking medicine which had lost its virtue.[3] Harriet Martineau, an exceedingly strong-minded woman, was restored to health by means of mesmerism, after long disablement by a pelvic tumor. The tumor was found in her body after death, but what of that? It had ceased to give her any trouble, and, therefore, for all practical purposes she may be reckoned as having been cured. Brodie restored many patients who were sick in bed by the simple process of bidding them get up and walk.[4]

[1] Smith, "Araucanians," p. 236.
[2] Brit. Med. Jour., June 1910, p. 1483.
[3] Dietetic and Hygienic Gazette, May 1911, p. 301.
[4] Brit. Med. Jour., June 1910, p. 1483.

There can be no question that the medicine man often succeeds in bringing about the recovery of the sick by influencing the mind, which in turn influences the body. Bourke writes, "The monotonous intonation of the savage doctor is not without good results, especially in such ailments as can be benefited by sleep, which such singing induces. On the same principle that babies are lulled to sleep by the crooning of their nurses, the sick will frequently be composed to a sound and beneficial slumber, from which they awake refreshed and invigorated. I can recall, among other cases, those of Chaundizi and Chemihuevi, both chiefs of the Apache, who recovered under the treatment of their own medicine men after our surgeons had abandoned the case. This recovery could be attributed only to the sedative effects of the chanting." [1] Mooney writes as follows to the same effect: "The faith of the patient has much to do with his recovery, for the Indian has the same implicit confidence in the shaman that the child has in a more intelligent physician. The ceremonies are well calculated to inspire this feeling, and the effect thus produced upon the mind of the sick man undoubtedly reacts favorably upon his physical organization." [2] Cockayne, in the preface to "Saxon Leechdoms," after speaking of the effect on the mind of the patient of exorcisms, prayers, sacrifices, conjurations, incantations, the use of charms and amulets, and other methods of treat-

[1] Bourke, "Medicine Men of the Apache," Bur. Eth., IX, pp. 464—465.
[2] Mooney, "Sacred Formulas of the Cherokees," Bur. Eth., VII, p. 323.

ment of the primitive doctor, adds: "The reader may enjoy his laugh at such devices, but let him remember that dread of death and wakeful anxiety must be hushed by some means, for they are very unfriendly to recovery from disease."[1]

In the cures of the medicine man, the hidden forces which produced the effect were in the patients themselves. The healing agency, be it medicine man, priest, or what not, was only the motive power that brought those forces into play. Of the nature and method of working of those forces, the medicine man had no idea. But modern scientists know very little more than the primitive doctor. The shaman unwittingly and unintentionally discovered and made use of those forces in spite of his illusory major premise. In effecting cures, his theory was to coerce the spirits. In recoveries of the same kind, the present theory is that faith is the active agent. When the desired result is brought about, it is, regardless of theory, his faith that makes the patient whole. It is said by neurologists that in cases where nerve power is deficient there is no more potent agent to operate in the interest of a sick person than his own faith. Future generations, perhaps, may discover the theory of the twentieth century to have been as fallacious as that of the medicine man. But there never can be any doubt that in both cases remarkable achievements have been attained.

SUMMARY. It has been found that the first conception of man concerning disease was that evil spirits had taken

[1] Cockayne, "Saxon Leechdoms," I, Preface, p. XI.

possession of the body.[1] This general notion expressed itself in different ways. After centuries of growth, experience, and intellectual development, man invoked special daimons as the explanation of diseases of the more pronounced and individualized type. The Hindus had temples dedicated to the goddess of small-pox, and the Romans had at least three shrines set apart to the goddess of fever, which, no doubt, was malaria. Lineal descendants of these shrines are found in Christendom. In the Middle Ages, for example, it was believed that St. Benedict interested himself in disease of the bladder, while hemorrhoids and other affections of the lower intestines were the specialty of St. Fiacre, whose relics were brought to the bedside of Richelieu, mortally ill with cancer of the rectum. At the present day, in the city of Rome, there is a Church dedicated to Our Lady of Fever.[2] The spirit notion of the causation of disease led naturally to a system of treatment, directed, when the conception of the spirits was that of hostility, to the avoidance or expulsion of the daimon intruder; and, when they came to be regarded as well disposed towards men, to a propitiation of the unseen powers. In the latter case, when sickness increased and abounded, it was thought that the gods had grown angry with their votaries. The only thing to do under such circumstances was to pacify and propitiate the angry spirits. Primitive man in this acted towards his divinities just as he would act towards earthly superiors whose

[1] Vide pp. 7—17.
[2] Brit. Med. Jour., Nov. 1909, p. 1549.

displeasure he had incurred. No new sentiment or line of action was introduced. Food, clothing, drink, incense, servants, wives, and other material possessions were offered as sacrifices to the powers of heaven to appease their anger, and render them well disposed towards the patient. Acts of propitiation consisted also of attitudes and language expressive of subordination on the part of the suppliant, in addition to the exaltation of the deities. From the positive method of the medicine man in dealing with spirits originated therapeutic agencies which have been applied in all subsequent ages of the history of the world, for example, prayer, incantation, conjuration, and blood-letting. The last named device was later rationalized, and used with a definite purpose in view. At the present day it is applied by the most progressive of physicians in cases of apoplexy, pneumonia, typhoid fever, and other complaints.[1] The method of avoidance or exorcism, or the negative method of the medicine man in dealing with spirits, was found to consist in making the usurped abode of the disease daimon as unpleasant as possible. To that end the patient was beaten, starved, drenched with every foul concoction that the savage could imagine, and was smoked with evil smelling substances; his body was pounded and kneaded; and frequently suction was used in order to extract the evil spirit. The fumigation treatment is illustrated by the story in the Apocrypha in which Tobias is said to have freed his bride from a daimon by putting the heart and liver of fish upon ashes and making a smoke

[1] Reference Hand Book to the Medical Sciences, II, p. 199.

therewith, "the smell when the evil spirit had smelled, he fled into the utmost part of Egypt." [1] In this same connexion it was pointed out that some of the methods of exorcism practiced by the medicine man survive even to this day, though with a different interpretation. The cupping glass, for example, belongs to uncivilized peoples. Our Indians frequently resorted to it. Cupping, as applied in the twentieth century, accomplishes exactly what the medicine man achieved when pretending to draw out the spirit of sickness by suction. Kneading the body, which has rationalized itself into massage, also harks back to shamanism. In the matter of medication, too, the practice of making the body such an uncomfortable habitat that the diabolical tenant would not remain, persisted long after the belief on which it was founded had ceased, and is not quite extinct at the present time. The horrible concoctions administered by the doctors of the Middle Ages might seem to have had for their purpose the expulsion of evil spirits, and the faith of the modern hospital patient in the efficacy of the medicine given is often in direct proportion to its nastiness. The disease daimon very frequently is pretended to be driven out by a superior spirit, whose assistance the medicine man alone knows how to secure. Amulets and charms, water and fire, came to be regarded as fetiches, because they were believed to be the temporary or permanent abodes of spirits. Since those fetiches contained powerful spirits, they were used

[1] Tobit, 6 : 9; 8 : 3.

in warding off, and in banishing inimical beings.
Hydrotherapy and cauterization were thus initiated.[1] The
charm or amulet is often a root or herb having medicinal
value when taken internally. In some cases the root or
herb is still in use as a medicine, although entirely apart
from any magical signification. In dualism one can also
discern the first dawn of the doctrine of signatures,
cures by spells and like expedients, which in one shape
or another, still to a large extent persist. The present
day explanation of cures of the latter description is that
of hypnotic suggestion. Suggestion also is responsible
for the success of Christian Science, mesmerism, prayer
cures, and faith healing.

So it was that primitive man, trying to secure immunity
from the ills and pains of life, turned for relief to the
special representative of the spirits responsible, according
to his philosophy, for those evils. The medicine man,
stimulated by a desire to maintain, retain, and fortify his
position, did his utmost to bring about the recovery of
the sufferer. He groped in the dark, but unwittingly,
unintentionally, and, in spite of wrong theories, he often
blundered upon scientific truth. In not a few cases he
possessed some knowledge of the pathology of disease,
and used a variety of efficacious remedies, many of which
have come into general use throughout the civilized world.

---

[1] Lippert, "Kulturgeschichte," II, p. 413.

CHAPTER VII

THE HISTORY OF SOME MEDICAL REMEDIES.

Cardinal Newman in his sermon on "The World's Benefactors," asks, "Who first discovered the medicinal herbs, which from the earliest times have been our resource against disease? If it was mortal man who thus looked through the vegetable and animal worlds, and discriminated between the useful and the worthless, his name is unknown to the millions whom he has thus benefited."[1] Doctor Benjamin Barton, in his "Collections for an Essay toward a Materia Medica in the United States," says, "The man who discovers one valuable new medicine is a more important benefactor to his species than Alexander, Caesar, or an hundred other conquerors. Even his glory, in the estimation of a truly civilized age, will be greater, and more lasting, than that of those admired ravagers of the world. I will venture to go further. All the splendid discoveries of Newton are not of so much real utility to the world as the discovery of the Peruvian bark, or of the powers of opium and mercury in the cure of certain diseases. If the distance of time or the darkness of history did not prevent us from ascertaining who first discovered the properties of the poppy, that 'sweet oblivious antidote' for alleviating pain,

[1] Newman, "Parochial and Plain Sermons," II, p. 5.

and for soothing, while the memory remains, those rooted
sorrows which disturb our happiness; if we could tell who
first discovered the mighty strength of mercury in
strangling the hydra of pleasures of generation; if
we could even ascertain who was the native of Peru,
that first experienced and revealed to his countrymen
the powers of the 'bark' in curing intermittent fevers,
would not the civilized nations of mankind, with one
accord, concur in erecting durable monuments of granite
and of bronze to such benefactors of the species?"[1]

Since the time of Newman and Barton, science has
progressed and knowledge has increased. A new science,
indeed, has arisen—the science of Anthropology—which by
disclosing, through a process of induction, the truth that
man universally reacts in a similar manner against a similar
environment, makes it unnecessary to remain longer in
ignorance as to the discoverers of the medicines that have
been of incalculable benefit to the race. This is not saying
that it is possible in every instance to learn the personal
name of the discoverer of each particular drug, or that in
the case of every article that has gained entrance to our
present official materia medica, any particular person
"looked through the vegetable and animal world and
discriminated between the useful and the worthless."
But if in general one can ascertain the manner of the
origination of the articles which Africa and America supply
to our pharmacopoeia,—since, "the same natural principle
by which the life of any individual epitomizes the life

[1] Op. cit., Lloyd Library, Bulletin, No. I, p. 43.

history of the race, from its lowest stages of development
to the highest, applies to the materia medica of the earth
at the present time," [1]— the inference is justified that the
articles which Europe and Asia furnish, in spite of the
fact that the personal name of the discoverer in many
instances is veiled in obscurity, must have originated in the
same general way.

At the close of the last chapter the statement was
made that the medicine man, in his efforts to propitiate
or exorcise the daimons of disease, often blundered upon
valuable therapeutical expedients, the value of which is
recognized by physicians of the present day.[2] Some of
these were mentioned, as the use of blood-letting, fire,
and water, expedients which later generations applied with
a different interpretation, rationalizing the use of water to
banish the daimons into hydrotherapy, the use of fire
into cauterization, and blood-letting into venesection.[3]
Speaking of the efforts of the medicine man to
bring about the recovery of his patient, and of his theories
and practices to secure that end, Mason says: "With this
knowledge fully before us, we are bound to own that
a great deal of experimental medicine and surgery were
early developed in spite of wrong theories. When a
Floridian Indian doctor scarified the forehead of a patient
with a shell and sucked therefrom the daimon of disease,
he was really cupping and leeching his sick man. When,

---

[1] True, "Folk Materia Medica," Jour. Am. Folklore, April 1901,
p. 107.
[2] Vide pp. 222 ff.
[3] Vide pp. 180 ff.

again, he compelled the patient to inhale the smoke of
tobacco or medicinal herbs, he was fumigating him, and
unwittingly discovering a little in bacteriology. These same
doctors had found out purgatives, and emetics, and
astringents to drive away with disgust the evil spirits;...
but the disease departed quite as soon for them as for us,
when the proper medicine was given." [1]

This statement leads to a consideration of the origin
of what were in all probability the first kinds of medicine,
and which, according to Professor Sumner, constituted, for
a time, the two great branches of the healing art, namely,
emetics and cathartics. Mooney says, "Many of the
Cherokees tried to ward off disease by eating the flesh of
the buzzard, which they believed to enjoy entire immunity
from sickness, owing to its foul smell, which keeps the
disease spirits at a distance." [2] Spencer writes, "The
primitive medicine man, thinking to make the body an
intolerable habitat for the daimon, exposed his patient
to this or that kind of alarming, painful, or disgusting
treatment... He produced under his nose atrocious
stenches, or made him swallow the most abominable
substances he could think of.... Now there is abundant
proof that, not only during medieval days, but in far
more recent days, the efficiency of medicines was associated
in thought with their disgustingness: the more repulsive
they were, the more effectual." [3]

[1] Mason, "Origins of Invention," p. 203.
[2] Mooney, "Sacred Formulas of the Cherokees," Bur. Eth., 1891,
    p. 334.
[3] Spencer, "Principles of Sociology," III, pp. 194—195.

It is the purpose here, with the thought of disgustingness in mind, to direct attention to the fact that the erroneous idea of the medicine man of banishing the intruder by this means led to the discovery of really efficacious remedies. For in his administration of vile-smelling and vile-tasting substances, he must, sooner or later, have lighted upon a root or herb, which, when taken internally, would produce nausea and vomiting. In some kinds of ailment, the stomach being thus rid of the toxins responsible for the disorder, relief would follow. Ethnography furnishes no specific instance indicating that emetics originated in this way. A quotation, however, from the "Pharmacologia" of Paris might go to show that scatalogic remedies yielded useful results in spite of wrong theories. It is as follows: "Among the poor of England, labor-pains used to be thought to be accelerated by a draught of the urine of the husband, and horse dung infused with wine was thought efficacious in expelling the placenta. But these produced the desired effect—or vomiting."[1] Since the ghost theory was responsible for scatalogic methods of treatment, and these, in cases of tocology, were productive of good results, though not in the way they were sought, the inference is plain that the medicine man, working on the same theory, and, therefore, thinking to disgust the spirit by subjecting the patient to nauseous treatment, would, from the very nature of things, administer a plant or root, which, although not driving out any daimon usurper,

[1] Op. cit., I, p. 33.

would cause improperly digested food to be expelled to the relief of the patient. The primitive doctor would no doubt continue to use the treatment with the magical purpose in view. But as long as he gave the proper medicine, good results would follow regardless of his theory. As societies grew, arts multiplied, and knowledge increased, wiser men would perceive that the root or herb produced physiological rather than animistic effects, and henceforth that remedy would be applied for a different purpose.

Bartels, writing along the same line, states that while the use of emetics is well known to primitive tribes, the reason for taking a substance which produces vomitory effects is not always medical, but sometimes prophylactic and even ritualistic.[1] At the medicine dance of the Navaho Indians in Arizona, every member of the tribe who wished to enter the medicine-hut had to take an emetic composed of fifteen kinds of plants, and had to vomit on a little pile of earth which, after certain ceremonies, was carried out of the hut.[2] It would seem, in this case, that vomiting was considered a necessary preparation for the person who desired to approach the god.[3] The coast Indians of southern Alaska are said to prepare themselves in a similar manner for ordeals and other religious ceremonies.[4] According to Myron Ells, the medicine man of the Twana Indians, before he began to treat a sick man, was accustomed to take an emetic,[5]

---

[1] Bartels, " Med. Naturvölker," p. 121.
[2] Ibid., p. 122.
[3] Ibid., p. 122.
[4] Ibid., p. 122.
[5] Ibid., p. 122.

apparently with the idea of rendering himself fit to come near the gods. These instances are mentioned not because they throw any light on the probable origin of the use of emetics, but in order to show that savage tribes understand that certain plants and roots have vomitory properties, and, in the second place, because their administration is sometimes connected with religion.

As to the prophylactic use of emetics, it is said that among the Karayás, vomiting with this end in view is provoked daily, and that the same custom is found in Ecuador.[1] Berdoe remarks, in this connexion, that "even the healthy among the Hindus were advised to be bled twice a year, to take a purgative once a month, and to take an emetic once a fortnight."[2]

Among primitive men, however, emetics are also taken for a physiological reason. Bourke writes, "All Indians know the benefit derived from relieving an overloaded stomach, and resort to titillation of the fauces with a feather to induce nausea. I have seen a Zuñi take great draughts of luke warm water, and then practice the above as a remedy in dyspepsia."[3] The Heidah Indians, and some tribes of the islands of the Pacific, use sea water for this purpose.[4] Among certain tribal groups, emetics are given in case of stomach troubles, and also in some infectious diseases.[5] By some of our Indians this expedient was used in order to remove poisons from

[1] Bartels, "Med. Naturvölker," p. 121.
[2] Berdoe, "Healing Art," p. 106.
[3] Bourke, "Medicine Men of the Apache," Bur. Eth., IX, p. 471.
[4] Bartels, "Med. Naturvölker," p. 121.
[5] Ibid., p. 123.

the stomach.[1] The Dakotas use the feather of a bird
with which to tickle the fauces and thus induce vomiting.[2]
Other savage tribes have discovered that decoctions made
from certain vegetables have a vomitory effect.[3]

It would be inexpedient to attempt the history of every
article classified in the materia medica of the present day
as an emetic. A better plan would seem to take the
case of a single drug, sketch in so far as possible an
account of its origin and history, and allow it to stand
as a typical example of other remedies of its class. This
section, therefore, will be limited to a discussion of a
drug than which a better could not be chosen as a
representative of its kind, namely, Cephaelis Ipecacuanha.
The habitat of the drug is Brazil. According to Tylor,
"ipecacuanha" "is a Brazilian word and is descriptive
of the nature of the drug: *ipe-caa-goene* means little
wayside-plant-emetic."[4] The word "cephaelis" is derived
from the Greek κεφαλή, and signifies a head.[5] The plant
grows most abundantly in the province of Matto Grosso,
Brazil,[6] and the root is dug throughout the year, but
"especially in the months of January and February, when it
is in bloom."[7] Before being administered as an emetic, in this
country at least, the root is ground to powder, and Lloyd,
quoting Lewis, says that "'in pulverizing considerable
quantities, the finer powder that flies off, unless great care

---

[1] Bartels, "Med. Naturvölker," p. 123.
[2] Ibid.
[3] Ibid.
[4] Tylor, "Anthropology," p. 330.
[5] Lloyd, "C. Ipecacuanha," Western Druggist, August 1897, p. 2.
[6] Ibid., p. 6. [7] Ibid., p. 5.

be taken to avoid it, is apt to afflict the operator with difficulty of breathing, spitting of blood, and bleeding at the nose, or swelling and inflammation of the eyes and face, and sometimes of the throat, adding that these symptoms disappear in a few days, either spontaneously or by the assistance of venesection."[1] As in the case of blood-letting,[2] the discovery of the medicinal properties of ipecacuanha has been traced to a medical beast story, which has it that the South American Indians gained their experience of its virtues from observing the habits of animals.[3] This story must likewise be relegated to the realm of myth and fable, thereby giving place to the more natural and credible explanation that a medicine man of a former generation, in his ambition to disgust an evil spirit, at some time happened to administer the ipecacuanha root. That was the right medicine in certain cases and so afforded relief. The fact that the patient was benefited would be sufficient to impress upon the mind of the primitive doctor the expediency of resorting to the use of the root on future occasions. He would transmit the knowledge of its habitat and ghost compelling power to future generations until at length its physiological effects were perceived and grasped. In a work called "His Pilgrimes," published in London by Samuel Purchas, in 1625, there is probably the first historical mention of ipecacuanha root.[4] This is a work

[1] Lloyd, "C. Ipecacuanha," Western Druggist, August 1897, p. 9.
[2] Vide pp. 183—184.
[3] Lloyd, "Hist. Veg. Drugs," Lloyd Library, Bulletin No. 18, p. 49.
[4] Ibid.

of five volumes, and contains accounts of travels, together with the natural history of foreign countries, purported to have been written by a number of different authors. From a treatise on Brazil, said to have been penned by a Jesuit Father, named Manoel Tristaon, who declared he had lived for a long time in that country, the following is quoted: "Igpecaya or pigaya is profitable for the bloudie fluxe. The stalk is a quarter long and the roots of another or more, it hath only foure or five leaves, it smelleth much wheresoever it is, but the smell is strong and terrible."[1] According to Flückiger and Handbury, the "igpecaya" thus described by Tristaon in 1625, was no doubt the drug now known as ipecacuanha.[2] A work entitled "Historia Nauralia Brasiliae" was published in Amsterdam, in 1648, by the traveller Piso, one chapter of which is devoted to a discussion of ipecacuanha. The author speaks of two kinds of plants, which have a similar use, but which differ in appearance. The root of one species, he says, is white in color, but the root of "Callicocca Ipecacuanha" is thin, tortuous, and of a brownish color. "In powder the dose is one drachm; in liquid the natives take two or more drachms. They use it as a purgative as well as an emetic, and nothing in that land could be found better for bloody flux." He further adds that the "natives prefer to use the liquid which they prepare as follows: They macerate the root and put it in water. After some time has elapsed they pour off and use the liquid.

[1] Purchas, "His Pilgrimes," IV, p. 1311.
[2] Flückiger and Handbury, "Pharmacographia," p. 370.

The residue they put through the same process again, but the resulting preparation is better suited to act as an astringent than as a purgative or emetic." Piso then dwells on the therapeutic virtues of the root—it detaches morbific matter from diseased places, and restores, by virtue of its astringent qualities, tonicity to the organs. Because of its emetic properties the drug removes poison from the system. The author closes by saying that the Brazilians preserve the root with religious earnestness, and that they were the first people to reveal its medicinal qualities.[1] According to Lloyd, the yellow species thus referred to is the ipecacuanha which today is recognized as official.[2] The drug, however, was not employed in Europe until 1672. At that date a travelling physician named Le Gras sold a quantity to a druggist in Paris.[3] Pomet, writing about that time, says, "I remember there was a quantity [of ipecacuanha] in the shop of M. Claquenelle," a Parisian apothecary, "which fell into the hands of his son-in-law, M. Poulain, who was likewise an apothecary."[4] But in those days such large doses were given that medicinally the drug was a failure. In 1680, a merchant named Garnier brought one hundred fifty pounds of the root, obtained in Spain, to Paris, and to insure its sale, enlisted the aid of a Dutch physician, J. A. Helvetius, (a graduate of the university of Rheims, and grandfather of the author of the book "De l'Esprit"),[5] who extensively advertised the drug

[1] Op. cit., chap. LXV, pp. 101–102.
[2] Lloyd, "Hist. Veg. Drugs," Lloyd Library, Bulletin No. 18, p. 50.
[3] Merat et De Lens, "Dict. de Mat. Med.," II, p. 465.
[4] Pomet, "Hist. Drugs," p. 47.
[5] Merat et De Lens, "Dict. de Mat. Med.," II, pp. 464–465.

under the name of "radix antidysenterica," keeping its
origin, however, a secret. The remedy soon gained such
reputation that Minister Colbert ordered that it have
official trial in the municipal hospital of Paris.[1] The
complete success of its use having been demonstrated, no less a person than the dauphin being
benefited by the drug, Louis XIV purchased the
secret from Helvetius for a thousand louis d'or, and
reserved to himself the exclusive right of selling it.[2]
His physician, Antonia d'Aquin, and his confessor,
François de Lachaise, meanwhile, had used their influence
to induce the king to acquire possession of the remedy
because they desired that the public might obtain
it as cheaply as possible.[3] Garnier maintained that
Helvetius had no right to all the profits of the transaction,
and brought suit to obtain his share. The case went to
court, the Châtelet of Paris deciding in favor of Helvetius.[4] The reputation of the medicament being established
in France it was introduced by Leibniz (1695) and by
Valentini (1698) into Germany, and by Friedrich Dekker,
in 1694, into Holland.[5] During the first part of the
eighteenth century the drug obtained good repute in
various parts of Germany, it being, for instance, an article
of "the authoritative drug list of the Silesian town of
Strehlen in 1724."[6] During the latter half of the eighteenth
century it became customary "to designate as ipecacuanha

[1] Lloyd, "Hist. Veg. Drugs," Lloyd Library, Bulletin No. 18, p. 50.
[2] Merat et De Lens, "Dict. Mat. Med.," II, pp. 464—465.
[3] Lloyd, "Hist. Veg. Drugs," Lloyd Library, Bulletin No. 18, p. 50.
[4] Ibid.   [5] Ibid.   [6] Ibid., p. 51.

any emetic plant, regardless of its botanical origin," and for that reason "the characteristics of the plant furnishing the true ipecacuanha root were almost forgotten."[1] For some cause there was much controversy, during that period, regarding the advantages of the drug.[2] About 1760, "Dover's Powder," a combination of ipecacuanha and opium, was introduced by Richard Brocklesby.[3] In 1764, a celebrated botanist in Santa Fe de Bogota, Mutis by name, sent a Peruvian emetic plant, which he thought was the true ipecacuanha root, to Linnaeus. The latter, believing the description of Piso regarding the true plant to fit the specimen sent him by Mutis, "accepted the statement of Mutis as correct," and "in 1781 gave it the name Psychotria Emetica, Mutis."[4] This error was corrected by Doctor Antonio Bernardino Gomez, who in 1800 returned to Lisbon from Brazil. In his memoir published at Lisbon in 1801, Gomez described accurately the true ipecacuanha plant, taking especial pains to distinguish it from Psychotria Emetica, Mutis, thus re-establishing "the nearly forgotten botanical character of the true ipecacuanha."[5] Gomez gave some specimens of the plant to a professor of botany at the university of Coimbra named Felix Avellar Brotero, who published an account of it in the Transactions of the Linnean Society for 1802, giving it the name Callicocca

---

[1] Lloyd, "Hist. Veg. Drugs," Lloyd Library, Bulletin No. 18, p. 51.
[2] Baas, "Hist. Medicine," p. 719.
[3] Ibid.
[4] Lloyd, "Hist. Veg. Drugs," Lloyd Library, Bulletin No. 18, p. 51.
   Ibid.

Ipecacuanha.[1] In 1814, a botanist, named Hectot, of Nantes, secured a copy of the essay of Gomez which he passed on to M. Tussac, "and the latter in publishing it, gave the drug the name Cephaelis Ipecacuanha, also laying stress on its distinction from Psychotria Emetica." [2] In 1820, a Frenchman by the name of A. Richard wrote a paper in which he called attention to the same distinction, but without giving due credit to Gomez. The result is that the drug is sometimes referred to as Cephaelis Ipecacuanha, A. Richard.[3] "The Pharmacopoeia Portugueze of 1875 gives credit to Dr. Gomez for his part in re-establishing the botanical source of the drug." [4] The remedy has had a place in nearly all pharmacopoeias since about 1750.[5]

It goes without saying that the medicine man or priest-physician in attending a patient whose illness was due to insufficient excretion, or similar cause, would sooner or later administer a noxious substance, which, although given with the intent of disgusting the spirit, would have the effect of a cathartic. Under some circumstances, that would be the right medicine, and the patient would improve. In this way the origin of cathartics is explained. The ancient Egyptians employed aloes to exorcise spirits [6] by means of the bitter taste and smell. The beginning of the use of this drug, no doubt, goes back to the time when the forefathers of the Egyptians were in the savage state and had medicine

[1] Trans. Linn. Soc., VI, p. 140.
[2] Lloyd, "Hist. Veg. Drugs," Lloyd Library, Bulletin No. 18, p. 51.
[3] Ibid.
[4] Lloyd, "C. Ipecacuanha," Western Druggist, Aug. 1897, p. 10.
[5] Ibid.
[6] Dyer, "Folk Lore of Plants," p. 77.

men. From its chemical composition aloes, when taken internally, had the same effect then as now, regardless of any theory. Primitive and semi-civilized peoples have likewise discovered other ways and means of purging. The Mincopies on the Andaman Islands, in case of constipation, eat the larvae of the bees found in the honey-combs.[1] The Winnebago Indians use as a purgative the bark of the white elder, if scraped off by the medicine man from the direction of the branches to the roots.[2] Sumner quotes Brunache that "'the Togbos' medical treatment for babies and children consisted of an excessive use of purging, by means of a clyster with infusion of herbs and peanut oil.'"[3] The Bilqulas use shark-oil as a cathartic, applying it by means of a sandal-wood pipe to which the wingbone of an eagle is fixed.[4] The Liberia negroes use a calabash as a clyster.[5] The Persians for a clyster use a very high funnel to which a bent pipe is fixed. This funnel is found in every Persian home. It is usually made of glass, in very wealthy families of silver, and may be dismounted for cleaning. Those people have very complicated prescriptions for carthartics. No Persian, even among ministers of state and high court officials, would dare transact any business on the important day when he takes his purgative.[6] MacCauley writes

[1] Bartels, "Med. Naturvölker," p. 121.
[2] Ibid.
[3] Brunache, "Cent. Africa," p. 135. Quoted by Sumner.
[4] Bartels, "Med. Naturvölker," p. 120.
[5] Ibid., pp. 120—121.
[6] Ibid.

of a Seminole festival in this manner: "The evening of the first day, the ceremonies of the 'black drink' are endured. This drink is said to have a nauseating smell and taste. It is probably a mixture similar to that used by the Creeks in the last century at a like ceremony. It acts as an emetic and cathartic, and the Indians believe that unless one drinks it, one will be sick at some time during the year."[1] "Some of the southern tribes" [of the North American continent], according to Catlin, "make a bitter and sickening drink, called 'Asíyahola' (the black drink), which they drink to excess for several days previous to the green corn feast. Everything is ejected from their stomachs and intestines, enabling them to commence with green corn upon an empty stomach."[2]

The use made of castor oil as a cathartic is extensive. A somewhat detailed account of its history may here be given. This drug is admittedly a very desirable laxative, despite the fact of its odor and taste having made it a by-word for offensiveness. Although there is no direct evidence that the use of castor oil as a cathartic originated in the efforts of the medicine man or priest to disgust the evil spirit, yet the first mention of the bean, from which the oil is extracted, is connected with religion. For in ancient Egypt the castor bean was held sacred, and was placed in sarcophagi in 4000, B. C. This evidently means that the ghosts of the dead were believed to have use for

[1] MacCauley, "Seminole Indians of Florida," Bur. Eth. V. p. 522.
[2] Catlin. After Sumner's Notes.

the spirit of the bean in the other world. The Egyptians called the bean "neter kaka," and the oil extracted was called "kiki." The Greeks changed the name to κίκινυμ, the Romans transliterating the word into "Kikinum," or "Cicinum," which in turn became "Ricinum," the present medical name.[1] The oil, from its supposed efficiency in assuaging the natural heat of the body, and from its reputed power to soothe the passions, was called by the French "Agnus Castus." For this reason the people of St. Kitt's, in the West Indies, "who were formerly blended with the French in that Island, called it Castor Oil."[2] The Papyrus Ebers (1552, B.C.) recommends the use of the seeds of the castor bean for a purgative and hair tonic, and the oil for boils and in the preparation of ointments.[3] Herodotus, according to Raubenheimer, says that the oil was prepared by "'crushing the seeds or boiling in water and skimming.'"[4] Hippocrates made an effort to remove the offensive odor and taste from the seeds and oil, so as to render them more palatable.[5] Pliny, in Book XXIII, chapter 4, writes, "'Castor oil taken with an equal quantity of hot water acts as a purgative on the bowels.'"[6] The Pen-Tsao of China, and the Susrata of ancient India both mention castor oil as a valuable medicine.[7] The Bower manuscript indicates that the drug was in use in ancient

---

[1] Raubenheimer, "Tasteless Castor Oil," p. 5.
[2] Paris, "Pharmacologia," I, pp. 59—60.
[3] Raubenheimer, "Tasteless Castor Oil," pp. 5—6.
[4] Ibid., p. 6.
[5] Ibid.
[6] Ibid.
[7] Ibid.

Turkestan.[1] For some reason the remedy was neglected during the Middle Ages, but Dr. Peter Canvane revived its use by publishing a book, about 1764, entitled, "Dissertation on Oleum Palmae Christi, sive Oleum Ricini." [2] Castor oil gained access to the London Pharmacopoeia of 1788, "and has since remained in universal use as the safest and surest purgative known to medicine." [3]

Another drug widely in use as a cathartic, but much less offensive to the taste, is what is popularly known as Cascara Sagrada. This is a Spanish name and signifies "sacred bark." [4] Concerning the laxative, Professor Lloyd writes, "Its journey from the aborigines to scientific use and therapeutic study appears to parallel the course of such drugs as coca, jalap, benzoin, and sassafras." [5] The botanical name of the tree from which the bark is obtained is "rhamnus purshiana," and it grows in the Pacific States of North America, chiefly in Oregon and California.[6] In some parts of California, in the early days, the Scriptural term "Shittim bark" was applied to the peel,[7] the local tradition connecting it with the Shittim wood of which the Hebrew ark was made. In 1877, Dr. J. H. Bundy, of Colusa, California, becoming impressed with the medicinal value of the bark, in a paper published in "New Preparations," later "The Therapeutic Gazette," recommended

[1] Raubenheimer, "Tasteless Castor Oil," pp. 6—7.
[2] Ibid., p. 7.
[3] Ibid.
[4] Lloyd, "Hist. Veg. Drugs," Lloyd Library, Bulletin No. 18, p. 70.
[5] Ibid., p. 69.
[6] Ibid., p. 68.
[7] Ibid., p. 70.

the drug under the name "cascara sagrada" "as a valuable remedy in the treatment of constipation."[1] In January 1878, Dr. Bundy wrote an article for the same publication, giving the "uses of fluid extract of 'cascara sagrada.'"[2] During that year no less than twenty contributions were printed in "New Preparations" by Dr. Bundy and other physicians on the subject of the bark and its use. This, together with the extensive advertising of the drug by Parke, Davis and Company, Detroit, Michigan, a wholesale drug company, served to arrest the attention of the profession, "and the remedy became a general favorite."[3] Within a reasonable length of time the remedy was in demand in all civilized countries, and was put into the United States Pharmacopoeia in 1890.[4] It is but fair to add that in his paper of 1878 Dr. Bundy stated, "A description of the Cascara I am unable to give at this time, but suffice it to say that it is a shrub, and in due time its botanical name will be known."[5] But Dr. Bundy, it appears, rested his case with that statement. In the fall of 1878, a partner of Dr. Bundy's, Dr. C. H. Adair, sent specimens of the bark, in addition to botanical specimens of the tree yielding it, to Professor John Uri Lloyd of Cincinnati, Ohio. These were examined by Mr. Curtis G. Lloyd, and identified as "rhamnus purshiana." Professor Lloyd, in a paper on "Some aspects of Western Plants," which he read before a

---

[1] Lloyd, "Hist. Veg. Drugs," Lloyd Library, Bulletin No. 18, pp. 68—69.
[2] Ibid., p. 69.
[3] Ibid., p. 68.
[4] Ibid.
[5] Ibid., p. 69.

meeting of the American Pharmaceutical Association, at Atlanta, Georgia, in November 1878, announced this fact, and thus the history of the drug was completed.[1]

Camphor is a remedy whose discovery goes back to its supposed efficacy in exorcising spirits. Among the Mohammedans this drug was held to be an infallible means of keeping off daimons by reason of its smell.[2] The inhabitants of Logone likewise believed in the spirit-banning influence of the smell of camphor, and, therefore, used it as an amulet.[3] The camphor tree was known to the Chinese writers as early as the sixth century of our era;[4] and Marco Polo, who visited China in the thirteenth century, saw many trees of this kind.[5] The English word camphor, is derived from the Arabian "cafur" or "canfur," which imports that our knowledge of the drug is derived from that people.[6] The earliest mention of camphor occurs in a poem by Imru-l-Kais, one of the oldest poems of the Arabic language, which was written at the opening of the sixth century.[7] At one time the drug was regarded as a rare and precious perfume, being mentioned on equal terms with ambergris, sandalwood, and musk, as a treasure "of the Sassanian dynasty of the kings of Persia."[8] "Possibly the first mention of camphor as a European medicine was by the Abbatissa Hildegard," in "De simplicibus medicamentis," Argen-

---

[1] Lloyd, "Hist. Veg. Drugs," Lloyd Library, Bulletin No. 18, p. 70.
[2] Nachtigal, "Sahara and Sudan," II, p. 527.
[3] Ibid.
[4] Baas, "Hist. Med.," p. 229.
[5] Lloyd, "Hist. Veg. Drugs," Lloyd Library, Bulletin No. 18, p. 13.
[6] Paris, "Pharmacologia," I, p. 67.
[7] Lloyd, "Hist. Veg. Drugs," Lloyd Library, Bulletin No. 18, p. 13.
[8] Ibid.

torati, 1533.[1] Since its introduction into the materia medica of civilized peoples, the drug has been used as a perfume constituent,[2] as an antiseptic, and as a nerve stimulant.[3]

It would appear that the use of iron as a medicine is to be traced back to belief in its power of spirit expulsion. Tylor writes, "The oriental jinn are in such deadly terror of iron, that its very name is a charm against them." [4] According to Mooney, "Among the Gaelic peasantry, fire, iron, and dung were the three great safeguards against the influence of fairies and the infernal spirits." [5] Tylor again says, "As to iron, demons are brought under the same category as elves and nightmares. Iron instruments keep them at bay, and especially iron horse-shoes have been chosen for this purpose, as the doors of many houses in Europe and America still show." [6] The Yakuts placed sharp tools made of iron under their beds, or put near by anything made of iron, in order to ward off the evil spirits that trouble people when asleep.[7] But it may be inquired, What has this to do with the internal use of iron as a medicine? As far as could be ascertained, the transition from the external to the internal use of this substance, with the spirit theory in mind, was made by the ancient Greeks. Dr. T. Lauder Brunton writes, "The Greeks,

---

[1] Lloyd, "Hist. Veg. Drugs," Lloyd Library, Bulletin No. 18, p. 13.
[2] Ibid., p. 13.
[3] "Useful Drugs," Prepared and issued by the Am. Med. Ass., p. 45.
[4] Tylor, "Prim. Cult.," I, p. 127.
[5] Mooney, "Medical Mythology of Ireland," Proceedings of Am. Phil. Soc., 1887, p. 141.
[6] Tylor, "Prim. Cult.," I, p. 127.
[7] Sumner, "Yakuts" Abridged from the Russian of Sieroshevski, J. A. I., XXXI. p. 105.

when a man was suffering from weakness and paleness, put a sword into a vessel of water and made the man drink the water. They thought the sword contained a spirit of some virtue that entered into the person and gave him strength, and so it had, especially if it were rusted to a great degree. If steel or iron is put into water, it gradually rusts, the steel slowly dissolves, so that the water becomes ferruginous. The Greeks therefore were correct in their treatment," [1] in spite of their theory. According to Berdoe, "the first instance in which a preparation of iron is known to have been prescribed in medicine" is when "Iphiclus having no children, asked Melampus to tell him how he could become a father." The Greek physician advised him "to take the rust from a knife, and drink it in water during ten days. The remedy was eminently successful." [2] Sulphate of iron, the same author says, "is mentioned in the Amera Cosha of the Hindus, and it was used by them as by the Romans, in the time of Pliny, in making ink." [3] Though the medical virtues of iron have been generally acknowledged from time immemorial, it has had a struggle for existence in this usage. It was thought by the ancients that wounds made by iron instruments would have difficulty in healing.[4] After the expulsion of the Tarquins, Porsena made the Romans agree not to use iron except in agriculture.[5] Avicenna (980—1037)

[1] Brunton, "Action of Medicines," p. 493.
[2] Berdoe, "Healing Art," p. 151.
[3] Ibid., p. 486.
[4] Paris, "Pharmacologia," I, p. 42.
[5] Ibid.

mentioned the drug in his text book on materia medica,[1] but advised the exhibition of a magnet, after it had been taken inwardly, to prevent any harmful results.[2] Iron as a remedy was first introduced into therapeutics by Paracelsus (1493—1541).[3] Basil Valentine, who probably lived about the close of the fifteenth century of the Christian era, says concerning sulphate of iron, "'when internally administered, it is a tonic and comforting to a weak stomach,' and 'externally applied it is an astringent and styptic.'"[4] A modern authority states that "the only therapeutic action attributable to the iron is the improvement in the number of red blood-cells, and in the amount of hemoglobin in them. For this purpose it is indicated in anemia, and in diseases of the blood in which anemia is a factor, such as leukemia."[5]

Spencer, quoting Petherick, says, "The Arabs suppose that 'in high fever.. the patient is possessed by the devil.'"[6] Berdoe writes, "The people of Tartary make a great puppet when fever is prevalent, which they call the Demon of Intermittent Fevers, and which when completed they set up in the tent of the patients."[7]

The one remedy in the pharmacopoeia of the civilized which is regarded as a specific against malarial fever is quinine. This is prepared from Peruvian bark, which, as the

[1] Baas, "Hist. Med.," p. 229.
[2] Paris, "Pharmacologia," I, p. 42.
[3] Baas, "Hist. Med.," p. 390.
[4] Paris, "Pharmacologia," I, p. 71.
[5] "Useful Drugs," Prepared and issued by the Am. Med. Ass., pp. 67—68
[6] Spencer, "Principles of Sociology," I, p. 246.
[7] Berdoe, "Healing Art," p. 31.

name implies, is imported from Peru. The native name for the bark is "quinia-quinia," or "medicine bark."[1] The Indians of the Matto-Grosso country consider red cinchona bark "a remedy for fevers."[2] In Ecuador, the bark is regarded as "a specific for fevers."[3] As to the discovery of the medicinal qualities of the drug, there is no reliable history. This is said to be due partly to the fact that it was the policy of the Spanish conquistadors to give as little credit as possible to the Indians for the many valuable products which they obtained from them, and partly to the fact that the natives were extremely secretive about the source of their medicines.[4] A legend regarding the discovery of the remedy is that a native of Peru who was attacked by fever, drank from a pool into which some of this bark had chanced to fall. Since the bark had imparted its medicinal properties to the water, he was cured.[5] Another legend has it that when the Spanish army was passing through the forests of Peru, about the time of the conquest, a soldier was seized by fever and abandoned to his fate. He drank from a pool of water where there grew a tree from which the bark is taken. He soon recovered, rejoined his regiment, and proclaimed the means of cure.[6] The daimon explanation of the discovery of the virtues of the bark would seem more

---

[1] Wellcome, "A visit to the Native Cinchona Forests," Proceedings Am. Pharm. Ass., 1879, p. 829.
[2] Ibid.
[3] Ibid.
[4] Ibid.
[5] Paris, "Pharmacologia," I, p. 23.
[6] Wellcome, "A visit to the Native Cinchona Forests," Proceedings Am. Pharm. Ass., 1879, p. 829.

simple. There is direct evidence that the savage attributes fever to spirit possession.[1] It is known that the natives of Ecuador and Peru resorted to the use of the bark in case of fever.[2] Putting these two facts together, what more reasonable than the supposition that the medicine man, in his efforts to expel the spirit, lighted upon the bark which effected a recovery? At any rate the Peruvians believe that the drug was known, and used as a remedy, at a much earlier date than when the Spaniards, under Pizarro, invaded their land.[3] And that the bark had some kind of religious significance among the Indians, is evidenced by this quotation from Wellcome: "I was informed that pieces of the bark had been discovered in some of the ancient tombs," [in Peru] "which is very probable." [4] This would seem to connect the use of the drug with the spirit theory. It was no doubt placed in the tombs in order that the departed might make use of its spirit against the spirits in the other world.

In the seventeenth century, when the Count of Chinchona was governor of Peru, at that time a Spanish colony, the Countess was taken by an attack of fever and seemed likely to die. The natives, hearing of the sickness of the foreign woman, gave to a Jesuit missionary, who worked among them, bark from a tree growing upon the mountain slopes, advising him to grind it to powder and give it to the sick woman at certain intervals. The countess recovered, and being of a philanthropic

[1] Vide p. 249.   [2] Vide p. 250.
[3] Wellcome, "A visit to the Native Cinchona Forests," Proceedings Am. Pharm. Ass., 1879, p. 830.   [4] Ibid.

disposition, she sent a quantity of the bark to Europe
for use among the poor. It effected the same recoveries in
Europe as in Peru, and so attracted much attention.[1]
It was at first known as "Jesuits' bark."[2] In the process
of time the bark and tree were botanically investigated by
Linnaeus, and named in honor of the house to which
the countess belonged, "chinchona," which name was
shortened to "cinchona."[3] It is now generally called
"cinchona bark," although sometimes the name "Peruvian
bark" is applied to it. According to Baas, the
first medical work to advise the use of Peruvian
bark was the "Vera Praxis ad Curationem Terti-
anae," written by Pietro Barba, a professor in Valladolid in 1642.[4] Francesco Torti (1658—1741) is said to
have introduced the drug into Italy.[5] The Edinburgh
Pharmacopoeia of 1730 says, "Cardinal de Lugo was the
first to bring the bark into France." That was in 1650, at
which time it was called "Jesuits' powder," "because the
Jesuits had the distribution of it, the Cardinal, who was
of their order, having left them a large quantity."[6] In
Salmon's "Practical Physic," published in 1692, one may
read, "'As a specific against all manner of ague, take
quinqum or Jesuits' bark, two drachms, beat it into
powder just about the time of using it, infuse it in a good

[1] True, Jour. Am. Folk Lore, April 1901, pp. 112 ff.
[2] Wellcome, "A visit to the Native Cinchona Forests," Proceedings of Am. Pharm. Ass., 1879, p. 829.
[3] True, Jour. Am. Folk Lore, April 1901, p. 112.
[4] Baas, "Hist. Med.," p. 544.
[5] Ibid., p. 719.
[6] Sanders, "Presidential Address," Proceedings Am. Pharm. Ass.,
1878, pp. 846—848.

draught of claret or other wine for the space of two hours, then give the patient both liquor and powder at once.'" [1] Not long after the introduction of the drug into France by the Jesuits it fell into neglect. Robert Tabor, according to one authority, in 1679,[2] and according to another writer, in 1706,[3] again established its reputation in that country by introducing it as a nostrum. He prepared a secret concoction said to be made of lemon juice, or Rhine wine, a small amount of opium, and cinchona, and was so successful in effecting cures in Paris that the government purchased his secret." [4] From about 1680 down to the eighteenth century, the medical world was divided as to the benefits to be derived from the administration of the remedy. It was condemned because "it did not evacuate the morbific matter," because "it bred obstructions in the viscera," because "it only bound up the spirits, and stopped the paroxysms for a time, and favored the translation of the peccant matter into the more noble parts." [5] "In a postscript to his work on 'Primitive Physic' published in 1747, John Wesley wrote, 'It is because they are not safe but extremely dangerous, that I have omitted the four Herculean medicines, opium, the bark, steel, and most of the preparations of quicksilver.'" [6] About the same time, a Dr. Tissot

[1] Sanders, " Presidential Address," Proceedings Am. Pharm. Ass., 1878, pp. 846–848.
[2] Baas, "Hist. Med.," p. 544.
[3] Sanders, Proceedings Am. Pharm. Ass., 1878, pp. 846—848.
[4] Baas, "Hist. Med.," p. 544.
[5] Paris, "Pharmacologia," I, p. 42.
[6] Sanders, " Presidential Address," Proceedings Am. Pharm. Ass., 1878, pp. 846–848.

strongly recommended the use of cinchona, especially in ague.[1] He was severely taken to task for this. An English writer who did not give his name, said in criticism of Tissot, "'with reference to his vehement recommendation of Peruvian bark as the only infallible remedy either for mortifications or intermittent fevers, he really seems transported with it, as do many physicians besides. It is not an infallible remedy either for the one or for the other. I have known pounds of it given to stop a mortification, yet the mortification spread till it killed the patient. I myself took pounds of it when I was young, for a common tertian ague, and I should have probably died of it, had I not been cured unawares by drinking largely of lemonade. I will be bold to say from my personal knowledge that there are other remedies which less often fail. I believe that the bark has cured six agues in ten. I know cobweb pills have cured nine in ten ... I object secondly, that it is far from being a safe remedy. This I affirm in the face of the sun, that it frequently turns an intermittent fever into a consumption. By this, a few years since, one of the most amiable young women I have known lost her life, and so did one of the healthiest young men in Yorkshire. I could multiply instances, but I need go no further than my own case. In the last ague which I had, the first ounce of the bark was, as I expected, thrown off by purging. The second, being mixed with salt of wormwood, stayed in my stomach, and just at the hour the

---

[1] Sanders, "Presidential Address," Proceedings Am. Pharm. Ass. 1878, pp. 846—848.

ague should have come, began a pain in my shoulder-blade. Quickly it shifted its place, began a little lower under my left breast and there fixed. In less than an hour I had a short cough, the pain and the fever continued without intermission, and every night soon after I lay down, came first a dry cough, for forty or forty-five minutes, then an impetuous one till something seemed to burst, and for half an hour more I threw up a thick fetid pus... In less than six hours it obstructed, inflamed, and ulcerated my lungs, and by the summary process brought me into the third stage of a true pulmonary consumption. Excuse me, therefore, if, escaped with the skin of my teeth, I say to all I have any influence over, wherever you have an intermittent fever, look at me, and beware of the bark.'" [1] The price at which the bark was sold serves to indicate the character of the various phases of the struggle through which it had to pass before it was admitted without question into the materia medica of Europe. When first introduced into France the remedy literally brought its weight in gold,[2] a price equal to about twenty dollars an ounce.[3] Sturmius, according to Paris, saw twenty doses of the powdered bark sold at Brussels for sixty florins, and adds that he would have paid that price for some doses, but the supply had given out.[4] In London, as late as 1680, the bark sold at eight pounds an ounce.[5] On the

[1] Sanders, "Presidential Address," Proceedings Am. Pharm. Ass. 1878, pp. 846—848.
[2] Baas, "Hist. Med.," p. 544.
[3] Proceedings Am. Pharm. Ass., 1879, p. 830.
[4] Paris, "Pharmacologia," I, p. 43.
[5] Baas, "Hist. Med.," p. 544.

other hand, Paris quotes Condamine to the effect that in 1690, "'several thousand pounds of the bark lay at Piura and Payta for want of a purchaser.'"[1] Baas states that to Sydenham belongs the greatest credit for introducing the bark into England; and that Peyer and Bernhard Valentini (1657—1729), a professor in the university of Giessen, were said to have been the first to employ it in Germany.[2] About 1757, according to Sanders, there is to be found "in a work on the commerce of the European settlements in America the following: 'This medicine,' [cinchona], 'as usual, was held in defiance for a good while by medical authorities, but after an obstinate defence they have thought proper at last to surrender. Notwithstanding all the mischiefs at first foreseen in its use, everybody knows that it is at this day innocently and efficaciously prescribed in a great variety of cases; for which reason it makes a considerable and valuable part of the cargo of the galleons.'"[3] In the latter part of the eighteenth century and the first part of the nineteenth, Fothergill, Werlhof and Torti, Johann Heinrich Rahn of Zürich, and Althof, a professor at Göttingen, had to carry on a continual fight to establish the advantages of the bark.[4] In 1854, Alfred Russell Wallace and Dr. Carl Hasskarl introduced the remedy into Dutch and English India. According to Baas that was a great service, for he says, "Without this humane and characteristically

[1] Paris, "Pharmacologia," I, p. 43.
[2] Baas, "Hist. Med.," p. 544.
[3] Sanders, "Presidential Address," Proceedings Am. Pharm. Ass. 1878, pp. 846—848.
[4] Baas, "Hist. Med.," p. 719.

professional act, cinchona and its preparations, particularly, under its recent abuse in medicine, would have finally disappeared from our store of drugs." [1]

It remains to be mentioned that, in 1820, the French chemists Pelletier and Caventou subjected the bark to a chemical analysis, and announced to the Academy of Sciences, Paris, that as a result of their experiments they had discovered its active principle, which in due time was called "quinine." [2]

It was stated in another chapter [3] that blood-letting is practiced by some savage tribes, with a different interpretation from that of propitiation, in that the inhabitants of the River Darling, New South Wales, give blood as nutrition to very weak patients. How near those primitive peoples came to reaching certain basic truths it is impossible to say. There is, however, authority for the statement that among civilized nations, arterial blood, dried and powdered, is recommended for use as a restorative; that blood is prescribed for persons suffering from anemia and poor nutrition; and that no less than fifteen preparations of blood are on sale in twentieth century pharmacies. [4]

The discovery of narcotics is to be traced neither to the positive nor to the negative methods—neither to propitiation nor exorcism—of the medicine man in the treatment of disease. In chapter II of this book it was

[1] Baas, "Hist. Med.," p. 846.
[2] Am. Jour. Pharmacy, Nov. 1905, p. 544.
[3] Vide p. 185.
[4] True, Jour. Am. Folk Lore, April 1901, p. 109.

shown that sometimes when the shaman is unable to present external proofs of being possessed by spirits, he resorts to the use of drugs, and in this manner feigns possession.[1] In this same connexion Spencer says, "Whether produced by fasting, fever, hysteria, or insanity, any extreme excitement is, by savage and semi-civilized peoples, ascribed to a possessing spirit. Similar is the interpretation of an unusual mental state caused by a nerve stimulant. It is thought that a supernatural being, contained in the solid or liquid swallowed, produces" [this mental state.][2] Speaking of Mohammedan opium-eaters, Vambéry says, "'What surprised me most was that these wretched people were regarded as eminently religious, of whom it was thought that from their love to God and the Prophet they had become mad, and stupefied themselves in order that in their excited state they might be nearer the Beings they loved so well.'"[3] Bourke writes, "The pranks and gibberish of the maniac or the idiot are solemnly treasured as outbursts of inspiration. Where such an exaltation can be produced by an herb, bulb, liquid, or food, the knowledge of such an excitant is kept as long as possible from the laity; and even after the general diffusion of a more enlightened intelligence has broadened the mental horizon of the devotee, these narcotics and irritants are 'sacred,' and the frenzies they induce are 'sacred' also... Mushroom, mistletoe, rue, ivy, mandrake, hemp, opium, and the stramonium

[1] Vide pp. 45—46. [2] Spencer, "Principles of Sociology," I, p. 355. [3] Ibid.

of the medicine man of the Hualpai Indians of Arizona,—
all may well be examined in the light of this proposition." [1]

Since "plants yielding intoxicating agents are supposed
by primitive peoples to contain spirits," [2] since it is thought
that when an individual is under the influence of intoxicants,
he is possessed by divinities, and since "the knowledge
of such excitant is kept as long as possible from the
laity," [3] "mushroom, mistletoe, rue, ivy, hemp, opium, and
stramonium," may reasonably have been discovered by
the medicine man in his efforts to induce a state of
religious ecstasy, thereby demonstrating to his constituents
the fact that a possessing spirit has descended upon him.
These drugs in due time would be taken up, investigated,
analyzed, named, and used with a new signification.

The typical narcotic whose history is to be sketched
in this chapter is opium. The name of the particular
medicine man who, in his ambition to appear
possessed, blundered upon this drug is not known.
Bartels says that, as far as he is aware, the drug
is never applied by savage tribes of the present time
for healing purposes, but rather with the idea of
inducing possession. [4] There are remedies used by
primitive races, however, with the intention of removing
pain, or of producing a kind of narcotization. The Tartars
and Cossacks on the Yenessei River prepare a decoction
made from the leaves of rhododendron chrysanthemum,

[1] Bourke, "Scatalogic Rites of all Nations," p. 97.
[2] Spencer, "Principles of Sociology," I, p. 358.
[3] Bourke, "Scatalogic Rites of all Nations," p. 97.
[4] Bartels, "Med. Naturvölker," p. 125.

which they get from the Koibals. They put the plant into a pot covered air-tight, and stew it in an oven. Thus they get a strong, bitter, brownish liquid which produces upon the patient a feverish heat, a kind of intoxication, and even unconsciousness.[1] Narcosis for the purpose of a surgical operation is recorded by Felkin to have been applied in Uganda. In that place a native surgeon performed the Caesarean operation upon a pregnant woman, after first producing partial stupor by means of banana-wine.[2] Since peoples at this stage of culture, therefore, are acquainted with the medicinal use of narcotics, it is a reasonable inference that, in spite of the fact that opium is not used by the savage of today with the idea of assuaging pain, yet some savage or semi-civilized individual in the far distant past must have experienced and revealed to his fellows "the properties of the poppy, that sweet oblivious antidote for alleviating pain," for "the discovery of the medical qualities of opium is lost in times gone by."[3] The English word "opium," according to the Oxford Dictionary, is derived from the Greek ὅπιον, or poppy juice.[4] Peters quotes Typhon Miquel as saying that the drug corresponds to the description of νήπενθες, which Helen gave to Telemachus, at the house of Menelaus, that he might forget his sorrows.[5] This conjecture, according to Peters, is supported by the fact that the formula for that beverage had been obtained from Polydamnos, wife of Thous of

[1] Bartels, "Med Naturvölker," p. 125.
[2] Ibid.
[3] Lloyd, "Hist. Veg. Drugs," Lloyd Library, Bulletin No. 18, p. 62.
[4] Op. Cit. p. 153.
[5] Peters, "Pictorial Pharmacy," p. 139.

Egypt.[1] Tincture of opium, or laudanum, therefore, "has been called Thebic Tincture."[2] The Hebrew books make no mention of the drug, though the poppy was cultivated in Western Asia in very ancient times, and probably even in historic times.[3] The properties of the plant were known in the time of Hippocrates,[4] and the Egyptians of Pliny's time used a liquor of the poppy for medical purposes.[5] Dioscorides, who lived in the second century of our era, distinguished between the juice obtained from the poppy capsule, and the extract obtained from the entire plant.[6] "Inasmuch as he describes how the capsule should be incised, and the juice collected, it is evident that he plainly refers to opium."[7] Theophrastus, in the first century, B. C., mentions the drug, as does Celsus, in the first century of the present era, and during the Roman sway, it was known as coming from Asia Minor.[8] It is conjectured that Mohammed's prohibition of wine led to extension of the use of opium in some parts of Asia.[9] At any rate the drug passed from Asia Minor to the Arabs, who took it to Persia, and even to more Eastern countries.[10] The Mohammedans introduced opium into India, "the earliest mention being by Barbosa, who visited Calicut, the port of export then being Aden, or

[1] Peters, "Pictorial Pharmacy," p. 139.
[2] Paris, "Pharmacologia," I, p. 24.
[3] De Candolle, "L' Origine des Plantes Cultivées," p. 320.
[2] Peters, "Pictorial Pharmacy," p. 139.
[5] De Candolle, "L' Origine des Plantes Cultivées," p. 320.
[6] Lloyd, "Hist. Veg. Drugs," Lloyd Library, Bulletin No. 18, p. 62.
[7] Ibid.
[8] Ibid.
[9] Ibid.
[10] Ibid.

Cambey." [1] Kämpfer, a German traveller, visited Persia in 1685, and described "the various kinds of opium then produced, stating that it was customary to mix the drug with various aromatics, such as nutmeg, cardamom, cinnamon, and mace, and even with ambergris; also with the red-coloring matter made of cannabis indica and the seeds of stramonium." [2] The *ching che chun ching* of the Chinese is said to date to a very early period in the Christian era, and perhaps to a time prior to that. It is a work of forty volumes, eight of which are devoted to Luy-Fang, or Pharmacology. In this "opium is recommended as an anodyne, and in dysentery." [3] Opium smoking began in China after the middle of the seventeenth century, and spread rapidly. [4] Lloyd can find no instance of the use of the drug in any form by the Turkish people of the present time, [5] though now as in the past the principle place of export of the opium poppy is Smyrna. [6] Heraclides of Tarentum, who lived about the third century, B. C., is said to have made use of the drug to procure sleep. [7] "In Europe, opium was not in times gone by one of the more costly drugs, being cheaper than camphor, rhubarb, or senna." [8] In the last half of the eighteenth,

[1] Lloyd, "Opium and its Compounds," Lloyd Bros. Drug Treatise, No. XXII, p. 4.
[2] Ibid.
[3] Therapeutic Monthly, Oct. 1901, p. 192.
[4] Lloyd, "Opium and its Compounds," Lloyd Bros. Drug Treatise, No. XXII, p. 5.
[5] Lloyd, "Hist. Veg. Drugs," Lloyd Library, Bulletin No. 18, p. 62.
[6] Lloyd, "Opium and its Compounds," Lloyd Bros. Drug Treatise, No. XXII, p. 4.
[7] Berdoe, "Healing Art," p. 201.
[8] Lloyd, "Opium and its Compounds," Lloyd Bros. Drug Treatise, No. XXII, p. 4.

and the first half of the nineteenth century, the advocates of this remedy had to fight to establish its advantages.[1] At the present time, opium and its alkaloids are in use in all civilized countries.[2]

The most important alkaloid of opium is morphine. The history of the discovery of morphine briefly stated is as follows: Paris quotes "Annales de Chimie," Vol. XLV, as saying that Doerosne first obtained a crystalline substance from opium in 1803, which dissolved in acids, but he did not determine its nature or properties.[3] The same author then says, giving as authority "Annales de Chimie," Vol. XCII, that in 1804, Seguin discovered another crystalline body in opium, and although describing most of its properties, he did not hint at its alkaline nature.[4] "Annales de Chimie," Vol. V., is then cited as authority for the statement that Sertürner at Eimbeck, Hannover, had contemporaneously with Doerosne and Seguin obtained these crystalline bodies, but it was not until 1817, "that he unequivocally proclaimed the existence of a vegetable alkali, and assigned to it the narcotic powers which distinguish the operation of opium."[5] Sertürner named this body "morphia,"[6] from Morpheus, the Greek god of sleep,[7] and it is said to be

[1] Baas, "Hist. Med.," p. 719.
[2] Lloyd, "Opium and its Compounds," Lloyd Bros. Drug Treatise, No. XXII, p. 4.
[3] Paris, "Pharmacologia," II, p. 244.
[4] Ibid.
[5] Ibid.
[6] Ibid.
[7] Park, "A Study of Medical Words," Yale Med. Jour., July 1902, p. 6.

the same as the essential salt noticed by Seguin.[1] The salt discovered by Doerosne was for a time mistaken for one of the salts of morphia, but, according to "Annales de Chimie," Vol V, M. Robiquet "pointed out its distinctive qualities," and it was thereafter denominated "Narcotine."[2]

Another drug, which owes its discovery to the efforts of the representatives of the imaginary environment to appear possessed, is Erythroxylon Coca. The coca shrub is indigenous to the eastern slope of the Andes, where, especially in Bolivia and Peru, it still grows wild. In recent times, however, the demand for coca has been so great that many acres of the plant are now under cultivation in those countries.[3] The leaves are the valuable portion. They resemble tea leaves in shape and size—oval-oblong, pointed, two or more inches long by about one in breadth, and having short, delicate footstalks.[4] Spencer, quoting Garcilasso de la Vega's "Royal Commentaries of the Incas," Vol. I, p. 88, says, "'The Peruvians still look upon it [coca] with feelings of superstitious veneration. In the time of the Incas it was sacrificed to the sun, the Huillac Umu, or high priest, chewing the leaf during the ceremony. Among the Chibchas, too, hayo [coca] was used as an inspiring agent by the priests.'"[5] There would seem, therefore, to be little room for doubt that the beginning of the knowledge of the effects of coca upon

[1] Paris, "Pharmacologia," II, p. 244.
[2] Ibid.
[3] Steele, Proceedings of Am. Pharm. Ass., 1878, p. 775.
[4] Ibid.
[5] Spencer, "Principles of Sociology," I, p. 358.

the physical organization is connected with religion. According to Mortimer, coca leaves were sometimes used in services of propitiation, as the following quotation from Lloyd will show: "'When the period for departure (on a perilous journey) actually arrives, the Indians throw coca in the air, just as did the Inca priests of old, to propitiate the gods of the mountains, who presumably do not wish their domains invaded.'" [1] The connexion of the plant with service to the gods is further attested by the fact that specimens of erythroxylon coca leaf have been obtained from the old Inca tombs of Peru,[2] and it is said to be the custom of the natives of that country, when they see a mummy, to kneel down with devotion and place around it a handful of coca leaves.[3]. The knowledge of the effects of the plant filtered down to the ranks of the laity, and was used with a different interpretation. This is evidenced by a quotation from the Jesuit Father Blas Valera, who, writing in 1609, said, "'It may be gathered how powerful the coca is in its effects on the laborer, from the fact that the Indians, who use it, become stronger and much more satisfied, and work all day without eating.'" [4] It is said that the Indian runners of the Andes, who of necessity had to carry as little food as possible, were accustomed to take with them a few coca leaves, and these sufficed to satisfy their hunger, and upon

---

[1] Lloyd, "Hist. Veg. Drugs," Lloyd Library, Bulletin No. 18, p. 19, Quoting W. G. Mortimer's "Hist. of Peru and Coca."
[2] Wellcome, Proceedings Am. Pharm. Ass., 1879, p. 830.
[3] Steele, Proceedings Am. Pharm. Ass., 1878, pp. 780 ff.
[4] Lloyd, "Hist. Veg. Drugs," Lloyd Library, Bulletin No. 18, p. 19, Quoting Blas Valera "Commentarios Reales."

such food they could undergo the most exhausting and exacting journeys.[1] A plant used so extensively in the native religious ceremonies necessarily fell under the hostile criticism of the early Spanish explorers, in whose opinion the sacerdotal employment of the leaves served to divert the heathen from the worship of the true God.[2] In 1567, accordingly, a Church council condemned coca as a "'worthless substance fitted for the misuse and superstition of the Indians,'"[3] and in 1569, "'the Spanish audience at Lima, composed of bishops from all parts of South America, denounced coca because, as they asserted, it was a pernicious leaf, the chewing of which the Indians supposed gave them strength, and was hence 'Un delusio del demonio.'"[4] All this, however, was of no avail. The Indians continued to use their national leaf, and the owners of plantations and mines, on account of its good effects on their laborers, came to its defence. But the Church, true to its conservative tendencies, did not give up until the last. It finally came, nevertheless, to regard the leaf highly, and recommended its introduction into Europe.[5] The fact that the chewing of coca leaves lessened the sense of fatigue, and imparted a feeling of well-being, attracted the attention of European travellers. Coca was first mentioned by Nicholas Monardes, of Seville,[6] who

---

[1] Lloyd, "Hist. Veg. Drugs," Lloyd Library, Bulletin No. 18, p. 19.
[2] Ibid.
[3] Steele, Proceedings Am. Pharm. Ass. 1878, pp. 780 ff.
[4] Lloyd, "Hist. Veg. Drugs," Lloyd Library, Bulletin No. 18, p. 19, Quoting Mortimer's "Hist. Peru and Coca."
[5] Steele, Proceedings Am. Pharm. Ass., 1878, pp. 781 ff.
[6] Baas, "Hist. Med.," p. 368.

in 1569 published an article on the drug, which was reproduced in 1577 in London.[1] A botanical description, written by Clusius, followed in 1605.[2] In 1793, Dr. Don Pedro Nolasco called attention to the advantages that might accrue from the introduction of the plant into European navies.[3] For many years, despite the experiences and recommendations of travellers, the reputed virtues of the drug were scouted as fabulous, or even ridiculed by the medical world of Europe.[4] Dr. H. A. Weddell and others, both prior and subsequent to the year 1850, attempted vainly to discover an energetic constituent of the drug. It was at first erroneously thought that the leaves of the plant owed their inherent properties (provided they had any) to some volatile principle. The only volatile base discovered was named "hydrine," but it "did not at all represent coca, and is no longer mentioned."[5] The fame and the reputed powers of coca, however, as well as the fact that it was creeping into the use of practicing physicians, led such chemists as Stanislas, Martin, Maisch, Lossin, Wöhler, and many others to subject the drug to repeated analyses, which resulted in such products as coca-wax, coca-tannic acid, and several alkaloidal bases.[6] In 1860, Dr. Albert Niemann, of Göttingen, Germany, assistant in the Laboratory of Professor Wöhler, succeeded in isolating an alkaloid to which he gave the name cocaine.[7]

[1] Lloyd, "Hist. Veg. Drugs," Lloyd Library, Bulletin No. 18, p. 18.
[2] Ibid.
[3] Steele, Proceedings Am. Pharm. Ass, 1878, pp. 781 ff.
[4] Lloyd, "Hist. Veg. Drugs," Lloyd Library, Bulletin No. 18, p. 18.
[5] Ibid. [6] Ibid., pp. 19—20.
[7] Lloyd, "Hist. Veg. Drugs," Lloyd Library Bulletin, No. 18, p. 20; Steele, Proceedings Am. Pharm. Ass., 1878, p. 785.

As in the case of quinine, ipecacuanha, and opium, cocaine has had a struggle to survive. English chemists, such as Dowdeswell, Murrell, and Garrard, subjected the alkaloid to chemical experimentation, the results of which Dowdeswell summed up in the London Lancet May 6, 1876, p. 667, as follows: "'It has not effected the pupil nor the state of the skin; it has caused neither drowsiness nor sleeplessness; assuredly it has occasioned none of those subjective effects so fervidly described and ascribed to it by others—not the slightest excitement, nor even the feeling of buoyancy and exhilaration, which is experienced from mountain air or a draught of spring water. This examination was commenced in the expectation that the drug would prove important and interesting physiologically, and perhaps valuable as a therapeutic agent. This expectation has been disappointed. Without asserting that it is positively inert, it is concluded from these experiments that its action is so slight as to preclude the idea of its having any value either therapeutically or popularly; and it is the belief of the writer, from observation upon the effect on the pulse, and other bodily organs, of tea, milk-and-water, and even plain water, hot, tepid, and cold, that such things may, at slightly different temperatures, produce a more decided effect than even large doses of coca, if taken at about the temperature of the body.'"[1] Similar observations were published by Dr. Roberts Bartholow in "The Therapeutic Gazette," July 1880, p. 280, who declared that coca

[1] Lloyd, "Hist. Veg. Drugs," Lloyd Library, Bulletin No. 18, pp. 21—22.

at its best "'acts like theine and caffeine as an indirect nutrient.'" [1] The scientific world of that day accepted the verdict of those investigators that coca and its alkaloid cocaine, were nothing more than mild caffeine-bearing stimulants, such as tea and coffee, and that far from possessing any important inherent quality, they were positively inert.[2] Since the investigations of Dowdeswell seemed incontrovertible, commercial enterprises concerned in the exploitation of coca suffered a severe loss. Shortly after its discovery, cocaine sold in New York at one dollar a grain,[3] but "the annual consumption in the middle and latter half of the nineteenth century of forty million pounds of coca, at a cost of ten million dollars," caused that "substance to take rank among the large economic blunders of the age."[4] The prospect very much disturbed the leading American manufacturing pharmacist of that time, Dr. Edward S. Squibb, of Brooklyn, New York, but be it said to his credit, since he was a painstaking chemist, he determined to "sacrifice his economic opportunities to his professional ideals, by accepting the findings of Dowdeswell and others, and by excluding preparations of coca from his pharmaceutical list."[5] It would not be consistent with the fundamental instincts of human nature, however, to sacrifice the source of such commercial advantages without a struggle. In 1882, Dr. Squibb contributed various articles to the "Ephemeris,"

[1] Lloyd, "Hist. Veg. Drugs," Lloyd Library, Bulletin No. 18, p. 22.
[2] Ibid., pp. 21—22.
[3] Steele, Proceedings Am. Pharm. Ass., 1878, p. 788.
[4] Squibb, Ephemeris, July 1884, p. 600 ff.
[5] Lloyd, "Hist. Veg. Drugs," Lloyd Library, Bulletin No. 18, p. 20.

Brooklyn, in which he communicated his decision to give up the manufacture of preparations of coca, but at the same time called attention to the fact that competent authorities might be conflicting and contradictory, in therapeutics as well as elsewhere, and expressed his belief that the seemingly economic blunder of exploiting coca might not have been a blunder after all.[1] Scarcely was this article given for publication before the scientific and professional world was confounded by the announcement "that a medical student named Koller, of Vienna, had discovered that a solution of hydrochlorate of cocaine was possessed of marvelous qualities as a local anesthetic." [2] This intelligence was published or referred to in every pharmaceutical and medical journal in America. Dr. D. Agnew in the "Medical Record," October 18, 1884, p. 438, wrote as follows: "'We have today used the agent in our clinic at the College of Physicians and Surgeons [New York] with most astonishing and satisfactory results. If future use should prove to be equally satisfactory, we will be in possession of an agent for the prevention of suffering in ophthalmic operations of inestimable value.'" [3] Dr. Squibb now began with zeal a new investigation of coca and its alkaloid, "his process of manufacture being yet a standard, and his writings on cocaine being yet an authority." [4] A great reaction followed in favor of the use of cocaine, and though, in the beginning, it was recommended only

[1] Squibb, Ephemeris, July 1884, p. 600 ff.
[2] Lloyd, "Hist. Veg. Drugs," Lloyd Library, Bulletin No. 18, p. 23.
[3] Ibid.
[4] Ibid., p. 24.

in operations on the cornea of the eye,[1] later experiments proved it to be efficacious in dentistry and minor surgical operations for dulling the ends of the sensory nerves and so adding greatly to the comfort of humanity.

Another of the greatest blessings to mankind was thus discovered as a result of religious ceremonials, later used by savages themselves for another purpose and after remaining a possession of nature people for many years, at last brought to the attention of the civilized world, tested, then used by scientists with a still different object in view, and finally admitted into the pharmacopoeia of cultured races.

In Africa, Asia, South America, and Australia, an extract is used for poisoning arrows, the source of which for the most part "is kept among the secrets of the medicine men or chiefs."[2] How the medicine men discovered their poisons is not clear. But that they do not always succeed in keeping the secret is evident. For it is told that "aconite has been widely employed as an arrow poison."[3] Aconite is still used for that purpose among the tribes of certain islands of the Pacific, and also among the Malay tribes of southeastern Asia. It was brought to the attention of explorers and travellers in those regions,[4] and was designated in the thirteenth century in a work published by the Welsh Manuscript Society, called "The Physicians of Myddvai,"

[1] Lloyd, "Hist. Veg. Drugs," Lloyd Library, Bulletin No. 18, pp. 23–24.
[2] Reference Handbook to Medical Sciences, I, p. 635.
[3] Flückiger and Handbury, "Pharmacographia," p. 8.
[4] True, Jour. Am. Folk Lore, April 1901, p. 113.

as a plant which every physician is to know.[1] Störck, of Vienna, introduced the drug into the regular practice of medicine, about 1762,[2] and now it is a well known remedy as a cardiac depressant, anti-pyretic, and diaphoretic.[3]

Strophanthus is another case in point. Though this plant was described by De Candolle in 1802, it was not until the early sixties that it came to the general notice of Europeans as being one of the arrow poisons used among the aborigines of western[4] and equatorial Africa, so deadly as to paralyze the heart at the slightest wound made by an arrow.[5] It is said that in Somaliland, Africa, the savage, in order to satisfy his mind as to the virulence of the poison, draws blood from his own body, pours it into a pool, and applies the poison to the lower end of the pool. Then he watches the coagulating effect from below upward.[6] Livingstone, the missionary, and Stanley, the explorer, upon observing the powerful effects of the drug, determined to have it chemically examined and tested. The result was that Sharpey in 1862, Pelikan in 1865, and Fraser in 1871, discovered that the strophanthus is a powerful cardiac agent,[7] and its alkaloid is now much lauded as a cardiac stimulant when given intravenously.

The calabar bean was brought to the attention of European explorers because of its use in ordeals. And

---

[1] Flückiger and Handbury, "Pharmacographia," p. 8.
[2] Ibid.
[3] "Useful Drugs," Prepared and issued by the American Medical Association, p. 13.
[4] Lloyd, "Hist. Veg. Drugs," Lloyd Library, Bulletin No. 18, p. 84.
[5] True, Jour. Am. Folk Lore, April 1901, p. 113.
[6] Lloyd, "Hist. Veg. Drugs," Lloyd Library, Bulletin No. 18, p. 85.
[7] Ibid.

concerning those ceremonies, it is said, "The administration of ordeals has been much in the hands of the priests, and they are more often than not worked on a theological basis. the intervention of a deity being invoked and assumed to take place even when the process is in its nature one of symbolic magic.... Among various drugs used in different parts of Africa are the mbundu root, and the calabar bean. The sorcerers who adminster this ordeal have in their hands a power of inflicting or remitting judicial murder, giving them boundless influence." [1] In the Niger Valley, when a person is accused of witchcraft or other grave crime, he is sentenced to eat the seeds of the calabar bean. If death follows, that is proof of the guilt of the accused.[2] The drug was first made known in England by Dr. W. F. Daniell, about 1840, and in 1846, he alluded to it in a paper read by him before an ethnological society.[3] In 1859, a missionary on the West Coast of Africa by the name of W. C. Thomson, sent a specimen of the plant to Professor Balfour of Edinburgh, "who figured it and described it as a type of a new genus." [4] Both before and after that date, the drug was chemically examined in the light of its use in the Niger valley, with the result that a new and valuable remedy for eye troubles,[5] and for certain exaggerated nervous conditions was discovered.[6]

[1] Encyc. Brit., Eleventh Edition, Vol. XX, pp. 173—174.
[2] True, Jour. Am. Folk Lore, April 1901, p. 113.
[3] Flückiger and Handbury, "Pharmacographia," p. 191.   [4] Ibid.
[5] "Useful Drugs," Prepared and issued by the American Medical Association, p. 106.
[6] True, Jour. Am. Folk Lore, April 1901, p. 113.

In his efforts to impress his people with the fact that he was possessed, or in his attempts to propitiate or exorcise the spirits, the medicine man thus blundered upon many remedies that were efficacious in certain combination of symptoms. Those remedies were transmitted from generation to generation, were communicated to other members of the caste, came into more frequent use, and finally obtained general recognition in the savage materia medica. By a process of selection, an empirical system of medicine grew up, by which the medicine man was able to treat successfully some classes of sickness, although without any intelligent idea of the process involved,[1] and in spite of illusory major premises. He also, as already has been said, discovered poisonous plants and herbs, which brought death to the accused at the ordeal, and on the tips of arrows carried venom to the veins of enemies. Later and more scientific ages took up the processes and results upon which the medicine man had blindly stumbled, applied them sometimes for the same, and sometimes for different purposes, and the issue is a complicated and elaborate system of medicine, capable in its entirety, according to modern science, of scientific explanation and demonstration, but which may appear to the scientist of the future as child-like and illogical as does the system of the savage to the investigator of the present day.[2]

In this connexion, Mrs. S. S. Allison says of the Similkameen Indians of British Columbia (p. 112 supra),

[1] Mooney, "Sacred Formulas of the Cherokees," Bur. Eth., VII, p. 328 ff.
[2] Ibid., pp. 323 ff.

"Setting aside the mysterious part, the doctors have some really valuable medicines. People apparently in the last stages of consumption have been cured by them. For blood-spitting they use a decoction of fibrous roots of the spruce, for rheumatism, the root of soap berry. The berry itself is used with success as a stomachic. A decoction of swamp poplar bark and spruce roots is used in syphilis. The wild-cherry bark and tansy root is much used by the women. The wild-cherry is used both as a tonic and expectorant, and is good for consumptives. There is a plant resembling the anemone, the root of which when bruised makes a powerful blister; and another resembling the geranium, the root of which will cure ringworm and dry up an old sore. The inner bark of the pine is used early in the spring when the sap is rising; the tree nettle is used as a physic, also as a wash for the hair, rendering it thick, soft, and glossy. Wild strawberry acts as an astringent." [1]

Mr. E. Palmer in "Notes on Some Australian Tribes," in the thirteenth volume of the Journal of the Anthropological Institute of Great Britain and Ireland, says that "the blacks appear to have possessed a considerable knowledge of indigenous plants," for use as food, for poisoning fish, "and also for healing and medicinal purposes." [2] One of the plants mentioned is Melaleuca Leucadendron, the young leaves of which are bruised in water and drunk for headache and colds. [3] Berdoe quotes

---

[1] Allison, "An Account of the Similkameen Indians of British Columbia," J. A. I., 1891, p. 311.

[2] Op. Cit., p. 310.

[3] Palmer, "Notes on Some Australian Tribes," J. A. I. XIII, p. 321.

Stillé to the effect that the oil from this tree
"'is of marked utility in cases of nervous vomiting,
nervous dysphagia, dyspnoea, and hiccup.'" [1] Among
some nature peoples, a wash is made from the bark
of the Excoecaria Parviflora or the gutta-percha tree, and
applied externally to all parts of the body for pains and
sickness.[2] The stems of Moschosma Polystachium are
bruised up in water and used for headache and fevers.[3]
The leaves and stems of Plectranthus Congestus are
employed as medicine.[4] The leaf of Pterocaulon Glan-
dulosus is crushed in water and applied for medical
purposes;[5] and Gnaphalium Luteo-album is among the
medicinal plants.[6] Concerning the last named plant Berdoe
says, "Several of this species are used in European
medicine in bronchitis and diarrhoea." [7] Eucalyptus Glo-
bulus is administered by the aborigines of Australia
as a remedy for intermittent fever.[8] Berdoe quotes
Stillé as saying "'the discovery of its virtues was acci-
dental. It is alleged that...the crew of a French man-
of-war, having lost a number of men with pernicious fever,
put into Botany Bay, where the remaining sick were
treated with eucalyptus and rapidly recovered.'" [9] In 1866,
Dr. Ramel of Valencia introduced the remedy to the

[1] Berdoe, "Healing Art," p. 34.
[2] J. A. I., XIII, p. 321.
[3] J. A. I., XIII, p. 323.
[4] Ibid., p. 322.
[5] Ibid.
[6] Ibid.
[7] Berdoe, "Healing Art," p. 34.
[8] Lloyd, "Hist. Veg. Drugs," Lloyd Library, Bulletin No. 18, p. 36.
[9] Berdoe, "Healing Art," p. 36.

Academy of Medicine, thus bringing the drug to the attention of the profession,[1] and the oil is now used as an antiseptic and expectorant.[2]

In 1535—1536, the Iroquois around Quebec treated members of the crew of Jacques Cartier, who had been taken with scurvy, with an infusion of the bark and leaves of the hemlock spruce. The treatment was a complete success.[3] In 1657, the same tribe recommended the sassafras leaf to the French at Onondaga for the closing of all kinds of wounds. It was tried for that purpose and pronounced "marvelous" in its effects.[4] Sanguinaria Canadensis,[5] or blood root, was used by our Indians for coloring their garments, and also as an application to indolent ulcers. The early settlers employed it for like purposes,[6] and after a time it attracted the attention of physicians. It was introduced finally into the United States Pharmacopoeia as a remedy for certain forms of dyspepsia, bronchitis, croup, and asthma.[7] Exogonium Purge, or jalap, is the gift of Mexico,[8] named for the city of Xalapa.[9] The early Spanish voyagers learned its cathartic properties from the natives,[10] and took large quantities

---

[1] Lloyd, "Hist. Veg. Drugs," Lloyd Library, Bulletin No. 18, p. 36.
[2] "Useful Drugs," Prepared and issued by the American Medical Association, p. 66.
[3] Garrison, "Hist. Med.," p. 21.
[4] Ibid.
[5] Bently, "New American Remedies," Pharmaceutical Journal, IV, pp. 263 ff.
[6] Lloyd, "Hist. Veg. Drugs," Lloyd Library, Bulletin No. 18, p. 73.
[7] Berdoe, "Healing Art," p. 37.
[8] Lloyd, "Hist. Veg. Drugs," Loyd Library, Bulletin No. 18, p. 51.
[9] Berdoe, "Healing Art," p. 38.
[10] Lloyd, "Hist. Veg. Drugs," Lloyd Library, Bulletin No. 18, p. 52.

of it in the sixteenth century to Europe. It stood
the test successfully, was botanically examined and
described by Coxe, of Philadelphia, about 1829,[1] and is
now recognized as a powerful purgative, in addition to
being "used for the purpose of removing water from
the tissues in the treatment of dropsy." [2]

The foregoing are merely a few examples of valuable
medical remedies that are used by primitive peoples, and
upon many of which science has placed the seal of its
approval.

Mooney, in his "Sacred Formulas of the Cherokees,"
employs a suggestive but naive method of showing how
some remedies originated, and how others doubtless
originated if we could project our knowledge far enough
into the past to discover it.[3] For that purpose he selects
the United States Dispensatory as an authority. Then
follows a list of twenty remedies upon which the medicine
men of the Cherokees had blundered. A comparison
between the Cherokee pharmacopoeia and the United
States Dispensatory shows, according to Mooney, that
about one third of those twenty remedies was correctly
used.[4]

It must be said, however, that after a diligent
comparison of 'the list of drugs named by Mooney with a
later edition of the United States Dispensatory the author

---

[1] Flückiger and Handbury, "Pharmacographia," p. 444.
[2] "Useful Drugs," Prepared and issued by the American Medical
Association, p. 50.
[3] Mooney, "Sacred Formulas of the Cherokees," Bur. Eth. VII,
pp. 323 ff.
[4] Ibid., p. 323.

found one of the five drugs which Mooney says were used by the Cherokees for the very purpose "for which it is best adapted," that is number twelve, or Hepatica Actiloba, not mentioned. Mooney probably used an earlier edition of the Dispensatory. As regards the other members of his list, Mooney is correct according to the later edition of the Dispensatory. Those drugs may not be applied to any great extent by the twentieth century practitioner. But they are down in the Dispensatory as possessing medical properties. Assuming, therefore, that the list given is a fair epitome of what the medicine men of the Cherokee Indians knew of the application of drugs as remedies, it is marvelous that in spite of the false reasoning by which they reached the results, in spite of their illusory major premises, and, one might almost say, in spite of themselves, nearly one third of the medicaments applied by those primitive doctors had, and still have, real medical properties.

It is not intended to assert that all the drugs in the pharmacopoeia of civilized people were discovered as the results of happy accident. Some remedies owe their origin to deliberate study and experiment. "It is difficult, however, to tell how far the use of drugs in modern practice is the result of scientific activity, and how far it is an inheritance from the folk remedies of former times. The former state grades into the latter." [1] But if one takes the experience of the Cherokee nation as a typical example,—and there is no reason why one should not, since it is the universal

[1] True, Jour. Am. Folk Lore, April 1901, p. 107.

tendency of man to react in a similar manner against
his environment,—the "recognized" drugs, the story of
whose origin is lost in the history of the tribes in which
they originated, must have come into use among primitive
peoples in the far distant past as a result of a series of
blunders on the part of the medicine man in treating sickness in accordance with the ghost theory. The primitive doctor to be sure applied many other drugs which
could not survive the test of time. Later and more
enlightened peoples separated the wheat from the chaff,
science attaching the signature of its authority to the
former, and the result is a fairly correct pharmacopoeia,
not the work of any one age or nation, but the product of
the blundering, criticism, and elimination of the centuries.

To Newman's inquiry,[1] therefore, "Who first discovered the medicinal herbs, which from earliest times have
been our resource against disease?" the answers may
be found in several writers, two of whom may be taken
as typical. Biart says, "Our materia medica owes tobacco,
gum-copal, liquid amber, sarsaparilla, resin of tecamaca,
jalap, and huaca to" the medicine men of "the Aztecs." [2]
Ratzel says: "Guiacum, ipecacuanha, and certain purgatives
....first became known through the Indian medicine
men." [3] To Barton's reflection, "If the distance of time
or the darkness of history did not prevent us from ascertaining who first discovered the properties of the poppy....
if we could tell who was that native of Peru that first

[1] Vide p. 227.
[2] Biart, "Aztecs," p. 285.
[3] Ratzel, "Hist. of Mankind," II, p. 155.

experienced and revealed to his countrymen the powers of the bark in curing intermittent fevers, would not the civilized nations of mankind with one accord concur in erecting durable monuments of granite and bronze to such benefactors of the species?"[1] replies may likewise be found. Waddle writes, "It was at first to the end of producing a state of religious ecstasy that the intoxicating mushroom, mistletoe, rue, ivy, mandrake, hemp, opium, and stramonium were used;"[2] and Bourke says that "the world owes a large debt to the medicine men of America, who first discovered the virtues of coca, sarsaparilla, jalap, cinchona, and guiacum."[3]

SUMMARY. It has been shown in this chapter that the medicine man, with the intent of dealing with the spirits, chanced to make use of roots or herbs with genuine remedial properties. He preserved and transmitted that knowledge. In course of the ages, those remedies were used with physiological rather than magical purposes in view. As time passed the useful drugs were differentiated from the worthless until ultimately a materia medica resulted. Business, scientific, and, not infrequently, religious interests have led members of civilized races to visit savage peoples. The remedies of the latter have arrested attention, have been tried and tested, and, in some

[1] Barton, "Collections for an Essay toward a Materia Medica in the United States," Lloyd Library, Bulletin No. I, p. 43.
[2] Waddle, "Miracles of Healing," Am. Jour. of Psychology, XX, p. 235.
[3] Bourke, "Medicine Men of the Apache," Bur. Eth., IX, p. 471.

cases, have gained entrance into the pharmacopoeia of the most highly cultured societies. The therapeutical agents to which men have been led by experimentation have been added, and the present elaborate materia medica has eventuated.

CHAPTER VIII

CONCLUSION.

It may be said by way of conclusion that a systematic study of the character and evolution of shamanism should not be without interest to the scientist.

The scientific principle that man, in a corresponding environment, although living in different regions of the earth, and at different stages of the history of the world, reacts in a similar manner, has received exemplification in this study. It has been shown that, as a result of his reaction, there has been developed a special representative of the imaginary environment, who, in spite of minor differences, is fundamentally one and the same the world over, call him by whatsoever name you choose. This intelligence should be illuminative to the sociologist.

Of particular interest to the physician and surgeon should be the knowledge of the connexion between his science and superstition. The noble profession of medicine had its beginning in the blind gropings of the medicine man in his efforts to expel or appease malicious or angry spirits. In Egypt those primitive notions and methods continued, and the empiricists, fettered by the conservatism of the cult, were content with the traditional prescriptions, handed down from generation to generation, not making any effort to develop the science other than the knowledge of embalming demanded. In Assyria no further advance was made; for the extraction of ominous livers of sheep was no more useful in teaching dissection to the Babylonians than was mummification adapted to impart that knowledge to the Hamites. On mounting a step or two higher, however, the Greeks are found laying a firmer foundation for practical medicine, and learning anatomy from dead, even from living bodies; and henceforth medicine leaves the apron strings of its mother, superstition, receiving, as time advanced, public hygiene from the Jews, and the beginnings of operative surgery from the Hindus.[1] Hippocrates taught that "no disease whatever came from the gods, but was in every instance traceable to a natural and intelligible cause."[2] Greek medicine, therefore, "was science in the making, with Roman medicine as an offshoot, Byzantium as a cold-storage plant, and Islam as travelling agent. The best side of mediaeval medicine was the organization of hospitals, sick nursing, medical legislation, and education."[3] The birth of anatomy as a science occured during the Renaissance period, and the same era marked the growth of surgery as a handicraft; the beginnings of pathology, instrumental diagnosis, and experimental surgery are to be traced to the eighteenth century; while—to the glory of the nineteenth century be it said—during that period scientific surgery was created, medicine as a science was organized, and advancement along every line was made.[4]

[1] Garrison, "Hist. Med.," p. 54.
[2] Berdoe, "Healing Art," p. 173.
[3] Garrison, "Hist. Med.," p. 594.
[4] Ibid.

Science thus has come out of superstition.[1] Medicine had its origin in the ghost theory of disease. That theory obtained until it was contradicted by later observation and criticism. Then another theory was advanced, which in turn was supplanted by another, until finally after centuries of blundering, stumbling, progressing, retrogressing, and again progressing, the germ theory, which is supposed to be the last word regarding the cause of disease, was advanced, our splendid system of the medical sciences following in its train.

Analogous to the origination of medicine in magic is that of chemistry in alchemy. The mediaeval alchemists taught that by means of the "philosopher's stone" baser metals could be transformed into gold. That theory caused many persons to spend their lives in search of the much-coveted object. The stone was not found, but as a result of the Herculean industry of those ancient savants, sulphuric acid, alcohol, and ammonia were discovered. The idea of the existence of the "philosopher's stone" must be called superstitious, but it led to the pursuit of truth by experiment. That method as the years passed was freed from its absurdities, and thus the science of chemistry has come from alchemy.[2]

Astronomy is another science that had its beginning in superstition.[3] The ancient Chaldeans believed the stars and planets to exercise such an influence over human life and events that they systematically observed and recorded

---

[1] Vide pp. 129 and 149.   [2] Tylor, "Anthropology," p. 328.   [3] Vide pp. 129—130.

the location of the heavenly bodies as indicating lucky and
unlucky days, as well as portending the coming of pestilence and the issues of battle. Even in comparatively
modern times, men of eminence along their special line of
activity, as, for example, Tycho Brahe and Kepler, have
disseminated the doctrine that the planets foretold the
destinies of men. That belief is called by later generations
superstition, but the fact remains that it led to observations
and calculations by which the motions of the planets themselves were foretold, and thus astrology prepared the
way for astronomy.[1]

Equally striking has been the evolution of the medicine
man in his character of religious leader. Since this subject
is to form the basis of a future discussion, it can only be
said here that in the capacity of priest the shaman was least
admirable. Whatever good he accomplished as physician
and counsellor, his efforts in interceding with the higher
powers were of course futile. But the medicine man
gradually became the teacher[2] of the young men of the
nation, and the almoner of the race. Almost down to the
present time, education and charity are largely in the
hands of the religious class. In this generation the Church
has shown a strong tendency, which is still growing, to
emphasize and strengthen its sociological work by means
of club rooms, gymnasiums, summer camps, schools and
colleges, medical missions, and welfare work in general.
Organized religion is thus still a great civilizing agency.

[1] Tylor, "Anthropology," p. 341.
[2] Spencer, "Principles of Sociology," German Edition, pp. 317—329.

Purely as religious teachers both clergymen and priests of this age have ideals so far above those of their sociological predecessor that the connexion between the old and the new would seem fanciful but for the investigations of science.

The beneficent effects of the dominance of the the medicine man are far from being exhausted in the foregoing recital. In the cosmic process of the centuries, the shaman and his associates unconsciously, unintentionally and incidentally, constituted a mighty socializing force. The scientific justification of the religious element in evolving society may be urged for the following reasons.

By maintaining a common propitiation of the deities, the exponents of religion have furnished a principle of societal cohesion. Worship of the same gods tends to unify a society.[1] The Ostyaks, for example, are said to be drawn together through using the same sacred places and yielding obedience to the same priest.[2]

Religious leaders have performed a social good by checking within tribes the tendencies to internal warfare. While they have frequently incited attacks on alien peoples and tribes of another religion, those leaders in the average case have checked hostilities between groups of the same blood and of the same religion.[3] The reproof of Moses to the Israelite who struck a brother slave in Egypt, "Wherefore smitest thou thy fellow?"[4] will occur to the reader as an illustration of this point.

---

[1] Spencer, "Principles of Sociology," III, pp. 96, 97, 141.
[2] Lathrop, "Descriptive Sociology," I, p. 456.
[3] Spencer, "Principles of Sociology," III, p. 141.   [4] Exodus, 2:13.

By strengthening the habit of self-restraint, the medicine man and his religious successors have done a praiseworthy work. When in return for their professional offices, the representatives of the gods demanded food, clothing, or other commodity, they compelled uncivilized peoples to give up something which was good to obtain some greater good. That discipline, enforced by shamanism, was of assistance in the development of foresight, or in other words, increased the willingness to sacrifice the present for the sake of the future. It is to be doubted whether any motive other than fear of the imaginary environment could so have strengthened the habit of self-restraint. And this habit is an essential factor for the regulation of conduct both for self benefit and for the interests of other people.[1]

The priest class has been of social service in that its members have approved of enforced labor, which is the only means of training men to apply themselves to tasks.[2] Savage peoples in the unregulated state do not have the principle of co-operation. This unity of effort is indispensable to fitness for societal life. Authority is necessary to establish co-operation. Undisciplined nature man can be made to work with his fellows by the application of only the most powerful means. The representative of the gods has exercised the strongest restraint possible in that he has impressed upon the minds of common men that if the commands of the deities are disobeyed, vengeance will most surely fall. Since the shaman

[1] Spencer, "Principles of Sociology," III, pp. 141—143.
[2] Ibid., III, p. 144.

is either the king, or has been forced into submission to the ruler, or works in co-operation with him, it can readily be seen that the religious leader has used his spiritual power to re-enforce political power. The application of coercion for societal good is clearly manifested in the development of the industrial organization. The building up of this institution would not have been possible except through hard, continuous labor. What other than a long-lasting and vigorous coercion could have compelled the idle and improvident savage to do useful work? And in this compulsion, shamanism was a powerful instrumentality.[1]

The medicine man, and the principles for which he stands, have always formed the conservative element in group, tribe, or nation. There is a place in every society for the spirit of stability. Shamanism, by the preservation of beliefs, sentiments, and usages, which by survival have been proved approximately fit for the requirements of the time, has been useful in maintaining and strengthening societal bonds, and, therefore, in conserving societal aggregates.[2]

The institution of shamanism has served a social purpose by forming a system for the regulation of conduct which co-operates with the civil administrative system. The prime requisite for societal progress is societal union. Nature man possesses so many anti-societal traits—impulsiveness, improvidence, an intolerance of restraint, a lack of sociality, an extended sense of blood revenge, a paucity of altruistic feelings, and an extreme resistance to change—

[1] Spencer, "Principles of Sociology," pp. 142—143.
[2] Ibid., III, p. 102.

which militate against societal co-operation, that nothing but an absolute submission to secular and sacred authority is strong enough to hold him in check.[1] Shamanism, therefore, has contributed to social progress in that it has co-operated with the civil power in enforcing submission to constituted political authority.[2] An illustration of this was observed by the writer at Bontoc, Mountain Province, Northern Luzon, Philippine Islands. A Bontoc Igorot was serving in the Constabulary when he sickened and died from pneumonia. At the funeral, his relatives, believing that he had been murdered by the Benguet Igorots, traditional enemies of their clan, nearly prevailed upon the Bontoc people to make a head-hunting raid upon the villages of Benguet for blood revenge. The authorities assembled the Bontoc priests and explained to them the real cause of the death. Those shamans then persuaded the angry relatives that their suspicions were unfounded, and the trouble was averted.

The shamanic class, furthermore, has aided social progress by demanding obedience, first to the deities and then to earthly rulers. This can be seen incidentally from the practical effects of the working of the taboo. Among savage peoples, tabooed articles are primarily those consecrated to a spirit. For an individual, therefore, to disregard a taboo is to rob the divinity.[3] Thus it is believed in New Zealand that both gods and man punish those who violate a taboo. The angry spirits inflict sickness and death; human

---

[1] Spencer, "Principles of Sociology," I, pp. 56—74. [2] Ibid., III, pp. 105—106. [3] Ibid., III, p. 144.

agencies visit upon the transgressor confiscation of property and expatriation or death. But terror of the gods is more effective in upholding the taboo than fear of men.[1] A mark, showing that a thing is the property of a god, may without difficulty be simulated. An offering with the sign of taboo upon it is by implication one that will eventually be sacrificed to a god. Since, however, the time when the sacrifice is to be made is not definite, there is a possibility that the consecration will not occur for a long period. Because of this postponement there would take place at times a simulated consecration of offerings, which men may not lawfully touch because they are tabooed, but which never will be sacrificed to the gods.[2] In Timor, for example, it is related that "a few palm leaves stuck outside a garden as a sign of the 'pomli' [taboo] will preserve its produce from thieves as effectually as the threatening notice of man-traps, spring-guns, or a savage dog would do for us."[3] Since it is always the medicine man or the ruler as medicine man, who makes sacrificial offerings, it will be seen that shamanism is responsible both for the taboo and for its beneficial influences.[4]

No single factor, it may be truthfully said, has more potently influenced the culture and shaped the destiny of society than the medicine man. In attempting to gain a true conception of the historical importance and development of a race, the one element which above all others

[1] Thompson, "The Story of New Zealand," I, p. 130.
[2] Spencer, "Principles of Sociology," III, p. 144.
[3] Wallace, "The Malay Archipelago," p. 196.
[4] Spencer, "Principles of Sociology," III, pp. 145-146.

demands closest attention and investigation is the power of the priest class. That the medicine man has frequently abused his opportunities is to be deplored. But in consideration of the social control which he has exercised, and in consideration of the fact that art, education, history, and science had their incipiency in the class to which he and his fellows belong, the verdict of impartial judgment must be that on the whole, whether consciously or unconsciously, the shaman has rendered a social service, the beneficial results of which are incalculable.

Another way of testing the relative merits of the priest class is by the standard of societal selection.[1] Every society which has survived has had medicine men. Social aggregations without priests could not compete with others of which those socializing agencies formed a part, and consequently gave way in the struggle before a superior foe.[2] Had shamanism been a social disadvantage rather than a social advantage, those societies in which it had place would have gone down in the contest with others where it did not exist, and the weaker aggregates together with their institutions would have perished. But the fact that it gave life to social groups proves the worth of the sacerdotal class.

It is thus seen that strength has come out of weakness; good out of evil; truth out of error. These words epitomize the story of the progress of the human race. Many wrong theories have been advocated, and many methods have

---

[1] Keller, "Societal Evolution," pp. 53—168.
[2] Spencer, "Principles of Sociology," pp. 148—149.

been of no avail to the purpose for which they were originally contemplated. In conjunction with his multitudinous mistakes, however, man of necessity has also blundered upon truth. The false has perished, while the true has survived. That process has been repeated time without end, until astronomy has eventuated from astrology, chemistry from alchemy, medicine from magic, nobler religious ideals and social betterment from fetichism—in other words, science, spiritual enlightenment, and societal advancement from superstition.

BIBLIOGRAPHY.

In the foregoing pages a painstaking effort has been made, by the footnotes, to give full credit wherever it is due. In addition, however, special mention may be made of a list of general works from which has been gleaned much of the data that constitute, so to speak, the background of this treatise. A list of these general works is first given.

Bartels, Max, Die Medizin der Naturvölker. Leipzig, 1893.

Fisher, Irving, Report on National Vitality. Bulletin Number 30 of the Committee of One Hundred on National Health. Washington, 1909.

Frazer, J. G., The Golden Bough. London, 1911, Twelve Volumes. Also New York, 1900, Three Volumes.

Gowers, W. R., Epilepsy and other Convulsive Diseases. Philadelphia, 1901.

Gumplowicz, L., Grundriss der Sociologie. Vienna, 1885.

Gumplowicz, L., Der Rassenkampf. Innsbruck, 1909.

Gumplowicz, L., Sociologie und Politik. Leipzig, 1892.

Keane, A. H., Ethnology. Cambridge, 1901.

Keller, Albert G., Societal Evolution. New York, 1915.

Lippert, J., Die Kulturgeschichte der Menschheit. Stuttgart, 1886.

McKay, W. J. S., Ancient Gynecology. New York, 1901.

Manson, P., Tropical Diseases. London, 1900.

Osborne, Oliver T., Introduction to Materia Medica and Pharmacology. New York, 1906.

Osborne, Oliver T., Handbook of Therapy (Editor). Chicago, 1912.

Schelenz, H., Geschichte der Pharmazie. Berlin, 1904.

Schmidt, E., Ausführliches Lehrbuch der pharmaceutischen Chemie. Marburg, 1901.

Solly, E., Medical Climatology. Philadelphia and New York, 1897.

Spencer, Herbert, Principles of Sociology. Volumes I and II, New York, 1908; Volume III, New York, 1897.
German Edition. Leipzig, 1897.

Sumner, William Graham, Folkways. Boston, 1907.

Tschirch, A., Handbuch der Pharmakognosie. Leipzig, 1909—1912.

Tylor, E. B., Anthropology. New York, 1893.

Tylor, E. B., Early History of Mankind. London, 1870.

Tylor, E. B., Primitive Culture. London, first Edition, 1865; second Edition, 1870.

Wetterstrand, O. G., Hypnotism and its Application to the Practice of Medicine. New York, 1899.

The following list contains books of a more specialized character.

Allen, A., and Thomson, T. H. R., Narrative of the Expedition to the River Niger in 1841. London, 1848.

Allen, Henry T., Atnatanas; natives of Copper River, Alaska. (In U. S. Smithsonian Institution. Annual Report, 1886, pt. 1. Washington, 1889, pp. 258-266).

Allison, Mrs. S. S., Account of the Similkameen Indians of British Columbia. (In Journal of Anthropological Institute of Great Britain and Ireland, 1891—1892, Vol. 21, pp. 305—318).

American Medical Association, Handbook of Useful Drugs. Chicago, 1913.

American Medical and Surgical Journal. St. Louis and Philadelphia.

American Journal of Pharmacy.

American Pharmaceutical Association, Proceedings of — — — Philadelphia.

Annals of Good Sainte Anne de Beaupré. Quebec, Canada.

Anstie, Francis E., Lectures on diseases of the nervous system. (Lecture VI, Lancet, Jan. 11, 1873, Vol. 1, pp. 39—41).

Aubrey, William H. S., The Natural and Domestic History of England. London, 1870—1880.

Australasian Association for the Advancement of Science. Sidney, 1892.

Apocrypha.

Astley, T., New General Collections of Voyages and Travels. London, 1745—1747.

Atkinson, T. W., Siberia, Oriental and Western. London, 1858.

Atlantic Monthly. Boston.

Baas, Johann H., Outline of the History of Medicine. Translation of Henry Handerson. New York, 1889.

B a c k h o u s e, James, A Narrative of a Visit to Australia. London, 1843.

B a c o n, Francis, Novum Organum. (In Rand's Modern Classical Philosophers, pp. 24—56. Boston and New York, 1908).

B a n c r o f t, Hubert H., The Native Races of the Pacific States of North America. New York, 1875—1876. Several other editions.

B a r t o n, Collections toward a Materia Medica in the United States. (In Lloyd Library, Bulletin Number 1).

B a r t r a m, William, Travels through North and South Carolina. London, 1792.

B a s t i a n, Adolf, Der Mensch in der Geschichte. Leipzig, 1860.

B e r d o e, Edward, The Origin and Growth of the Healing Art. London, 1893.

B e v e r l y, R., Histoire de la Virginie. Paris, 1707.

B i a r t, Lucien, The Aztecs. Translation, Chicago, 1892.

B i s h o p, Isabella Bird, Among the Tibetans. New York, 1894.

B i s h o p, Isabella Bird, Korea and Her Neighbors. New York, Chicago, and Toronto, 1898.

B l a c k, W. G., Folk Medicine: A Chapter in the History of Culture. London, 1883.

B o a s, Franz, Central Eskimo. (In United States Bureau of Ethnology, Sixth and Seventh Annual Reports, 1884—1885; 1885—1886. Washington, 1890—1891, pp. 399—675; 301—409). Also in Popular Science Monthly, Vol. 57, p. 631 ff.

B o u r k e, John G., The Medicine Men of the Apache. (In United States Bureau of Ethnology, Ninth Annual Report, 1887—1888. Washington, 1892, pp. 443—617).

B o u r k e, John G., Scatologic Rites of All Nations. Washington, 1891.

B o y l e, Frederick, Adventures among the Dyaks of Borneo. London, 1865.

Brand, John, Observations on Popular Antiquities of Great Britian. Revised by H. E. Elles. London, 1901.

Brasseur de Bourbourg, Charles E., Histoire des Nations Civilisées du Mexique et de l'Amérique-Centrale, etc. Paris, 1857—1859.

Brett, W. H., Indian Tribes of Guiana. London, 1868.

Brinton, Daniel G., The Myths of the New World. New York, 1868; Third Edition, Philadelphia, 1896.

Brinton, Daniel G., Religions of Primitive Peoples. New York, 1897.

Brinton, Daniel G., Nagualism. Philadelphia, 1894.

British Association for the Advancement of Science. London.

British Medical Journal. London.

Brugsch-Bey, Henry, History of Egypt under the Pharaohs. Edited by Philip Smith. London, 1881.

Brunton, T. L., Action of Medicines. New York, 1899.

Brunton, T. L., Pharmacology and Therapeutics. London, 1880.

Buchanan, James, Sketches of the History, Manners and Customs of North American Indians. London, 1824.

Bureau of Ethnology. Reports and Bulletins of —— Washington.

Burton, Richard F., Mission to Gelele, King of Dahomey. London, 1864.

Burton, Richard F., The City of the Saints. London, 1861.

Burton, Robert, Anatomy of Melancholy. London, 1806.

Cabello de Balboa, Miguel, Histoire du Pérou. (In Ternaux-Compans, Henri, Voyages... Vol. 15. Paris, 1837—1841).

Caldwell, R., On Demonolatry in Southern India. (In Anthropological Society of Bombay, Journal, Vol. I, 1886, pp. 91—105).

California, University of, Publications in American Archaeology and Ethnology, Vol. 5.

Callaway, Canon, and Bishop, Religious Systems of the Amazulu. Folk Lore Society Publications, Vol. 15. London, 1884.

Campbell, J., The Wild Tribes of Central Africa. (In Transactions of Ethnological Society. London, Vol. 7, p. 153).

Candolle, Adolphe, De l'Origine des Plantes Cultivées. Paris, 1883.

Catholic World, New York.

Catlin, George, Letters and Notes on the Manners and Customs and Conditions of the North American Indians, London, 1841.

Cator, Dorothy, Every-day Life among the Head-Hunters. New York, 1905.

Cérémonies et Coutumes Religieuses des Peuples Idolâtres. Vol. 6. Amsterdam, 1735.

Christian, F. W., The Caroline Islanders. London, 1899.

Clemens, Samuel, Christian Science. New York, 1907.

Cockayne, T. O., Saxon Leechdoms, Wort-Cunning, and Star Craft. London, 1864—1866.

Codrington, R. H., The Melanesians. Oxford, 1891.

Congrès International d'Archéologie Préhistorique et d'Anthropologie. Moscou.

Connolly, R. M., Social Life in Fanti-Land. (In Anthropological Institute of Great Britain and Ireland, Journal, 1896—1897, Vol. 26, pp. 128—153).

Contributions to North American Ethnology, Washington, 1877—1893.

Cook, James, A Voyage to the Pacific Ocean... 1776-1780. London, 1784.

Crantz, D., Historie von Grönland bis 1779. Leipzig, 1780. Translation, London, 1820.

Curr, E. M., The Australian Race. Melbourne, 1886-1887.

Dalton, Edward T., Descriptive Ethnology of Bengal. Calcutta, 1872.

Dalton, Henry G., History of British Guiana, London, 1855.

Dawson, James, Australian Aborigines in the Western District of Victoria. Melbourne, 1881.

Dealy, James J. and L. F. Ward, A Text-book of Sociology. New York, 1905.

De Groot, J. J. M., The Religious System of China. Leide, 1892—1910.

Dellenbaugh, The North American Indians of Yesterday. New York, 1901.

Dennys, N. B., Folk-Lore of China. London, 1876.

Dietetic and Hygienic Gazette. New York and Philadelphia.

Dixon, The Chimariko Indians and Language. (In University of California Publications in American Archeology and Ethnology. Vol. 5, pp. 303 ff.).

Dixon, Some Aspects of American Shamanism. (Journal of American Folk Lore, January, 1908, pp. 1-2 ff.).

Dobrizhoffer, Martin, An Account ot the Abipones, an Equestrian People of Paraguay. Translation, London, 1822.

Doolittle, Justus, Social Life of the Chinese. New York, 1865. Revised by Edwin P. Hood, London, 1868.

Dorman, R. R., The Origin of Primitive Superstitions. Philadelphia and London, 1881.

Dowd, Jerome, The Negro Races. A Sociological Study. New York, 1907.

Dunglinson, Richard J., History of Medicine. Philadelphia, 1872.

Dupuis, C. F., Origine de tous les Cultes. Edition used was not dated.

Dyer, Folk-Lore of Plants. New York, 1899.

Ebers, G., Egypt. Edition used was not dated.

Edkins, Joseph, Religion in China. London, 1893.

Ella, S., Samoa. (In Australasian Association for the Advancement of Science. Fourth Meeting, 1892. Report, Sydney, 1892, pp. 620—645).

Ellis, A. B., Tshi-Speaking Peoples. London, 1887.

Ellis, A. B., Ewe-Speaking Peoples of the Slave Coast of West Africa. London, 1890.

Ellis, A. B., Yoruba-Speaking Peoples of the Slave Coast of West Africa. London, 1894.

Ellis, Havelock, Man and Woman. London, 1894.

Ellis, William, Polynesian Researches. London, 1859.

Ellis, William, History of Madagascar. London, 1858.

Ellis, William, Journal of a Tour around Hawaii. Boston, 1825.

Emerson, Ellen Russel, Indian Myths. Boston, 1884.

Encyclopedia Britannica.

English Bible. (Revised version).

Ephemeris. Brooklyn.

Erman, Adolph, Life in Ancient Egypt. Translated by H. M. Tirard, London, 1894.

Ethnological Society, Transactions of — — United States. London, 1869.

Fairmount Park Art Association, Thirty-second Annual Report.

Falkner, Thomas, A Description of Patagonia, Hereford, 1774.

Fawcett, Fred, On the Saoras (or Savaras), an Aboriginal Hill People of the Eastern Ghats of the Madras Presidency. (In Anthropological Society of Bombay, Journal. 1886, Vol. 1, pp. 206—272).

Fitzroy, Robert, Narrative of the Expedition and Surveying Voyage of the Beagle. London, 1839—1840.

Fletcher, The Hako, A Pawnee Ceremony. (In United States Bureau of Ethnology, Washington, 1904, pp. 14 ff.).

Fletcher-Laflesche, The Omaha Tribe. (In United States Bureau of Ethnology, Washington, 1911, pp. 580 ff.).

Flückiger, F. A., and Handbury, Daniel, Pharmacography. London, 1879.

Garcilaso de la Vega, Royal Commentaries of the Incas. London, 1869—1871.

Garrison, F. H., History of Medicine. Philadelphia, 1914.

Gill, W. W., Myths and Songs from the South Pacific, London, 1876.

Gilmour, J., Among the Mongols. London, 1883.

Grey, George, Journals of Two Expeditions of Discovery in Australia. London, 1841.

Grimm, Teutonic Mythology. Translation of Stallybrass, London, 1880—1883.

Grote, George, History of Greece. Fourth Edition, London, 1846—1856.

Guhl, E., and Koner, W., Life of the Greeks and Romans. Translation of Hüfer, New York, 1875.

Hakluyt, R., Voyages. London, 1850.

Hale, Horatio, Northwestern Tribes of Canada. (In British Association for the Advancement of Science. Fifty-ninth Meeting, Report, 1889, London, 1890, pp. 797—925).

Hallberg, C. S. N., Some Ancient Pharmacists. Chicago, 1903.

Harper's Weekly, New York.

Hearne, Samuel, Voyage... du Fort du Prince de Galles dans la Baie de Hudson á l'Océan Nord. Paris, 1799.

Herodotus, Works. Various Editions.

Herrera, Antonio de, General History of the Continent and Isles of America. Translation of Stevens, London, 1725—1726.

Hoffman, W. J., The Midewiwin or "Grand Medicine Society" of the Ojibway. (In United States Bureau of Ethnology. Seventh Annual Report, 1885-1886. Washington, 1891, pp. 143—300).

Hoffman, W. J., The Menomini Indians. (In United States Bureau of Ethnology, Washington, 1896, pp. 98 ff.).

Homer, Iliad.

Homer, Odyssey.

Howitt, A. W., Native Tribes of South Eastern Australia. London, 1904.

Howitt, A. W., On Australian Medicine Men. (In Anthropological Institute of Great Britian and Ireland, Journal, 1886, Vol. 16, pp. 23—58).

Huc, Evariste Régis, Travels in Tartary, Thibet, and China. Translation of Hazlitt, London, 1844, 1845, 1856.

Huchinson, George Thompson, (Editor), The Living Races of Mankind. New York, 1902.

Hunter, W. W., The Indian Empire. London, 1893.

Index Medicus, Washington, 1879—1899; 1903—1921.

International Congress of Anthropologists, Chicago.

Jastrow, Joseph, Fact and Fable in Psychology. Boston and New York, 1900.

Johns, C. A., Flowers of the Field. London, 1853.

Journal of American Folk Lore.

Journal of the American Medical Association. Chicago.

Journal of Anthropological Institute of Great Britian and Ireland. London.

Journal of the Anthropological Society of Bombay. Bombay.

Journal of the Asiatic Society of Bengal. Calcutta.

Keating, William H., Narrative of the Expedition to the Source of St. Peter's River, under the Command of S. H. Long. Philadelphia, 1824.

Keller, Albert G., Homeric Society. New York, 1902.

Keller, Albert G., Societal Evolution. New York, 1915.

Kingsley, M. H., Travels in West Africa. New York, 1897.

Kingsley, M.H., West African Studies. New York, 1899.

Laflesche, Who was the Medicine Man? (In Thirty-second Annual Report of the Fairmount Park Art Association, pp. 10 ff.).

Lancet and Observer. Cincinnati.

Lancet. London.

Lathrop, R. G., Descriptive Sociology. 1859.

Laurie, J., Aneityum, New Hebrides. (In Australasian Association for the Advancement of Science. Fourth Meeting, 1892. Report, Sydney, 1892, pp. 708—717).

Le Clerc, Daniel, Histoire de la Medicine. La Haye, 1729.

Lee, Frederick George, Glimpses of the Supernatural. London, 1875.

Lehmann, A., Aberglaube und Zauberei. Stuttgart, 1898.

Leland, Charles G., Gypsy Sorcery and Fortune Telling. New York, 1891.

Lenormant, F., Chaldean Magic. London, 1877.

Linnean Society, Transactions of, New York.

Livingstone, David, Travels in South Africa. New York, 1858.

Lloyd, John U., Cephaelis Ipecacuanha. (In Western Druggist, 1897).

Lloyd, John U., History of Vegetable Drugs. (In Bulletin Number 18 of the Lloyd Library, Cincinnati).

Lloyd, John U., Opium and its Compounds. (In Drug Treatise Number 22 of the Lloyd Library, Cincinnati).

Lubbock, John, Origin of Civilization. New York, 1870.

MacCauley, Clay, Seminole Indians of Florida. (In United States Bureau of Ethnology, Fifth Annual Report, 1883—1884. Washington, 1887, pp. 469-531).

MacDonald, James, East Central African Customs. (In Anthropological Institute of Great Britain and Ireland, Journal, 1893, Vol. 22, pp. 99—122).

Maeterlink, Maurice, The Life of the Bee. Translation of Alfred Sutro. Pocket Edition, London, 1910.

Mallery, Garrick, Picture Writing of American Indians. (In United States Bureau of Ethnology, Tenth Annual Report, 1888—1889. Washington, 1893).

Man, E. H., On Andamanese and Nicobarese Objects. (In Anthropological Institute of Great Britain and Ireland, Journal, 1881—1882, Vol. 11, pp. 268-294).

Mariner, William, An Account of the Natives of the Tongo Islands. London, 1817.

Martin, Carl, Über die Eingeborenen von Chiloe. (In

Zeitschrift für Ethnologie, Jahrg. 1877, Band 9, pp. 161—181).

Martius, C. F. Ph. v., Von dem Rechtszustande unter den Ureinwohnern Brasiliens. München, Leipzig, 1832.

Mason, Otis T., Origins of Invention. London, 1895.

Maspero, G., Dawn of Civilization in Egypt and Chaldea. London, 1897, Third Edition.

Maspero, G., Peuples de l'Orient Classique. Paris, 1899.

Maspero, G., Life in Egypt and Assyria. London, 1892.

Masson, Charles, Afghanistan, the Punjab, and Kalât. Edition used was not dated.

Matthews, The Mountain Chant. (In United States Bureau of Ethnology, Washington, 1888, pp. 444 ff.).

Matthews, The Night Chant, A Navaho Ceremony. (In Memoirs of American Museum of Natural History, pp. 40 ff.).

Meiners, C., Allgemeine Kritische Geschichte der Religionen. Hannover, 1807.

Memoirs of American Museum of Natural History.

Mendieta, Gerónimo de, Historia Eclesiástica Indiana. Mexico, 1870.

Merat, J. F., et de Lens, A. J., Dictionnaire Universel de Matière Médicale. Bruxelles, 1837.

Metcalf, R. Life of Vincenz Priessnitz. London, 1898.

Middendorf, E. W., Wörterbuch des Runa simi oder der Keshua Sprache. Leipzig, 1890.

Minnesota Historical Collections. St. Paul, 1860—1908.

Mockler-Ferryman, A. F., British Nigeria. London and New York, 1902.

Mollien, Gaspard T., Travels in the Interior of Africa to the Sources of the Senegal and Gambia. Translation, London, 1820.

Monier-Williams, Brahmanism and Hinduism. New York, 1891.

Mooney, James, The Ghost-Dance Religion. (In United States Bureau of Ethnology, Fourteenth Annual Report, 1892—1893, part. 2, pp. 980 ff. Washington, 1896).

Mooney, James, Medical Mythology of Ireland. (In American Philosophical Society, Proceedings, 1887. Philadelphia, 1887, pp. 136—166).

Mooney, James, Sacred Formulas of the Cherokees. (In United States Bureau of Ethnology, Seventh Annual Report, 1885—1886. Washington, 1890, pp. 307—409).

Morley, H., Life of Cornelius Agrippa. London, 1856.

Munsey's Magazine, New York.

Müller, J. G., Geschichte der Amerikanischen Urreligionen. Basel, 1867, Second Edition.

Müller, Max, Lecture on the Science of Religion. New York, 1872.

Myers, Philip V. N., Ancient History. Boston, 1888. Several other Editions.

Nachtigall, Gustav, Sahara and the Sudan. Berlin, 1879—1881.

Nansen, Fridtjof, Eskimo Life. Translation, London, 1893.

Nassau, R. Hamill, Fetichism in West Africa. London and New York, 1904.

Neill, E. D., Dakota Land and Dakota Life. (In Minnesota Historical Collections, 1872, Vol. 1, pp. 254-294).

Newman, Albert Henry, A Manual of Church History. Philadelphia, 1900—1903.

Newman, John Henry, Parochial and Plain Sermons. London and New York, 1902.

New Sydenham Society, Lexicon of Medicine. By H. Power and L. W. Sedwick, London, 1881.

New York Medical and Surgical Journal. New York.

Nineteenth Century Magazine. London and New York.

Oldfield, Augustus, On the Aborigines of Australia.

(In Ethnological Society of London. Transactions, 1865, n.s., Vol. 3, pp. 215—298).

Orbigny, D', Alcide D., L'Homme Américain. (In Voyages dans l'Amérique. Paris, 1839).

Palmer, Edward, Notes on Some Australian Tribes. (In Anthropological Institute of Great Britain and Ireland, Journal, 1884, Vol. 13, pp. 276—334).

Pane, Ramon, Antiquities of the Indians. (In Bourne's Columbus, Ramon Pane, and the Beginnings of American Anthropology. Worcester, 1906).

Paris, J. A., Pharmacologia. London, 1812, Second Edition; also New York, 1824.

Park, Roswell, An Epitome of the History of Medicine. Philadelphia, 1897.

Parkman, F., The Jesuits of North America. Boston, 1867.

Pascal, B., Thoughts of — — Wright's Translation. New York, 1861.

Pennsylvania Medical Journal, Athens, Philadelphia.

Peters, Hermann, Pictorial History of Ancient Pharmacy. Translation of Netter, Chicago, 1899, Second Edition; Third Edition, Chicago, 1902.

Petrie, W. M. F., Ten Years Digging in Egypt. London, 1892.

Pettigrew, Superstitions Connected with the History and Practice of Medicine. London, 1844.

Pharmaceutical Review, Milwaukee.

Philadelphia Medical Journal, Philadelphia.

Pinkerton, John, General Collection of Voyages and Travels. London, 1808—1814.

Piso, William, Historia Naturalium Brasiliae. Amsterdam, 1648.

Plinius, Caius Secundus, Historia Naturalia. London, 1855.

Pomet, Pierre, Histoire Générale des Drogues, Simples et Composes. Paris, 1694.

Popular Science Monthly, Philadelphia.

Powers, S., The Tribes of California. (In Contributions to North American Ethnology, Vol. 3, pp. 160 ff. Washington, 1877).

Prayer Book.

Proceedings of the American Philosophical Society. Philadelphia.

Purchas, Samuel, His Pilgrimes. London, 1625-1626.

Rambles in the Deserts of Syria. London, 1864.

Ratzel, Friedrich, History of Mankind. Translation of A. J. Butler from the Second German Edition, New York, 1896.

Raubenheimer, Otto, Tasteless Castor Oil. Buffalo. Not dated.

Réclus, Élie, Primitive Folk. New York, 1891.

Reed, W. A., Negritos of Zambales, Manila, 1904.

Reference Hand Book of the Medical Sciences. Third Edition, New York, 1913-1914.

Rhys, John, Welsh Fairies. (In Nineteenth Century Magazine, October 1891 Vol. 30, pp. 564—574).

Roth, Henry Ling, Natives of Sarawak and British North Borneo. New York, 1896.

Roth, Henry Ling, Great Benin: Its Customs and Manners. Halifax, England, 1903.

Roth, W. E., Superstition, Magic, and Medicine. (In North Queensland Ethnography. Brisbane, 1903, Bulletin, Number 5, pp. 9 ff.).

Routledge, W. Scoresby, With a Prehistoric People, the Akikuyu of British East Africa. London, 1910.

Rowlatt, E. R., Report of an Expedition to the Mishmée Hills to the North East of Sudyah. (In Asiatic Society of Bengal, Journal, January—June 1845, Vol. 14, pp. 477—495).

Royle, J. F., Materia Medica and Therapeutics. London, 1847.

Russell, Frank, Pima Indians. (In United States Bureau of Ethnology, Twenty-sixth Annual Report, 1904—1905. Washington, 1908, pp. 3—390).

St. John, C. W. G., Short Sketches of the Wild Sports and History of the Highlands. London, 1849.

St. John, Spencer, Life in the Forests of the Far East. London, 1862.

Salmon, William, Synopsis of Medicine. London, 1671.

Salverte, E., Philosophy of Magic. London, 1846.

Schoolcraft, Henry R., Historical and Statistical Information Respecting the Indian Tribes of the United States. London, 1853—1856. Philadelphia, 1851—1857.

Schultze, Fritz, Der Fetischismus. Leipzig, 1871.

Scientific Monthly. Garrison, New York.

Shooter, J., The Kaffirs of Natal and Zulu Country. London, 1857.

Smirnov, J., Le Cannibalisme et les Sacrifices Humaines chez les Ancêtres des Finnois Orientaux. (In Congrés International d'Archéologie Préhistorique et d'Anthropologie, XI, 1892, Moscou, pp. 315-322).

Smith, Edmund R., The Araucanians. London, 1855.

Smith, W. R., Dictionary of Greek and Roman Antiquities. London, 1890.

Smith, W. Robertson, Lectures on the Religion of the Semites. London, 1894.

Smith, W. R., Dictionary of Greek and Roman Biography and Mythology. London, 1849.

Smithsonian Institution Reports. Washington.

Smyth, R. Brough, The Aborigines of Victoria. London and Melbourne, 1878.

Southey, R., The Doctor. New York, 1836. Numerous other Editions.

Spencer, Walter B., and Gillen, F. J., Native Tribes of Central Australia, New York, 1899.

Sprengel, Kurt, Histoire de la Médicine. Paris, 1815.

Stanley, John M., Portraits of North American Indians. (In United States Smithsonian Institution. Smithsonian Miscellaneous Collections, Vol. 2, Washington, 1852. Publication Number 53).

S t e i n e n, Karl von den, Shingu Tribes. (In Berlin Museum for 1888).

S t e i n e n, Karl von den, Unter den Naturvölkern Zentral-Brasiliens. Berlin, 1894.

S t i l l e and M a i c h, National Dispensatory. Philadelphia, 1879.

S t r a c k, H. L., The Jew and Human Sacrifice. Translation, London and New York, 1909.

S u m n e r, William G., The Yakuts, Abridged from the Russian of Sieroshevski. (In Anthropological Institute of Great Britain and Ireland, Journal, January—June 1901, Vol. 31, pp. 65—110).

T a n n e r, J., Narrative of the Capture and Adventures of John Tanner. New York, 1830.

T a y l o r, W. C., History of New Zealand. London, 1840.

T e r n a u x-C o m p a n s, Henri, Voyages. Paris, 1807.

T h e r a p e u t i c M o n t h l y. Philadelphia.

T h o m p s o n, Arthur S., The Story of New Zealand, Past and Present. London, 1859.

T h u r s t o n, E., Ethnographic Notes in South India. Madras, 1906.

T r u e, Rodney, H., Folk Materia Medica. (In Journal of American Folklore, April—June 1901, Vol. 14, pp. 105—114).

T u c k e y, James K., Narrative of an Expedition to the River Zaire. London, 1818.

T u r n e r, George, Nineteen Years in Polynesia. London, 1861.

T u r n e r, George, Samoa, A Hundred Years and Long Before. London, 1844.

U n i t e d S t a t e s B u r e a u o f E t h n o l o g y, Reports, of — —. Washington.

U s e f u l D r u g s: A Publication of the American Medical Association. Chicago, 1913.

V á m b é r y, A., Sketches of Central Asia. London, 1868.

V e n e g a s, Miguel, Histoire Naturelle et Civile de la Californie. Paris, 1767.

W a d d l e, Charles W., Miracles of Healing. (In American Journal of Psychology, April 1909, Vol. 20, pp. 219—268).

W a l l a c e, A. R., The Malay Archipelago. 1872.

W e l l c o m e, Henry S., A Visit to Native Cinchona Forests of South America. (In American Pharmaceutical Association, Twenty-seventh Annual Meeting, 1879. Proceedings, Philadelphia, 1880. Vol. 27, pp. 814—830).

W e l s h, Herbert, Report of a Visit to the Grand Sioux Reserve, Dakota, in 1883. Philadelphia, 1883.

W i l k i n s o n, J. G., Manners and Customs of the Ancient Egyptians. London, 1878.

W i l l i a m s, T., and James C a l v e r t, The Fiji and the Fijians. London, 1858; New York, 1859.

W i l s o n, J. L., Western Africa; Its History, Condition, and Prospects. New York, 1856.

W i l s o n, John L., West African Tribes. London, 1856.

W i n t e r b o t t o m, Thomas, Account of the Native Africans in the Neighborhood of Sierra Leone. London, 1803.

W o o d, Dispensatory of the United States. Philadelphia, 1912.

W o o d, Natural History of Man. London, 1870.

Y a l e   M e d i c a l   J o u r n a l. New Haven, Connecticut.

Z e i t s c h r i f t   f ü r   E t h n o l o g i e. Berlin.

Z e i t s c h r i f t   f ü r   K l e i n e   M e d i z i n. Berlin.

INDEX OF NAMES.

Note. — References are to numbers of pages.

INDEX OF SUBJECTS.

Note. — References, unless otherwise indicated, are to numbers of pages.

* (w.) = Medicine woman.

*(w.) = Medicine woman.

ERRATA.

When this book was going through the press the author,
assisted by many scholars and proof readers, in a painstaking endeavor to avoid all errors, read fifteen different
copies of proof sheets. Absolute accuracy, however, in a
work of this character is so difficult that on reading a
corrected copy of the text, after the plates had been
made, despite all precautions taken, many inaccuracies
were found to have crept into the book. The only recourse
under the circumstances is to append the following errata.

Page 8, line 14: Instead of "Itongo" read . . . . **"Amatongo."**
Page 10, line 13: Instead of "Togans" read . . . . . **"Tongans."**
Page 11, footnote 5: Instead of "Page 93" read . . . **"Page 73."**
Page 12, footnote 2: Instead of "Page 179" read . . . **"Page 199."**
Page 14, line 10: Instead of "only" read . . . **"in the first line."**
Page 14, line 23: Instead of "Anisgi'na" read . . . . **"Anisgína."**
Page 15, line 10: Instead of "and then burning the whole in a secret
    place" read **"which is then buried in some secret place."**
Page 16, line 12: Instead of "Kernai" read . . . . . . **"Kurnai."**
Page 27, line 14: Instead of "Bilquila" read . . . . . **"Bilqula."**
Page 30, line 14: Instead of "Makjarawaint" read . **"Mukjarawaint."**
Page 30, line 15: Instead of "Watgo" read . . . . . . **"Wotjo."**
Page 30, line 15: Instead of "the necessary" read . **"a desirable."**
Page 33, footnote 1: Instead of "Depuis" read . . . **"Dupuis."**
Page 33, footnote 3: Instead of "Naturvöker" read . **"Naturvölker."**
Page 36, line 12: Instead of "will present the necessary
    qualifications" read **"undergoes the bodily castigations
    indispensable for it."**
Page 36, footnote 3: Instead of "p. 179" read . . . . . **"p. 79."**
Page 37, footnote 1: Instead of "Meyers" read . . . . . **"Myers."**
Page 39, line 19: Instead of "a god" read . . . . **"the divinity."**
Page 41, line 15: Instead of "imyanga" read . . . . . **"inyanga."**
Page 41, line 23: Instead of "Dieyerie" read . . . . . . **"Dieri."**
Page 42, line 6: Instead of "medicine man" read **"medicine woman."**
Page 42, line 6: Instead of "his" read . . . . **"her."**
Page 45, line 6: Instead of "olloliuhqui" read . . . **"ololiuhqui."**
Page 45, footnote 5: Read . . . . **"pp. 7-9."**
Page 46, line 23: Instead of "Malanau" read . . . . **"Milanau."**
Page 48, line 21: Instead of "the representatives"
    read . . . . **"the female representatives."**
Page 49, line 12: Read **"the amadhlozi or amatongo, the ghosts,"** etc.
Page 50, line 5: Instead of "tormgarsuk" ... "tormgak"
    read . . . . **"torngarsuk"** ... **"torngak."**
Page 50, footnote 2: Instead of "Crantz" read . . . . . **"Cranz."**
Page 50, footnote 2: Instead of "p. 194" read . . . . **"pp. 268-9."**
Page 53, line 6: Read . . . . **"invoking a tornaq or flying,"** etc.
Page 53, line 7: Instead of "distinct" read . . . . . **"distant."**
Page 54, lines 11 ff.: Remove quotation marks.
Page 56, line 27: Instead of "from the lodges of women"
    read . . . . **"from the menstrual lodges of women."**
Page 57, footnote 1: Instead of "XXVII" read . . . . . **"XXVI."**
Page 58, lines 9 ff.: Remove quotation marks.

328

Page 59, line 13: Read . . . "African and Indonesian tribes ..."·
Page 62, line 18, to p. 66, line 5: Only the parts within quotation marks are taken literally from the text of Ellis.
Page 67, line 19: Instead of "Ki tshi Man ido" read "Kitshi Manido."
Page 77, footnote ²: Instead of "p. 469" read . . . . · "p. 284."
Page 77, footnote ⁸: Instead of "American Shamanism" read . . . . "The American Shaman."
Page 78, line 16: Instead of "Tapantunnuasu" read "Topantunuasu."
Page 78, line 19: Read "of all women only medicine women are allowed," etc.
Page 80, lines 1 ff.: Only the words within quotation marks are taken literally from the text.
Page 82, line 20 ff.: (the same).
Page 83, line 6: (the same).
Page 84, line 22: Instead of "gods of ancestral spirits" read . . . . "gods or ancestral spirits."
Page 86, line 23: Read . . . "to steal away to dig up the horns."
Page 86, lines 24-25: Inclose the words "which ... (till) . . . . wanderings" in [ ].
Page 88, line 11: Instead of "Kolmyck" read . . . . "Kolymsk."
Page 88, footnote ²: Instead of "American Shamanism" read . . . . "The American Shaman."
Page 92, line 5: Instead of "Indians" read . . . . . . "negroes."
Page 97, footnote ¹: See also Ellis, "Ewe-Speaking Peoples," p. 146.
Page 97, line 19: Instead of "superior powers" read . . . . "superhuman powers."
Page 98, footnote ²: Instead of "p. 589" read . . . . · "p. 580."
Page 99, line 24: Instead of "uncared for" read . . . . "unkept."
Page 104, lines 9-10: It is an error of Bartels to say that the Mide-societies spread over a great part of the U. S. So far as is known, the "Midewiwin" existed only among the Algonquin tribes of the Great Lakes, especially among the Ojibway and Menomini.
Page 104, line 17: Instead of "assist" read . . . . . . "assists."
Page 104, line 23: Inclose "they contemplate coming" in [ ].
Page 105, line 25: Inclose medicine men in [ ].
Page 109, lines 7-10: Remove quotation marks.
Page 111, line 6: Instead of "Dieyeri" read . . . . . "Dieri."
Page 111, line 7: Instead of "America" read . . . "Australia."
Page 117, line 16: Read "The Algonquin tribes, especially the Sacs and Foxes, (who belong to this linguistic stock)," etc.
Page 117, footnote ⁴: Instead of "Smithsonian Contributions, II, p. 38" read . . "Smithsonian Miscellaneous Collections, II, No. 53."
Page 118, line 5: Instead of "new comer" read . . . "newcomer."
Page 119, line 21: Instead of "Thlinkeets" read . . . . "Tlinkits."
Page 121, line 16: Read "In some parts of Africa," etc.
Page 122, lines 7-28: Remove quotation marks.
Page 122, footnote ¹: Instead of "pp. 142-146" read . . . "p. 142."
Page 122, footnote ²: Read . . . . "Ibid. p. 144."
Page 123, line 26: Instead of "Sahaptain" read . . . "Sahaptin."
Page 124, footnote ¹: Omit "and 57."
Page 133, line 17: Instead of "gomera" read . . . . "gommera."
Page 133, line 21: Instead of "Mangia" read . . . . "Mangaia."
Page 133, line 22: Instead of "Tauna" read . . . . . "Tanna."
Page 134, lines 20-21: Instead of "Hitzilopochtil" read "Huitzilopochtli, the divine king or celestial leader of the Aztec pantheon, is reputed," etc.

Page 137, lines 10-13: Remove quotation marks.
Page 138, line 11: Instead of "Caquingue" read . . . . "Angola."
Page 140, line 9: Instead of "below" read . . . . . "around."
Page 140, lines 20 and 22: Instead of "Hap-od-no" read "Hop-od-no."
Page 140, line 21: Instead of "Indians" read . . . . . "Yokuts."
Page 142, line 17: Instead of "wommers" read . . . "wommera."
(Wommera = a throwing stick).

Page 143, line 22: Instead of "Lemnig-Lennape" read "Lenni-Lennape."
Page 145, line 21: Instead of "Pe-i-men" read . . . "Pee-ai-men,"
or "Piai-men." (cf. p. 146, line 4).

Page 146, line 12 and footnote 6: Instead of "MacCurdy" read "Thalbitzer."
Page 146, footnote 6: Instead of "p. 652" read . . "pp. 448, 450."
Page 147, footnote 1: Instead of "p. 692" read . . . . . "p. 592."
Page 155, line 2 ff.: Read "novices, realizing the dangers attendant upon it as upon the military profession, nevertheless seldom forsook the vocation."

Page 162, line 26, to p. 163, line 5: Remove quotation marks.
Page 163, line 8: Instead of "Mascotin" read . . . . "Mascoutin."
Page 163, footnote 1: Read "Smithsonian Report, 1886, Part 1", etc.
Page 164, lines 10-14: . . . . Remove quotation marks.
Page 164, footnote 2: Read . . . . "p. 124."
Page 164, footnote 3: Read . . . . "Ibid. p. 125."
Page 169, line 6: Instead of "quartz, crystals" read "quartz crystals."
Page 171, line 21: Read . . . . "the ancestral spirits."
Page 172, footnote 3: Instead of "Sprengle" read . . "Sprengel."
Page 182, line 20: Instead of "state god" read . . "national God."
Page 182, line 23: Instead of "household gods" read "national God."
Page 183, line 1: Instead of "household gods" read "national God."
Page 184, line 25: Instead of "branches" read . . . . "bunches."
Page 187, line 10: Instead of "agglutin-ating" read "aggluti-nating."
Page 191, line 10: Instead of "Kernai" read . . . . . "Kurnai."
Page 193, line 2: Instead of "Gillan" read . . . . . . "Gillen."
Page 194, footnote 2: Instead of "1888" read . . . . . "1887."
Page 196, line 16: Instead of "stepps" read . . . . , "steppes."
Page 200, footnote 1: Instead of "pp. 221—232" read "pp. 221 and 232."

Page 217, line 6: Instead of יְהוָֹה read . . . . יְהוָֹה

Page 217, line 7: Instead of יְהוָֹה צְבָאוֹת . . . . אֱלֹהָי . . .
read . . . . אֱלֹהָי . . . יְהוָֹה צְבָאוֹת

Page 217, footnote 1, line 3: Instead of יְהוָֹה read . . . . יְהוָֹה

Page 217, footnote 1, line 4: Instead of יְהוָֹה צְבָאוֹת read יְהוָֹה צְבָאוֹת
Page 217, footnote 1, line 3: Instead of "Jehova" read. "Jehovah."
Page 221, line 4—10: . . . . Remove quotation marks.
Page 221, line 11: Instead of "Chaundizi" read . . "Chaundezi."
Page 221, line 12: Instead of "Chemihuevi" read "Chemihuevi-Sal."
Page 233, line 19: Instead of "a Zuñi" read . . . . . "Zuñi."
Page 233, line 21: Instead of "Heidah" read . . . . . "Haidah."
Page 234, footnote 2: Read . . . . "Ibid. p. 121."

Page 236, line 5 and 12: Instead of "Tristaon" read . . "Tristaõ."
Page 236, line 14: Instead of "Nauralia" read . . "Naturalium."
Page 242, line 2—8: . . . . Remove quotation marks.
Page 246, footnote 2: Read . . . . "Sahara und Sudan."
Page 279, line 3: Read . . . . "Hepatica acutiloba."

330

Page 297, line 18: Instead of "Beverly" read . . . . "Beverley."
Page 297, line 27ff: Read . . "Sixth Annual Report, 1884—1885, Washington 1888, pp. 399—675."
Page 298, line 2: Read . . . . "Britain."
Page 298, line 21: Instead of "London" read . . . "New York."
Page 298, line 30: Instead of "Cabello de Balboa" read "Cevallo de Balboa."
Page 299, line 3: Instead of "1884" read . . . . . . "1870."
Page 299, line 32: Read "Cranz, D., Historie von Grönland. Barby 1765."
Page 300, line 15: Read "Some Aspects of the American Shaman."
Page 301, line 26: Read . . . "The Hako, A Pawnee Ceremony, etc."
Page 301, line 26: Instead of "pp. 14 ff." read . . . . "pp. 5 ff."
Page 301, line 31: Instead of "pp. 580 ff." read . . . "pp. 17 ff."
Page 302, line 27: Instead of "Ojibway" read . . . . "Ojibwa."
Page 302, line 32: Instead of "pp. 98 ff." read . . . . "pp. 3 ff."
Page 303, line 4: Instead of "Huchinson" read . . "Hutchinson."
Page 303, line 17: Instead of "Britian" read . . . . . "Britain."
Page 303, lines 27 and 29: Instead of "New York" read "London."
Page 304, lines 10-11: Read "Livingstone, David, Missionary Travels and Researches in South Africa. London 1857."
Page 304, line 36: Instead of "Tongo" read . . . . . "Tonga."
Page 305, line 15: Instead of "1888, pp. 444 ff." read "1887, pp. 379 ff."
Page 305, line 17-18: Put after "History" . . . . . "Vol. VI."
Page 306, line 10-11: Instead of "1890, pp. 307—409" read "1891, pp. 301—409."
Page 306, line 20: Read "Nachtigal, Gustav, Sahara und Sudan."
Page 307, line 15: Read . . . "The Jesuits in North America."
Page 308, line 1-2: Omit . . . . "pp. 160 ff."
Page 308, lines 21-22: Read "Great Benin. Its Customs, Arts and Horrors."
Page 310, lines 13—14: Read "Tanner, J., Narrative of Captivity and Adventures among the Indians in North America."
Page 311, line 24: Instead of "1870" read . . . . . . "1874."
Page 311, line 27: Instead of "Kleine" read . . . . "Klinische."
Page 313, *Col. 2: Put between "Andes" and "Annamites," "Angola, 138."
Page 314, Col. 1, line 4: Instead of "Bilquila" read . . "Bilqula."
Page 314, Col. 2, line 13: Instead of "Dieyerie" read . . "Dieri."
Page 315, Col. 2, line 19: Instead of "Heidah" read . . "Haidah."
Page 315, Col. 2, line 21-22: Omit . . . . "Loango 92."
Page 315, Col. 2, line 26: Instead of "Sahaptain" read "Sahaptin."
Page 316, Col. 1, line 6: Instead of "Kernai" read . . "Kurnai."
Page 316, Col. 1, line 18: Instead of "Lemnig" read . . . . "Lenni."
Page 316, Col. 1, line 23: Instead of "72, 135, 164" read "72, 92, 135, 164."
Page 316, Col. 1, line 32: Instead of "Makjarawaint" read "Mukjarawaint."
Page 316, Col. 1, line 37: Instead of "Mangia" read "Mangaia."
Page 316, Col. 1, line 44: Instead of "Mascotin" read "Mascoutin."
Page 317, Col. 2, line 27: Instead of "Tapantunnuasu" read "Topantunuasu."
Page 317, Col. 2, line 32: Instead of "Tauna" read . . "Tanna."
Page 317, Col. 2, line 35: Instead of "Thlinkeets" read "Tlinkits."
Page 317, Col. 2, line 40: Instead of "Togans" read . "Tongans."
Page 318, Col. 2, line 2: Instead of "Watgo" read . . . "Wotjo."

*Col. = column.

A CATALOG OF SELECTED
DOVER BOOKS
IN ALL FIELDS OF INTEREST

A CATALOG OF SELECTED DOVER
BOOKS IN ALL FIELDS OF INTEREST

CONCERNING THE SPIRITUAL IN ART, Wassily Kandinsky. Pioneering work by father of abstract art. Thoughts on color theory, nature of art. Analysis of earlier masters. 12 illustrations. 80pp. of text. 5⅜ x 8½.   23411-8

ANIMALS: 1,419 Copyright-Free Illustrations of Mammals, Birds, Fish, Insects, etc., Jim Harter (ed.). Clear wood engravings present, in extremely lifelike poses, over 1,000 species of animals. One of the most extensive pictorial sourcebooks of its kind. Captions. Index. 284pp. 9 x 12.   23766-4

CELTIC ART: The Methods of Construction, George Bain. Simple geometric techniques for making Celtic interlacements, spirals, Kells-type initials, animals, humans, etc. Over 500 illustrations. 160pp. 9 x 12. (Available in U.S. only.)   22923-8

AN ATLAS OF ANATOMY FOR ARTISTS, Fritz Schider. Most thorough reference work on art anatomy in the world. Hundreds of illustrations, including selections from works by Vesalius, Leonardo, Goya, Ingres, Michelangelo, others. 593 illustrations. 192pp. 7⅛ x 10¼.   20241-0

CELTIC HAND STROKE-BY-STROKE (Irish Half-Uncial from "The Book of Kells"): An Arthur Baker Calligraphy Manual, Arthur Baker. Complete guide to creating each letter of the alphabet in distinctive Celtic manner. Covers hand position, strokes, pens, inks, paper, more. Illustrated. 48pp. 8¼ x 11.   24336-2

EASY ORIGAMI, John Montroll. Charming collection of 32 projects (hat, cup, pelican, piano, swan, many more) specially designed for the novice origami hobbyist. Clearly illustrated easy-to-follow instructions insure that even beginning papercrafters will achieve successful results. 48pp. 8¼ x 11.   27298-2

THE COMPLETE BOOK OF BIRDHOUSE CONSTRUCTION FOR WOODWORKERS, Scott D. Campbell. Detailed instructions, illustrations, tables. Also data on bird habitat and instinct patterns. Bibliography. 3 tables. 63 illustrations in 15 figures. 48pp. 5¼ x 8½.   24407-5

BLOOMINGDALE'S ILLUSTRATED 1886 CATALOG: Fashions, Dry Goods and Housewares, Bloomingdale Brothers. Famed merchants' extremely rare catalog depicting about 1,700 products: clothing, housewares, firearms, dry goods, jewelry, more. Invaluable for dating, identifying vintage items. Also, copyright-free graphics for artists, designers. Co-published with Henry Ford Museum & Greenfield Village. 160pp. 8¼ x 11.   25780-0

HISTORIC COSTUME IN PICTURES, Braun & Schneider. Over 1,450 costumed figures in clearly detailed engravings–from dawn of civilization to end of 19th century. Captions. Many folk costumes. 256pp. 8⅜ x 11¾.   23150-X

STICKLEY CRAFTSMAN FURNITURE CATALOGS, Gustav Stickley and L. & J. G. Stickley. Beautiful, functional furniture in two authentic catalogs from 1910. 594 illustrations, including 277 photos, show settles, rockers, armchairs, reclining chairs, bookcases, desks, tables. 183pp. 6½ x 9¼.   23838-5

AMERICAN LOCOMOTIVES IN HISTORIC PHOTOGRAPHS: 1858 to 1949, Ron Ziel (ed.). A rare collection of 126 meticulously detailed official photographs, called "builder portraits," of American locomotives that majestically chronicle the rise of steam locomotive power in America. Introduction. Detailed captions. xi+ 129pp. 9 x 12.   27393-8

AMERICA'S LIGHTHOUSES: An Illustrated History, Francis Ross Holland, Jr. Delightfully written, profusely illustrated fact-filled survey of over 200 American lighthouses since 1716. History, anecdotes, technological advances, more. 240pp. 8 x 10¾.
25576-X

TOWARDS A NEW ARCHITECTURE, Le Corbusier. Pioneering manifesto by founder of "International School." Technical and aesthetic theories, views of industry, economics, relation of form to function, "mass-production split" and much more. Profusely illustrated. 320pp. 6⅛ x 9¼. (Available in U.S. only.)   25023-7

HOW THE OTHER HALF LIVES, Jacob Riis. Famous journalistic record, exposing poverty and degradation of New York slums around 1900, by major social reformer. 100 striking and influential photographs. 233pp. 10 x 7⅞.   22012-5

FRUIT KEY AND TWIG KEY TO TREES AND SHRUBS, William M. Harlow. One of the handiest and most widely used identification aids. Fruit key covers 120 deciduous and evergreen species; twig key 160 deciduous species. Easily used. Over 300 photographs. 126pp. 5⅜ x 8½.   20511-8

COMMON BIRD SONGS, Dr. Donald J. Borror. Songs of 60 most common U.S. birds: robins, sparrows, cardinals, bluejays, finches, more—arranged in order of increasing complexity. Up to 9 variations of songs of each species.
Cassette and manual 99911-4

ORCHIDS AS HOUSE PLANTS, Rebecca Tyson Northen. Grow cattleyas and many other kinds of orchids—in a window, in a case, or under artificial light. 63 illustrations. 148pp. 5⅜ x 8½.   23261-1

MONSTER MAZES, Dave Phillips. Masterful mazes at four levels of difficulty. Avoid deadly perils and evil creatures to find magical treasures. Solutions for all 32 exciting illustrated puzzles. 48pp. 8¼ x 11.   26005-4

MOZART'S DON GIOVANNI (DOVER OPERA LIBRETTO SERIES), Wolfgang Amadeus Mozart. Introduced and translated by Ellen H. Bleiler. Standard Italian libretto, with complete English translation. Convenient and thoroughly portable—an ideal companion for reading along with a recording or the performance itself. Introduction. List of characters. Plot summary. 121pp. 5¼ x 8½.   24944-1

TECHNICAL MANUAL AND DICTIONARY OF CLASSICAL BALLET, Gail Grant. Defines, explains, comments on steps, movements, poses and concepts. 15-page pictorial section. Basic book for student, viewer. 127pp. 5⅜ x 8½.   21843-0

THE CLARINET AND CLARINET PLAYING, David Pino. Lively, comprehensive work features suggestions about technique, musicianship, and musical interpretation, as well as guidelines for teaching, making your own reeds, and preparing for public performance. Includes an intriguing look at clarinet history. "A godsend," *The Clarinet,* Journal of the International Clarinet Society. Appendixes. 7 illus. 320pp. 5⅜ x 8½. 40270-3

HOLLYWOOD GLAMOR PORTRAITS, John Kobal (ed.). 145 photos from 1926-49. Harlow, Gable, Bogart, Bacall; 94 stars in all. Full background on photographers, technical aspects. 160pp. 8⅜ x 11¼. 23352-9

THE ANNOTATED CASEY AT THE BAT: A Collection of Ballads about the Mighty Casey/Third, Revised Edition, Martin Gardner (ed.). Amusing sequels and parodies of one of America's best-loved poems: Casey's Revenge, Why Casey Whiffed, Casey's Sister at the Bat, others. 256pp. 5⅜ x 8½. 28598-7

THE RAVEN AND OTHER FAVORITE POEMS, Edgar Allan Poe. Over 40 of the author's most memorable poems: "The Bells," "Ulalume," "Israfel," "To Helen," "The Conqueror Worm," "Eldorado," "Annabel Lee," many more. Alphabetic lists of titles and first lines. 64pp. 5$\frac{3}{16}$ x 8¼. 26685-0

PERSONAL MEMOIRS OF U. S. GRANT, Ulysses Simpson Grant. Intelligent, deeply moving firsthand account of Civil War campaigns, considered by many the finest military memoirs ever written. Includes letters, historic photographs, maps and more. 528pp. 6⅛ x 9¼. 28587-1

ANCIENT EGYPTIAN MATERIALS AND INDUSTRIES, A. Lucas and J. Harris. Fascinating, comprehensive, thoroughly documented text describes this ancient civilization's vast resources and the processes that incorporated them in daily life, including the use of animal products, building materials, cosmetics, perfumes and incense, fibers, glazed ware, glass and its manufacture, materials used in the mummification process, and much more. 544pp. 6⅛ x 9¼. (Available in U.S. only.) 40446-3

RUSSIAN STORIES/RUSSKIE RASSKAZY: A Dual-Language Book, edited by Gleb Struve. Twelve tales by such masters as Chekhov, Tolstoy, Dostoevsky, Pushkin, others. Excellent word-for-word English translations on facing pages, plus teaching and study aids, Russian/English vocabulary, biographical/critical introductions, more. 416pp. 5⅜ x 8½. 26244-8

PHILADELPHIA THEN AND NOW: 60 Sites Photographed in the Past and Present, Kenneth Finkel and Susan Oyama. Rare photographs of City Hall, Logan Square, Independence Hall, Betsy Ross House, other landmarks juxtaposed with contemporary views. Captures changing face of historic city. Introduction. Captions. 128pp. 8¼ x 11. 25790-8

AIA ARCHITECTURAL GUIDE TO NASSAU AND SUFFOLK COUNTIES, LONG ISLAND, The American Institute of Architects, Long Island Chapter, and the Society for the Preservation of Long Island Antiquities. Comprehensive, well-researched and generously illustrated volume brings to life over three centuries of Long Island's great architectural heritage. More than 240 photographs with authoritative, extensively detailed captions. 176pp. 8¼ x 11. 26946-9

NORTH AMERICAN INDIAN LIFE: Customs and Traditions of 23 Tribes, Elsie Clews Parsons (ed.). 27 fictionalized essays by noted anthropologists examine religion, customs, government, additional facets of life among the Winnebago, Crow, Zuni, Eskimo, other tribes. 480pp. 6⅛ x 9¼. 27377-6

FRANK LLOYD WRIGHT'S DANA HOUSE, Donald Hoffmann. Pictorial essay of residential masterpiece with over 160 interior and exterior photos, plans, elevations, sketches and studies. 128pp. 9¼ x 10¾. 29120-0

THE MALE AND FEMALE FIGURE IN MOTION: 60 Classic Photographic Sequences, Eadweard Muybridge. 60 true-action photographs of men and women walking, running, climbing, bending, turning, etc., reproduced from rare 19th-century masterpiece. vi + 121pp. 9 x 12. 24745-7

1001 QUESTIONS ANSWERED ABOUT THE SEASHORE, N. J. Berrill and Jacquelyn Berrill. Queries answered about dolphins, sea snails, sponges, starfish, fishes, shore birds, many others. Covers appearance, breeding, growth, feeding, much more. 305pp. 5¼ x 8¼. 23366-9

ATTRACTING BIRDS TO YOUR YARD, William J. Weber. Easy-to-follow guide offers advice on how to attract the greatest diversity of birds: birdhouses, feeders, water and waterers, much more. 96pp. 5³⁄₁₆ x 8¼. 28927-3

MEDICINAL AND OTHER USES OF NORTH AMERICAN PLANTS: A Historical Survey with Special Reference to the Eastern Indian Tribes, Charlotte Erichsen-Brown. Chronological historical citations document 500 years of usage of plants, trees, shrubs native to eastern Canada, northeastern U.S. Also complete identifying information. 343 illustrations. 544pp. 6½ x 9¼. 25951-X

STORYBOOK MAZES, Dave Phillips. 23 stories and mazes on two-page spreads: Wizard of Oz, Treasure Island, Robin Hood, etc. Solutions. 64pp. 8¼ x 11. 23628-5

AMERICAN NEGRO SONGS: 230 Folk Songs and Spirituals, Religious and Secular, John W. Work. This authoritative study traces the African influences of songs sung and played by black Americans at work, in church, and as entertainment. The author discusses the lyric significance of such songs as "Swing Low, Sweet Chariot," "John Henry," and others and offers the words and music for 230 songs. Bibliography. Index of Song Titles. 272pp. 6½ x 9¼. 40271-1

MOVIE-STAR PORTRAITS OF THE FORTIES, John Kobal (ed.). 163 glamor, studio photos of 106 stars of the 1940s: Rita Hayworth, Ava Gardner, Marlon Brando, Clark Gable, many more. 176pp. 8⅜ x 11¼. 23546-7

BENCHLEY LOST AND FOUND, Robert Benchley. Finest humor from early 30s, about pet peeves, child psychologists, post office and others. Mostly unavailable elsewhere. 73 illustrations by Peter Arno and others. 183pp. 5⅜ x 8½. 22410-4

YEKL and THE IMPORTED BRIDEGROOM AND OTHER STORIES OF YIDDISH NEW YORK, Abraham Cahan. Film Hester Street based on *Yekl* (1896). Novel, other stories among first about Jewish immigrants on N.Y.'s East Side. 240pp. 5⅜ x 8½. 22427-9

SELECTED POEMS, Walt Whitman. Generous sampling from *Leaves of Grass*. Twenty-four poems include "I Hear America Singing," "Song of the Open Road," "I Sing the Body Electric," "When Lilacs Last in the Dooryard Bloom'd," "O Captain! My Captain!"–all reprinted from an authoritative edition. Lists of titles and first lines. 128pp. 5³⁄₁₆ x 8¼. 26878-0

THE BEST TALES OF HOFFMANN, E. T. A. Hoffmann. 10 of Hoffmann's most important stories: "Nutcracker and the King of Mice," "The Golden Flowerpot," etc. 458pp. 5⅜ x 8½.   21793-0

FROM FETISH TO GOD IN ANCIENT EGYPT, E. A. Wallis Budge. Rich detailed survey of Egyptian conception of "God" and gods, magic, cult of animals, Osiris, more. Also, superb English translations of hymns and legends. 240 illustrations. 545pp. 5⅜ x 8½.   25803-3

FRENCH STORIES/CONTES FRANÇAIS: A Dual-Language Book, Wallace Fowlie. Ten stories by French masters, Voltaire to Camus: "Micromegas" by Voltaire; "The Atheist's Mass" by Balzac; "Minuet" by de Maupassant; "The Guest" by Camus, six more. Excellent English translations on facing pages. Also French-English vocabulary list, exercises, more. 352pp. 5⅜ x 8½.   26443-2

CHICAGO AT THE TURN OF THE CENTURY IN PHOTOGRAPHS: 122 Historic Views from the Collections of the Chicago Historical Society, Larry A. Viskochil. Rare large-format prints offer detailed views of City Hall, State Street, the Loop, Hull House, Union Station, many other landmarks, circa 1904-1913. Introduction. Captions. Maps. 144pp. 9⅜ x 12¼.   24656-6

OLD BROOKLYN IN EARLY PHOTOGRAPHS, 1865-1929, William Lee Younger. Luna Park, Gravesend race track, construction of Grand Army Plaza, moving of Hotel Brighton, etc. 157 previously unpublished photographs. 165pp. 8⅞ x 11¾.   23587-4

THE MYTHS OF THE NORTH AMERICAN INDIANS, Lewis Spence. Rich anthology of the myths and legends of the Algonquins, Iroquois, Pawnees and Sioux, prefaced by an extensive historical and ethnological commentary. 36 illustrations. 480pp. 5⅜ x 8½.   25967-6

AN ENCYCLOPEDIA OF BATTLES: Accounts of Over 1,560 Battles from 1479 B.C. to the Present, David Eggenberger. Essential details of every major battle in recorded history from the first battle of Megiddo in 1479 B.C. to Grenada in 1984. List of Battle Maps. New Appendix covering the years 1967-1984. Index. 99 illustrations. 544pp. 6½ x 9¼.   24913-1

SAILING ALONE AROUND THE WORLD, Captain Joshua Slocum. First man to sail around the world, alone, in small boat. One of great feats of seamanship told in delightful manner. 67 illustrations. 294pp. 5⅜ x 8½.   20326-3

ANARCHISM AND OTHER ESSAYS, Emma Goldman. Powerful, penetrating, prophetic essays on direct action, role of minorities, prison reform, puritan hypocrisy, violence, etc. 271pp. 5⅜ x 8½.   22484-8

MYTHS OF THE HINDUS AND BUDDHISTS, Ananda K. Coomaraswamy and Sister Nivedita. Great stories of the epics; deeds of Krishna, Shiva, taken from puranas, Vedas, folk tales; etc. 32 illustrations. 400pp. 5⅜ x 8½.   21759-0

THE TRAUMA OF BIRTH, Otto Rank. Rank's controversial thesis that anxiety neurosis is caused by profound psychological trauma which occurs at birth. 256pp. 5⅜ x 8½.   27974-X

A THEOLOGICO-POLITICAL TREATISE, Benedict Spinoza. Also contains unfinished Political Treatise. Great classic on religious liberty, theory of government on common consent. R. Elwes translation. Total of 421pp. 5⅜ x 8½.   20249-6

MY BONDAGE AND MY FREEDOM, Frederick Douglass. Born a slave, Douglass became outspoken force in antislavery movement. The best of Douglass' autobiographies. Graphic description of slave life. 464pp. 5⅜ x 8½. 22457-0

FOLLOWING THE EQUATOR: A Journey Around the World, Mark Twain. Fascinating humorous account of 1897 voyage to Hawaii, Australia, India, New Zealand, etc. Ironic, bemused reports on peoples, customs, climate, flora and fauna, politics, much more. 197 illustrations. 720pp. 5⅜ x 8½. 26113-1

THE PEOPLE CALLED SHAKERS, Edward D. Andrews. Definitive study of Shakers: origins, beliefs, practices, dances, social organization, furniture and crafts, etc. 33 illustrations. 351pp. 5⅜ x 8½. 21081-2

THE MYTHS OF GREECE AND ROME, H. A. Guerber. A classic of mythology, generously illustrated, long prized for its simple, graphic, accurate retelling of the principal myths of Greece and Rome, and for its commentary on their origins and significance. With 64 illustrations by Michelangelo, Raphael, Titian, Rubens, Canova, Bernini and others. 480pp. 5⅜ x 8½. 27584-1

PSYCHOLOGY OF MUSIC, Carl E. Seashore. Classic work discusses music as a medium from psychological viewpoint. Clear treatment of physical acoustics, auditory apparatus, sound perception, development of musical skills, nature of musical feeling, host of other topics. 88 figures. 408pp. 5⅜ x 8½. 21851-1

THE PHILOSOPHY OF HISTORY, Georg W. Hegel. Great classic of Western thought develops concept that history is not chance but rational process, the evolution of freedom. 457pp. 5⅜ x 8½. 20112-0

THE BOOK OF TEA, Kakuzo Okakura. Minor classic of the Orient: entertaining, charming explanation, interpretation of traditional Japanese culture in terms of tea ceremony. 94pp. 5⅜ x 8½. 20070-1

LIFE IN ANCIENT EGYPT, Adolf Erman. Fullest, most thorough, detailed older account with much not in more recent books, domestic life, religion, magic, medicine, commerce, much more. Many illustrations reproduce tomb paintings, carvings, hieroglyphs, etc. 597pp. 5⅜ x 8½. 22632-8

SUNDIALS, Their Theory and Construction, Albert Waugh. Far and away the best, most thorough coverage of ideas, mathematics concerned, types, construction, adjusting anywhere. Simple, nontechnical treatment allows even children to build several of these dials. Over 100 illustrations. 230pp. 5⅜ x 8½. 22947-5

THEORETICAL HYDRODYNAMICS, L. M. Milne-Thomson. Classic exposition of the mathematical theory of fluid motion, applicable to both hydrodynamics and aerodynamics. Over 600 exercises. 768pp. 6⅛ x 9¼. 68970-0

SONGS OF EXPERIENCE: Facsimile Reproduction with 26 Plates in Full Color, William Blake. 26 full-color plates from a rare 1826 edition. Includes "The Tyger," "London," "Holy Thursday," and other poems. Printed text of poems. 48pp. 5¼ x 7. 24636-1

OLD-TIME VIGNETTES IN FULL COLOR, Carol Belanger Grafton (ed.). Over 390 charming, often sentimental illustrations, selected from archives of Victorian graphics—pretty women posing, children playing, food, flowers, kittens and puppies, smiling cherubs, birds and butterflies, much more. All copyright-free. 48pp. 9¼ x 12¼. 27269-9

PERSPECTIVE FOR ARTISTS, Rex Vicat Cole. Depth, perspective of sky and sea, shadows, much more, not usually covered. 391 diagrams, 81 reproductions of drawings and paintings. 279pp. 5⅜ x 8½. 22487-2

DRAWING THE LIVING FIGURE, Joseph Sheppard. Innovative approach to artistic anatomy focuses on specifics of surface anatomy, rather than muscles and bones. Over 170 drawings of live models in front, back and side views, and in widely varying poses. Accompanying diagrams. 177 illustrations. Introduction. Index. 144pp. 8⅜ x11¼. 26723-7

GOTHIC AND OLD ENGLISH ALPHABETS: 100 Complete Fonts, Dan X. Solo. Add power, elegance to posters, signs, other graphics with 100 stunning copyright-free alphabets: Blackstone, Dolbey, Germania, 97 more–including many lower-case, numerals, punctuation marks. 104pp. 8⅛ x 11. 24695-7

HOW TO DO BEADWORK, Mary White. Fundamental book on craft from simple projects to five-bead chains and woven works. 106 illustrations. 142pp. 5⅜ x 8. 20697-1

THE BOOK OF WOOD CARVING, Charles Marshall Sayers. Finest book for beginners discusses fundamentals and offers 34 designs. "Absolutely first rate . . . well thought out and well executed."–E. J. Tangerman. 118pp. 7¾ x 10⅝. 23654-4

ILLUSTRATED CATALOG OF CIVIL WAR MILITARY GOODS: Union Army Weapons, Insignia, Uniform Accessories, and Other Equipment, Schuyler, Hartley, and Graham. Rare, profusely illustrated 1846 catalog includes Union Army uniform and dress regulations, arms and ammunition, coats, insignia, flags, swords, rifles, etc. 226 illustrations. 160pp. 9 x 12. 24939-5

WOMEN'S FASHIONS OF THE EARLY 1900s: An Unabridged Republication of "New York Fashions, 1909," National Cloak & Suit Co. Rare catalog of mail-order fashions documents women's and children's clothing styles shortly after the turn of the century. Captions offer full descriptions, prices. Invaluable resource for fashion, costume historians. Approximately 725 illustrations. 128pp. 8⅜ x 11¼. 27276-1

THE 1912 AND 1915 GUSTAV STICKLEY FURNITURE CATALOGS, Gustav Stickley. With over 200 detailed illustrations and descriptions, these two catalogs are essential reading and reference materials and identification guides for Stickley furniture. Captions cite materials, dimensions and prices. 112pp. 6½ x 9¼. 26676-1

EARLY AMERICAN LOCOMOTIVES, John H. White, Jr. Finest locomotive engravings from early 19th century: historical (1804–74), main-line (after 1870), special, foreign, etc. 147 plates. 142pp. 11⅜ x 8¼. 22772-3

THE TALL SHIPS OF TODAY IN PHOTOGRAPHS, Frank O. Braynard. Lavishly illustrated tribute to nearly 100 majestic contemporary sailing vessels: Amerigo Vespucci, Clearwater, Constitution, Eagle, Mayflower, Sea Cloud, Victory, many more. Authoritative captions provide statistics, background on each ship. 190 black-and-white photographs and illustrations. Introduction. 128pp. 8⅞ x 11¾. 27163-3

LITTLE BOOK OF EARLY AMERICAN CRAFTS AND TRADES, Peter Stockham (ed.). 1807 children's book explains crafts and trades: baker, hatter, cooper, potter, and many others. 23 copperplate illustrations. 140pp. 4⅝ x 6.   23336-7

VICTORIAN FASHIONS AND COSTUMES FROM HARPER'S BAZAR, 1867–1898, Stella Blum (ed.). Day costumes, evening wear, sports clothes, shoes, hats, other accessories in over 1,000 detailed engravings. 320pp. 9⅜ x 12¼. 22990-4

GUSTAV STICKLEY, THE CRAFTSMAN, Mary Ann Smith. Superb study surveys broad scope of Stickley's achievement, especially in architecture. Design philosophy, rise and fall of the Craftsman empire, descriptions and floor plans for many Craftsman houses, more. 86 black-and-white halftones. 31 line illustrations. Introduction 208pp. 6½ x 9¼.   27210-9

THE LONG ISLAND RAIL ROAD IN EARLY PHOTOGRAPHS, Ron Ziel. Over 220 rare photos, informative text document origin (1844) and development of rail service on Long Island. Vintage views of early trains, locomotives, stations, passengers, crews, much more. Captions. 8⅞ x 11¾.   26301-0

VOYAGE OF THE LIBERDADE, Joshua Slocum. Great 19th-century mariner's thrilling, first-hand account of the wreck of his ship off South America, the 35-foot boat he built from the wreckage, and its remarkable voyage home. 128pp. 5⅜ x 8½.
40022-0

TEN BOOKS ON ARCHITECTURE, Vitruvius. The most important book ever written on architecture. Early Roman aesthetics, technology, classical orders, site selection, all other aspects. Morgan translation. 331pp. 5⅜ x 8½.   20645-9

THE HUMAN FIGURE IN MOTION, Eadweard Muybridge. More than 4,500 stopped-action photos, in action series, showing undraped men, women, children jumping, lying down, throwing, sitting, wrestling, carrying, etc. 390pp. 7⅞ x 10⅝.
20204-6 Clothbd.

TREES OF THE EASTERN AND CENTRAL UNITED STATES AND CANADA, William M. Harlow. Best one-volume guide to 140 trees. Full descriptions, woodlore, range, etc. Over 600 illustrations. Handy size. 288pp. 4½ x 6⅜.   20395-6

SONGS OF WESTERN BIRDS, Dr. Donald J. Borror. Complete song and call repertoire of 60 western species, including flycatchers, juncoes, cactus wrens, many more—includes fully illustrated booklet.   Cassette and manual 99913-0

GROWING AND USING HERBS AND SPICES, Milo Miloradovich. Versatile handbook provides all the information needed for cultivation and use of all the herbs and spices available in North America. 4 illustrations. Index. Glossary. 236pp. 5⅜ x 8½.
25058-X

BIG BOOK OF MAZES AND LABYRINTHS, Walter Shepherd. 50 mazes and labyrinths in all—classical, solid, ripple, and more—in one great volume. Perfect inexpensive puzzler for clever youngsters. Full solutions. 112pp. 8⅛ x 11.   22951-3

PIANO TUNING, J. Cree Fischer. Clearest, best book for beginner, amateur. Simple repairs, raising dropped notes, tuning by easy method of flattened fifths. No previous skills needed. 4 illustrations. 201pp. 5⅜ x 8½. 23267-0

HINTS TO SINGERS, Lillian Nordica. Selecting the right teacher, developing confidence, overcoming stage fright, and many other important skills receive thoughtful discussion in this indispensible guide, written by a world-famous diva of four decades' experience. 96pp. 5⅜ x 8½. 40094-8

THE COMPLETE NONSENSE OF EDWARD LEAR, Edward Lear. All nonsense limericks, zany alphabets, Owl and Pussycat, songs, nonsense botany, etc., illustrated by Lear. Total of 320pp. 5⅜ x 8½. (Available in U.S. only.) 20167-8

VICTORIAN PARLOUR POETRY: An Annotated Anthology, Michael R. Turner. 117 gems by Longfellow, Tennyson, Browning, many lesser-known poets. "The Village Blacksmith," "Curfew Must Not Ring Tonight," "Only a Baby Small," dozens more, often difficult to find elsewhere. Index of poets, titles, first lines. xxiii + 325pp. 5⅜ x 8¼. 27044-0

DUBLINERS, James Joyce. Fifteen stories offer vivid, tightly focused observations of the lives of Dublin's poorer classes. At least one, "The Dead," is considered a masterpiece. Reprinted complete and unabridged from standard edition. 160pp. 5³⁄₁₆ x 8¼. 26870-5

GREAT WEIRD TALES: 14 Stories by Lovecraft, Blackwood, Machen and Others, S. T. Joshi (ed.). 14 spellbinding tales, including "The Sin Eater," by Fiona McLeod, "The Eye Above the Mantel," by Frank Belknap Long, as well as renowned works by R. H. Barlow, Lord Dunsany, Arthur Machen, W. C. Morrow and eight other masters of the genre. 256pp. 5⅜ x 8½. (Available in U.S. only.) 40436-6

THE BOOK OF THE SACRED MAGIC OF ABRAMELIN THE MAGE, translated by S. MacGregor Mathers. Medieval manuscript of ceremonial magic. Basic document in Aleister Crowley, Golden Dawn groups. 268pp. 5⅜ x 8½. 23211-5

NEW RUSSIAN-ENGLISH AND ENGLISH-RUSSIAN DICTIONARY, M. A. O'Brien. This is a remarkably handy Russian dictionary, containing a surprising amount of information, including over 70,000 entries. 366pp. 4½ x 6⅛. 20208-9

HISTORIC HOMES OF THE AMERICAN PRESIDENTS, Second, Revised Edition, Irvin Haas. A traveler's guide to American Presidential homes, most open to the public, depicting and describing homes occupied by every American President from George Washington to George Bush. With visiting hours, admission charges, travel routes. 175 photographs. Index. 160pp. 8¼ x 11. 26751-2

NEW YORK IN THE FORTIES, Andreas Feininger. 162 brilliant photographs by the well-known photographer, formerly with *Life* magazine. Commuters, shoppers, Times Square at night, much else from city at its peak. Captions by John von Hartz. 181pp. 9¼ x 10¾. 23585-8

INDIAN SIGN LANGUAGE, William Tomkins. Over 525 signs developed by Sioux and other tribes. Written instructions and diagrams. Also 290 pictographs. 111pp. 6⅛ x 9¼. 22029-X

ANATOMY: A Complete Guide for Artists, Joseph Sheppard. A master of figure drawing shows artists how to render human anatomy convincingly. Over 460 illustrations. 224pp. 8⅜ x 11¼. 27279-6

MEDIEVAL CALLIGRAPHY: Its History and Technique, Marc Drogin. Spirited history, comprehensive instruction manual covers 13 styles (ca. 4th century through 15th). Excellent photographs; directions for duplicating medieval techniques with modern tools. 224pp. 8⅜ x 11¼. 26142-5

DRIED FLOWERS: How to Prepare Them, Sarah Whitlock and Martha Rankin. Complete instructions on how to use silica gel, meal and borax, perlite aggregate, sand and borax, glycerine and water to create attractive permanent flower arrangements. 12 illustrations. 32pp. 5⅜ x 8½. 21802-3

EASY-TO-MAKE BIRD FEEDERS FOR WOODWORKERS, Scott D. Campbell. Detailed, simple-to-use guide for designing, constructing, caring for and using feeders. Text, illustrations for 12 classic and contemporary designs. 96pp. 5⅜ x 8½. 25847-5

SCOTTISH WONDER TALES FROM MYTH AND LEGEND, Donald A. Mackenzie. 16 lively tales tell of giants rumbling down mountainsides, of a magic wand that turns stone pillars into warriors, of gods and goddesses, evil hags, powerful forces and more. 240pp. 5⅜ x 8½. 29677-6

THE HISTORY OF UNDERCLOTHES, C. Willett Cunnington and Phyllis Cunnington. Fascinating, well-documented survey covering six centuries of English undergarments, enhanced with over 100 illustrations: 12th-century laced-up bodice, footed long drawers (1795), 19th-century bustles, 19th-century corsets for men, Victorian "bust improvers," much more. 272pp. 5⅝ x 8¼. 27124-2

ARTS AND CRAFTS FURNITURE: The Complete Brooks Catalog of 1912, Brooks Manufacturing Co. Photos and detailed descriptions of more than 150 now very collectible furniture designs from the Arts and Crafts movement depict davenports, settees, buffets, desks, tables, chairs, bedsteads, dressers and more, all built of solid, quarter-sawed oak. Invaluable for students and enthusiasts of antiques, Americana and the decorative arts. 80pp. 6½ x 9¼. 27471-3

WILBUR AND ORVILLE: A Biography of the Wright Brothers, Fred Howard. Definitive, crisply written study tells the full story of the brothers' lives and work. A vividly written biography, unparalleled in scope and color, that also captures the spirit of an extraordinary era. 560pp. 6⅛ x 9¼. 40297-5

THE ARTS OF THE SAILOR: Knotting, Splicing and Ropework, Hervey Garrett Smith. Indispensable shipboard reference covers tools, basic knots and useful hitches; handsewing and canvas work, more. Over 100 illustrations. Delightful reading for sea lovers. 256pp. 5⅜ x 8½. 26440-8

FRANK LLOYD WRIGHT'S FALLINGWATER: The House and Its History, Second, Revised Edition, Donald Hoffmann. A total revision–both in text and illustrations–of the standard document on Fallingwater, the boldest, most personal architectural statement of Wright's mature years, updated with valuable new material from the recently opened Frank Lloyd Wright Archives. "Fascinating"–*The New York Times*. 116 illustrations. 128pp. 9¼ x 10¾. 27430-6

PHOTOGRAPHIC SKETCHBOOK OF THE CIVIL WAR, Alexander Gardner. 100 photos taken on field during the Civil War. Famous shots of Manassas Harper's Ferry, Lincoln, Richmond, slave pens, etc. 244pp. 10⅝ x 8¼. 22731-6

FIVE ACRES AND INDEPENDENCE, Maurice G. Kains. Great back-to-the-land classic explains basics of self-sufficient farming. The one book to get. 95 illustrations. 397pp. 5⅜ x 8½. 20974-1

SONGS OF EASTERN BIRDS, Dr. Donald J. Borror. Songs and calls of 60 species most common to eastern U.S.: warblers, woodpeckers, flycatchers, thrushes, larks, many more in high-quality recording. Cassette and manual 99912-2

A MODERN HERBAL, Margaret Grieve. Much the fullest, most exact, most useful compilation of herbal material. Gigantic alphabetical encyclopedia, from aconite to zedoary, gives botanical information, medical properties, folklore, economic uses, much else. Indispensable to serious reader. 161 illustrations. 888pp. 6½ x 9¼. 2-vol. set. (Available in U.S. only.) Vol. I: 22798-7
Vol. II: 22799-5

HIDDEN TREASURE MAZE BOOK, Dave Phillips. Solve 34 challenging mazes accompanied by heroic tales of adventure. Evil dragons, people-eating plants, blood-thirsty giants, many more dangerous adversaries lurk at every twist and turn. 34 mazes, stories, solutions. 48pp. 8¼ x 11. 24566-7

LETTERS OF W. A. MOZART, Wolfgang A. Mozart. Remarkable letters show bawdy wit, humor, imagination, musical insights, contemporary musical world; includes some letters from Leopold Mozart. 276pp. 5⅜ x 8½. 22859-2

BASIC PRINCIPLES OF CLASSICAL BALLET, Agrippina Vaganova. Great Russian theoretician, teacher explains methods for teaching classical ballet. 118 illus-trations. 175pp. 5⅜ x 8½. 22036-2

THE JUMPING FROG, Mark Twain. Revenge edition. The original story of The Celebrated Jumping Frog of Calaveras County, a hapless French translation, and Twain's hilarious "retranslation" from the French. 12 illustrations. 66pp. 5⅜ x 8½. 22686-7

BEST REMEMBERED POEMS, Martin Gardner (ed.). The 126 poems in this superb collection of 19th- and 20th-century British and American verse range from Shelley's "To a Skylark" to the impassioned "Renascence" of Edna St. Vincent Millay and to Edward Lear's whimsical "The Owl and the Pussycat." 224pp. 5⅜ x 8½. 27165-X

COMPLETE SONNETS, William Shakespeare. Over 150 exquisite poems deal with love, friendship, the tyranny of time, beauty's evanescence, death and other themes in language of remarkable power, precision and beauty. Glossary of archaic terms. 80pp. 5³⁄₁₆ x 8¼. 26686-9

THE BATTLES THAT CHANGED HISTORY, Fletcher Pratt. Eminent historian profiles 16 crucial conflicts, ancient to modern, that changed the course of civiliza-tion. 352pp. 5⅜ x 8½. 41129-X

THE WIT AND HUMOR OF OSCAR WILDE, Alvin Redman (ed.). More than 1,000 ripostes, paradoxes, wisecracks: Work is the curse of the drinking classes; I can resist everything except temptation; etc. 258pp. 5⅜ x 8½. 20602-5

SHAKESPEARE LEXICON AND QUOTATION DICTIONARY, Alexander Schmidt. Full definitions, locations, shades of meaning in every word in plays and poems. More than 50,000 exact quotations. 1,485pp. 6½ x 9¼. 2-vol. set.

Vol. 1: 22726-X
Vol. 2: 22727-8

SELECTED POEMS, Emily Dickinson. Over 100 best-known, best-loved poems by one of America's foremost poets, reprinted from authoritative early editions. No comparable edition at this price. Index of first lines. 64pp. 5³⁄₁₆ x 8¼. 26466-1

THE INSIDIOUS DR. FU-MANCHU, Sax Rohmer. The first of the popular mystery series introduces a pair of English detectives to their archnemesis, the diabolical Dr. Fu-Manchu. Flavorful atmosphere, fast-paced action, and colorful characters enliven this classic of the genre. 208pp. 5³⁄₁₆ x 8¼. 29898-1

THE MALLEUS MALEFICARUM OF KRAMER AND SPRENGER, translated by Montague Summers. Full text of most important witchhunter's "bible," used by both Catholics and Protestants. 278pp. 6⅝ x 10. 22802-9

SPANISH STORIES/CUENTOS ESPAÑOLES: A Dual-Language Book, Angel Flores (ed.). Unique format offers 13 great stories in Spanish by Cervantes, Borges, others. Faithful English translations on facing pages. 352pp. 5⅜ x 8½. 25399-6

GARDEN CITY, LONG ISLAND, IN EARLY PHOTOGRAPHS, 1869–1919, Mildred H. Smith. Handsome treasury of 118 vintage pictures, accompanied by carefully researched captions, document the Garden City Hotel fire (1899), the Vanderbilt Cup Race (1908), the first airmail flight departing from the Nassau Boulevard Aerodrome (1911), and much more. 96pp. 8⅞ x 11¾. 40669-5

OLD QUEENS, N.Y., IN EARLY PHOTOGRAPHS, Vincent F. Seyfried and William Asadorian. Over 160 rare photographs of Maspeth, Jamaica, Jackson Heights, and other areas. Vintage views of DeWitt Clinton mansion, 1939 World's Fair and more. Captions. 192pp. 8⅞ x 11. 26358-4

CAPTURED BY THE INDIANS: 15 Firsthand Accounts, 1750-1870, Frederick Drimmer. Astounding true historical accounts of grisly torture, bloody conflicts, relentless pursuits, miraculous escapes and more, by people who lived to tell the tale. 384pp. 5⅜ x 8½. 24901-8

THE WORLD'S GREAT SPEECHES (Fourth Enlarged Edition), Lewis Copeland, Lawrence W. Lamm, and Stephen J. McKenna. Nearly 300 speeches provide public speakers with a wealth of updated quotes and inspiration–from Pericles' funeral oration and William Jennings Bryan's "Cross of Gold Speech" to Malcolm X's powerful words on the Black Revolution and Earl of Spenser's tribute to his sister, Diana, Princess of Wales. 944pp. 5⅜ x 8⅜. 40903-1

THE BOOK OF THE SWORD, Sir Richard F. Burton. Great Victorian scholar/adventurer's eloquent, erudite history of the "queen of weapons"–from prehistory to early Roman Empire. Evolution and development of early swords, variations (sabre, broadsword, cutlass, scimitar, etc.), much more. 336pp. 6⅛ x 9¼. 25434-8

AUTOBIOGRAPHY: The Story of My Experiments with Truth, Mohandas K. Gandhi. Boyhood, legal studies, purification, the growth of the Satyagraha (nonviolent protest) movement. Critical, inspiring work of the man responsible for the freedom of India. 480pp. 5⅜ x 8½. (Available in U.S. only.) 24593-4

CELTIC MYTHS AND LEGENDS, T. W. Rolleston. Masterful retelling of Irish and Welsh stories and tales. Cuchulain, King Arthur, Deirdre, the Grail, many more. First paperback edition. 58 full-page illustrations. 512pp. 5⅜ x 8½. 26507-2

THE PRINCIPLES OF PSYCHOLOGY, William James. Famous long course complete, unabridged. Stream of thought, time perception, memory, experimental methods; great work decades ahead of its time. 94 figures. 1,391pp. 5⅜ x 8½. 2-vol. set. Vol. I: 20381-6 Vol. II: 20382-4

THE WORLD AS WILL AND REPRESENTATION, Arthur Schopenhauer. Definitive English translation of Schopenhauer's life work, correcting more than 1,000 errors, omissions in earlier translations. Translated by E. F. J. Payne. Total of 1,269pp. 5⅜ x 8½. 2-vol. set. Vol. 1: 21761-2 Vol. 2: 21762-0

MAGIC AND MYSTERY IN TIBET, Madame Alexandra David-Neel. Experiences among lamas, magicians, sages, sorcerers, Bonpa wizards. A true psychic discovery. 32 illustrations. 321pp. 5⅜ x 8½. (Available in U.S. only.) 22682-4

THE EGYPTIAN BOOK OF THE DEAD, E. A. Wallis Budge. Complete reproduction of Ani's papyrus, finest ever found. Full hieroglyphic text, interlinear transliteration, word-for-word translation, smooth translation. 533pp. 6½ x 9¼. 21866-X

MATHEMATICS FOR THE NONMATHEMATICIAN, Morris Kline. Detailed, college-level treatment of mathematics in cultural and historical context, with numerous exercises. Recommended Reading Lists. Tables. Numerous figures. 641pp. 5⅜ x 8½. 24823-2

PROBABILISTIC METHODS IN THE THEORY OF STRUCTURES, Isaac Elishakoff. Well-written introduction covers the elements of the theory of probability from two or more random variables, the reliability of such multivariable structures, the theory of random function, Monte Carlo methods of treating problems incapable of exact solution, and more. Examples. 502pp. 5⅜ x 8½. 40691-1

THE RIME OF THE ANCIENT MARINER, Gustave Doré, S. T. Coleridge. Doré's finest work; 34 plates capture moods, subtleties of poem. Flawless full-size reproductions printed on facing pages with authoritative text of poem. "Beautiful. Simply beautiful."–*Publisher's Weekly.* 77pp. 9¼ x 12. 22305-1

NORTH AMERICAN INDIAN DESIGNS FOR ARTISTS AND CRAFTSPEOPLE, Eva Wilson. Over 360 authentic copyright-free designs adapted from Navajo blankets, Hopi pottery, Sioux buffalo hides, more. Geometrics, symbolic figures, plant and animal motifs, etc. 128pp. 8⅜ x 11. (Not for sale in the United Kingdom.) 25341-4

SCULPTURE: Principles and Practice, Louis Slobodkin. Step-by-step approach to clay, plaster, metals, stone; classical and modern. 253 drawings, photos. 255pp. 8⅛ x 11. 22960-2

THE INFLUENCE OF SEA POWER UPON HISTORY, 1660–1783, A. T. Mahan. Influential classic of naval history and tactics still used as text in war colleges. First paperback edition. 4 maps. 24 battle plans. 640pp. 5⅜ x 8½. 25509-3

THE STORY OF THE TITANIC AS TOLD BY ITS SURVIVORS, Jack Winocour (ed.). What it was really like. Panic, despair, shocking inefficiency, and a little heroism. More thrilling than any fictional account. 26 illustrations. 320pp. 5⅜ x 8½. 20610-6

FAIRY AND FOLK TALES OF THE IRISH PEASANTRY, William Butler Yeats (ed.). Treasury of 64 tales from the twilight world of Celtic myth and legend: "The Soul Cages," "The Kildare Pooka," "King O'Toole and his Goose," many more. Introduction and Notes by W. B. Yeats. 352pp. 5⅜ x 8½. 26941-8

BUDDHIST MAHAYANA TEXTS, E. B. Cowell and others (eds.). Superb, accurate translations of basic documents in Mahayana Buddhism, highly important in history of religions. The Buddha-karita of Asvaghosha, Larger Sukhavativyuha, more. 448pp. 5⅜ x 8½. 25552-2

ONE TWO THREE . . . INFINITY: Facts and Speculations of Science, George Gamow. Great physicist's fascinating, readable overview of contemporary science: number theory, relativity, fourth dimension, entropy, genes, atomic structure, much more. 128 illustrations. Index. 352pp. 5⅜ x 8½. 25664-2

EXPERIMENTATION AND MEASUREMENT, W. J. Youden. Introductory manual explains laws of measurement in simple terms and offers tips for achieving accuracy and minimizing errors. Mathematics of measurement, use of instruments, experimenting with machines. 1994 edition. Foreword. Preface. Introduction. Epilogue. Selected Readings. Glossary. Index. Tables and figures. 128pp. 5⅜ x 8½. 40451-X

DALÍ ON MODERN ART: The Cuckolds of Antiquated Modern Art, Salvador Dalí. Influential painter skewers modern art and its practitioners. Outrageous evaluations of Picasso, Cézanne, Turner, more. 15 renderings of paintings discussed. 44 calligraphic decorations by Dalí. 96pp. 5⅜ x 8½. (Available in U.S. only.) 29220-7

ANTIQUE PLAYING CARDS: A Pictorial History, Henry René D'Allemagne. Over 900 elaborate, decorative images from rare playing cards (14th–20th centuries): Bacchus, death, dancing dogs, hunting scenes, royal coats of arms, players cheating, much more. 96pp. 9¼ x 12¼. 29265-7

MAKING FURNITURE MASTERPIECES: 30 Projects with Measured Drawings, Franklin H. Gottshall. Step-by-step instructions, illustrations for constructing handsome, useful pieces, among them a Sheraton desk, Chippendale chair, Spanish desk, Queen Anne table and a William and Mary dressing mirror. 224pp. 8⅛ x 11¼. 29338-6

THE FOSSIL BOOK: A Record of Prehistoric Life, Patricia V. Rich et al. Profusely illustrated definitive guide covers everything from single-celled organisms and dinosaurs to birds and mammals and the interplay between climate and man. Over 1,500 illustrations. 760pp. 7½ x 10⅛. 29371-8

Paperbound unless otherwise indicated. Available at your book dealer, online at **www.doverpublications.com**, or by writing to Dept. GI, Dover Publications, Inc., 31 East 2nd Street, Mineola, NY 11501. For current price information or for free catalogues (please indicate field of interest), write to Dover Publications or log on to **www.doverpublications.com** and see every Dover book in print. Dover publishes more than 500 books each year on science, elementary and advanced mathematics, biology, music, art, literary history, social sciences, and other areas.